KNOWING POVERTY

Critical Reflections on Participatory Research and Policy

Edited by
Karen Brock and Rosemary McGee

EARTHSCAN

Earthscan Publications Ltd
London • Sterling, VA

First published in the UK and USA in 2002
by Earthscan Publications Ltd

ISBN: 1 85383 894 2 paperback
      1 85383 899 3 hardback

Typesetting by JS Typesetting Ltd, Wellingborough, Northants
Printed and bound in the UK by Creative Print and Design Wales, Ebbw Vale
Cover design by Danny Gillespie

For a full list of publications please contact:

Earthscan Publications Ltd
120 Pentonville Road, London, N1 9JN, UK
Tel: +44 (0)20 7278 0433
Fax: +44 (0)20 7278 1142
Email: earthinfo@earthscan.co.uk
Web: **www.earthscan.co.uk**

22883 Quicksilver Drive, Sterling, VA 20166-2012, USA

Earthscan is an editorially independent subsidiary of Kogan Page Ltd and
publishes in association with WWF-UK and the International Institute for
Environment and Development

A catalogue record for this book is available from the British Library

Library of Congress Cataloging-in-Publication Data

Knowing poverty : critical reflections on participatory research and policy / edited
by Karen Brock and Rosemary McGee.
       p. cm.
   Includes bibliographical references and index.
   ISBN 1-85383-899-3 (cloth) – ISBN 1-85383-894-2 (pbk.)
     1. Economic assistance, Domestic. 2. Poverty. 3. Participant observation.
  I. Brock, Karen. II. McGee, Rosemary

HC79.P63 K56 2002
362.5'07'23–dc21

2002002847

CONTENTS

LIST OF FIGURES, TABLES AND BOXES

FIGURES

TABLES

BOXES

ABOUT THE CONTRIBUTORS

Ahmed Adan has worked with ActionAid Somaliland since May 1993 in various posts. He studied agriculture at Somaliland National University, and lectured there from 1989 until 1990, when he was forced to leave for his home town in the north. He played a role in conflict resolution between Somaliland clans in the early 1990s.

Aklilu Kidanu is a social development researcher with particular interest in the relationship between poverty and health, particularly reproductive health including HIV/AIDS. His current research focuses on family planning and reproductive health service-delivery programmes in the three major regions of Ethiopia.

Anne Rademacher is a joint-degree candidate in Anthropology and Environmental Studies at Yale University. Her research interests include international conservation-development initiatives, urban ecology and cultural politics in South Asia. Her recent work explores the social and cultural dimensions of urban river conservation initiatives in Kathmandu, Nepal.

Carrie Turk is currently working for the World Bank in Hanoi, Viet Nam. She is a poverty specialist with an interest in pro-poor macro policy-making and the development of stronger links between policy and participatory processes/research. Currently, this includes supporting work on government strategies to reduce poverty; informing work on making public expenditure more pro-poor; work in making budget and expenditure information more transparent and readily accessible; and coordinating participatory research in poor urban areas.

Haroon Yusuf is an agricultural economist with a special interest in rural livelihoods. His background is in work with pastoralist communities on achieving self-reliance in managing natural resources, and in peace-building after prolonged internal conflict. He is currently working with ActionAid in Somaliland on the development of community-based organizations.

Jenny Yates is a socio-economist specializing in rural livelihoods. She is currently working with DFID on the monitoring and evaluation of rural livelihoods projects. She previously worked with Oxfam GB in northern Mozambique, developing and managing a food security and livelihoods programme focusing on farmer association development and marketing.

Karen Brock is a social scientist with particular interest in policies for poverty reduction and natural resource management. Recent work has looked at the impact of participatory poverty assessments on pro-poor policy; methodological innovation and complementarity in poverty assessments; information, knowledge, narrative and discourses in policy processes; and agropastoral livelihoods in Africa.

Leonard Okello is a social development worker and pro-poor policy advocate, with particular interest in people's participation in local governance, policy formulation and programme implementation. His background is in working with marginalized communities, internally displaced people and refugees in Africa.

Marcus Melo is a political scientist with research interests in public policy, particularly social policy, decentralization and institutional analysis. His recent publications include *Reforma do Estado e Mudança Institucional no Brasil* (1999).

Paul Shaffer is a political economist specializing in the interdisciplinary analysis of poverty. His ongoing research projects focus on the interdisciplinary analysis of poverty dynamics, the development of national poverty monitoring systems in Rwanda, and the interdisciplinary impact evaluation of UN poverty projects in Myanmar.

Petia Kabakcheiva is a lecturer on sociology of the civil sector and social regulation, University of Sofia, Bulgaria. She has authored several university sociology textbooks. Her recent research projects focus on Bulgarian civil society, the decentralization of political decision-making and the role of participatory action and research in this process, local authorities and European structures.

Raj Patel is currently completing his PhD on resistance to economic liberalization in Zimbabwe at Cornell University's Department of Rural Sociology. He is a researcher with SEATINI in Harare and co-editor of *The Voice of the Turtle*.

Robert Chambers is a social scientist with special interest in the development and spread of participatory approaches, behaviours and methods, and perceptions of poverty, illbeing and wellbeing. He is the author of *Putting the Last First* (1983) and *Whose Reality Counts?* (1997).

Rosemary McGee is a social development specialist with a background in anthropological research on poverty and policy, work on poverty assessment methodologies, and policy advocacy in international NGOs. Recent projects focus on civil society participation in national poverty reduction processes and poverty knowledge and policy processes in Uganda.

EDITORS'
ACKNOWLEDGEMENTS

THE EDITORS GRATEFULLY acknowledge funding from the Department for International Development (DFID) in the UK, the Swedish International Development Cooperation Agency (Sida) and the Swiss Agency for Development and Cooperation (SDC) that allowed us to spend time working on *Knowing Poverty*, and to commission work for several of the chapters.

We would also like to thank all our colleagues in the Participation Group at the Institute of Development Studies (IDS), University of Sussex, for their support throughout the process of making this book. Particular gratitude is due to Jane Stevens for her midwifery skills in the publication process, Kelly Greene for preparatory work on the manuscript and John Gaventa, Robert Chambers and Andrea Cornwall for personal and intellectual encouragement. Andy Norton, currently with the Overseas Development Institute, has been a consistent source of support for us both. Our co-authors around the world, some of whom we have never met in person, have all been tremendously patient and supportive throughout the long process of editing, and we have learned a great deal from working with them.

In addition we each have personal debts of gratitude to acknowledge:

While it is impossible to name all the people who have helped me navigate the journey that this book has represented, I would like to give particular thanks to Chris Whitmore and Jane Stevens for giving me a home, to Raj Patel for his infectious faith in the possible, to James Keeley for keeping a parallel path and, most especially, to Tessa Hodsdon and Edwin Rowe for believing, for so long.

Karen Brock

A range of people in far-flung places have urged and helped me, consciously and unconsciously, throughout the sometimes daunting process of translating the experience of fieldwork into the distant and abstract form of development literature, in the hopes that it can somehow make a difference. I want to thank especially Pacho de Roux SJ, Bernardo Molina, the people of Uribe in Colombia and my family.

Rosemary McGee

LIST OF ACRONYMS AND ABBREVIATIONS

ABC	attitude and behaviour change
CAP	community action plan
CAS	Country Assistance Strategy (World Bank)
CBO	community based organization
CDRN	Community Development Resource Network
CGE	computer general equilibrium
CIDA	Canadian International Development Agency
CPR	common property resource
CSO	civil society organization
DFID	Department for International Development (UK)
GoU	Government of Uganda
GRET	Groupe de Recherche et d'Echanges Technologiques
GRIP	Grassroots Immersion Programme (World Bank)
HDI	Human Development Initiative
HDIBS	Human Development Initiative Baseline Survey
HEPR	Hunger Eradication and Poverty Reduction (national programme, Viet Nam)
HIPC	Highly Indebted Poor Countries (World Bank)
IDS	Institute of Development Studies (University of Sussex, UK)
IMF	International Monetary Fund
LSMS	Living Standards Measurement Study (World Bank)
MFPED	Ministry of Finance, Planning and Economic Development (Uganda)
MoLG	Ministry of Local Government (Uganda)
MTEF	Medium-term expenditure framework (Uganda)
NGO	non-governmental organization
NRS	North Rakine State (Myanmar)
PA	poverty assessment
PAF	Poverty Action Fund (Uganda)

PEAP	Poverty Eradication Action Plan (Uganda)
PLA	participatory learning and action
PMA	Plan for the Modernization of Agriculture (Uganda)
PPA	participatory poverty assessment
PRA	participatory rural appraisal
PRSP	Poverty Reduction Strategy Papers (World Bank and IMF)
SACB	Somalia Aid Coordination Body
SAM	Social Accounting Matrix
SCBO	Sanaag Community Based Organization (Somaliland)
SDC	Swiss Agency for Development and Cooperation
SEWA	Self-Employed Women's Association (India)
Sida	Swedish International Development Cooperation Agency
SNM	Somali National Movement
SOSOTEC	self-organizing systems on the edge of chaos
SSD	Studies in Social Deprivation
TCBO	Toghdeer Community Based Organization
UN	United Nations
UNDESA	United Nations Department of Economic and Social Affairs
UNDP	United Nations Development Programme
UNHCR	United Nations High Commission for Refugees
UPPAP	Uganda Participatory Poverty Assessment Project
VIP	Village Immersion Programme (World Bank)
WDR	*World Development Report*
ZEIS	Zonas Especiais de Interes Social (Brazil)

Introduction:
Knowing poverty:
Critical reflections
on participatory
research and policy

Karen Brock[1]

THE USE OF participatory research methods to provide policy-makers with information about poor people's perspectives on poverty became increasingly common during the 1990s. This book presents a series of reflections about participatory poverty research, and the contribution it has made to the process of making policy for poverty reduction. Our aim is to learn from recent and ongoing processes, and to draw lessons for the improvement of future practice.

During the course of the 1980s and 1990s, participation has entered the development mainstream. The 1990s witnessed a shift in the functions and applications of participatory methodologies, adding a focus on participatory research for policy to the project-based activities that were dominant in the 1980s. Much of this effort to bring participation and policy closer together has focused on the issue of poverty, in particular the co-production with poor people of information about poverty which reflects their perspectives.

This book examines not only how participatory research has influenced the way that poverty is framed and understood, but also how that under-standing has been acted on in processes of making policy for poverty reduction. It shows that diverse ways of knowing poverty are part of contemporary poverty reduction policies, and that understanding these better can contribute to improvements both in the content and process of poverty reduction policy. The authors come from a range of backgrounds and disciplines. The reflections they present are concerned with different elements of the relationship between participation and policy. The range of questions they pose are varied: technical, ethical, operational, political and methodological. Through raising their concerns and dilemmas, they highlight areas of current practice from which lessons can be learned, and key emerging issues for future work.

THE CONVERGENCE OF PARTICIPATION AND POVERTY REDUCTION POLICY

The relationship between participation and poverty reduction policy must be seen in the context of shifting discourses of development. Such discourses represent both the way in which the value and purpose of participation are interpreted by powerful development actors, and the shaping of agendas concerning valid strategies and policy instruments for poverty reduction.

Cornwall, reviewing the relationship between participation and development, notes an important divergence of positions concerning the nature of that relationship:

> *For some, the proliferation of the language of 'participation' and 'empowerment' within the mainstream is heralded as the realization of a long-awaited paradigm shift in development thinking. For others, however, there is less cause for celebration. Their concerns centre on the use of participation as a legitimating device that draws on the moral authority of claims to involve the poor to place the pursuit of other agendas beyond reproach. According to this perspective, much of what is hailed as 'participation' is a mere technical fix that leaves inequitable global and local relations of power, and with it the root causes of poverty, unchallenged.* (2000, p1)

The conviction that engaging with mainstream development policy processes offers an opportunity for participatory practices to have a wider impact – the first position Cornwall outlines – has been a major driver of methodological and operational innovations in poverty reduction policy processes, particularly those emanating from multinational development institutions.

Such innovations can be typified by the development of participatory poverty assessments (PPAs), a term that emerged in the early 1990s in the World Bank to describe field-based research exercises designed to contribute to country poverty assessments (PAs). PAs were carried out in most borrower countries during the 1990s; they relied heavily on the quantitative analysis of household survey data to produce consumption-based poverty lines and national poverty profiles, and were important mechanisms for turning the poverty reduction agenda of international development actors into poverty reduction policies at the national level. Although they were policy instruments of the World Bank, as Norton and colleagues note they 'formed a major part of the analytical work sponsored by the donor community in the early to mid-1990s' (2001, p10).

PPAs were developed and introduced as a result of arguments within and outside the World Bank, which advocated a broadening of conventional poverty assessment approaches. This agenda owed a great deal to participatory and social science research during the 1980s, and the critiques it made of household survey methods. It emphasized the multidimensional and dynamic nature of poverty, and the need for field methods that would capture these phenomena from the perspectives of poor people. This conceptual challenge to the orthodoxy of poverty measurement has given rise to methodological questions and dilemmas, particularly concerning the relationship between qualitative and quantitative information and their respective roles in policy. Paul Shaffer (Chapter 2) focuses on some of these methodological issues, which were raised at the interface of different poverty assessment methods during a recent United Nations Development Programme (UNDP) sponsored PPA in Myanmar.

From early experiences in sub-Saharan Africa in the early 1990s, PPAs spread widely within and outside the World Bank.[2] A range of development actors, particularly the UNDP and European bilateral donors, supported PPA processes in many countries of the South, with varying levels of scope and impact. The first wave of PPAs consisted principally of research exercises using participatory methods, which formed the basis of reports aimed at informing both World Bank lending strategies and national policy-makers about poor people's perspectives on poverty. McGee and Norton note, however, that from the outset, the case for PPAs has consisted not only of the broadening of the conceptual agenda of poverty assessment, but also a stress on 'the right of the poor to participate in defining and analysing the phenomenon and processes of poverty as these affect them' (1999, p28). Nonetheless, early PPAs placed their strongest emphasis on increasing the breadth, quality and relevance of information supplied to policy-makers, to contribute to poverty reduction strategies that are better at meeting the needs of poor people.

PPA design and rationale evolved throughout the 1990s. As the practice and experience of PPAs has widened far beyond the framework of World Bank poverty assessments, a third element of rationale become explicit, which 'stresses the opportunities inherent in the PPA process itself to open up spaces in which poor people's perspectives can influence policy-makers' perspectives and practices' (McGee with Norton, 1999, p27). The emergence of 'second-generation' PPAs has been marked by lengthier processes, which have been carefully designed to maximize policy influence through institutional embedding, and are linked to other consultative processes within and outside national governments. The ongoing Uganda PPA is an example of this second generation of practice, and is discussed in Chapter 3 by Jenny Yates and Leonard Okello. The rationale behind second-generation PPAs builds on earlier arguments, but the additional stress on opening spaces for the representation of poor people's perspectives embodies a realization that influencing policy involves far more than the provision of information. Therefore it addresses both the structure of the policy process and the attitudes and behaviours of policy-makers as individuals. The importance of understanding how individuals – particularly policy-makers – learn and change is the subject of reflection in Rosemary McGee's chapter.

As well as developments in theory and practice at the country level, PPA methods have also been used for cross-country comparative studies, aimed at influencing poverty reduction policy at the global level. The largest of these studies, the World Bank's Voices of the Poor, not only carried out fieldwork in 23 countries, but reviewed findings from World Bank PPAs and other participatory research on poverty;[3] it is the largest study of its type to date.[4] The study was carried out to inform the World Development Report 2000, and thus aimed to influence the bastions of development orthodoxy. The multiple components of the study offer rich sources for reflection. Different parts of the Voices of the Poor process form the focus of three of our chapters. Anne Rademacher and Raj Patel reflect on their involvement in analysing the findings of World Bank PPAs. Robert Chambers writes about the experience of being one of a team of writers responsible for producing a book of findings from Consultations with the Poor, the 23-country comparative study of poverty. The authors of Chapter 4, six of whom were in-country researchers for Consultations with the Poor, examine the nature and extent of local impacts of the study in Brazil, Bulgaria, Ethiopia, Somaliland and Viet Nam, one year after it was completed.

As our range of case studies demonstrates, proponents of Cornwall's first perspective on the role of participation in development have enacted their position by applying participatory methodologies to research, and to opening up spaces in the policy process for the articulation of poor people's views and priorities. What, then, of Cornwall's second perspective on participation and development, which sees the adoption of participation on an increasingly wide scale as a legitimization of the activities of powerful development actors, and as a technical shift that does not challenge dominant power relations? Adopting this second position implies understanding participation as part of wider changes in the structures and rhetoric of development. Further, it suggests an examination of structural changes which have allowed invited participation in policy-making processes, and an analysis of the underlying factors that form boundaries to the kind of action that can arise from such participation.

Parallel to the evolution of PPAs outlined above, significant shifts have occurred in discourses of poverty reduction, responding both to development policy failures and to the articulation of alternative development perspectives. The failure of structural adjustment to reduce poverty in sub-Saharan Africa, and the debt crisis of the 1980s, allowed poverty reduction to return to the centre-stage of development for the first time since the mid-1970s. Together with this change of development focus came a widening of the frame of poverty reduction, which saw issues of social and institutional development increasingly forming part of the narratives of economic growth and poverty reduction which characterize development orthodoxy. There has been a second, related shift towards the recognition of a wider range of development actors, who have been invited to participate in poverty reduction initiatives.[5] Alternative agendas on human development, participation and rights have contributed to both of these changes, as have processes of globalization, which have created not only new policy frameworks and interest groups but also new mechanisms for articulating voice.[6]

One effect of these structural transformations has been a new focus on the policy process itself as an integral part of the domain which external development actors explicitly aim to influence with their interventions. Donor agencies' interpretation of their own roles in development is increasingly moving away from the traditional strategy of the direct invest-ment of resources in poverty reduction initiatives, towards facilitating 'broad based pro-poor change in public policy' (Norton et al, 2001, p13).

What, then, do we understand by the word 'policy'? A linear view of policy has been mainstream in public administration and development since the 1950s. From this perspective, policy formulation and implementation are seen as separate processes. This model has been variously described as decision-oriented and top-down, and as resting on the assumptions that rational actions underlie decision-making, and that an optimal policy is possible (Clay and Schaffer, 1984; Schaffer, 1984; Keeley and Scoones, 1999). Although the linear model of policy has been widely criticized, not least for obscuring the extent to which policy is shaped through interactions between various actors at multiple levels as it is translated into action, it remains a remarkably prevalent mindset in development practice. It is congruent with a technical approach to development and orthodox poverty assessment methods, in the sense that it privileges expert and scientific knowledge (McGee and Brock, 2001).

Alternative perspectives on policy suggest that it is more than just a simple process of stating concerns and selecting a strategy: other things matter (Clay and Schaffer, 1984). For some, this has led to a focus on the complexities

of implementation (Lipsky, 1980; Thomas and Grindle, 1990). An imple-
mentation-orientated model of policy is described as being incremental,
overlapping, bottom-up and containing a vision of a direct role for citizens
in the creation of policy (Keeley and Scoones, 1999). For others, it is most
important to see policy as a complex configuration of interest and interactions
between a range of differently positioned actors whose agency matters
(Grindle and Thomas, 1991).

As well as looking at processes of policy-making and the nature of relationships between actors in those processes, it is important to take account of what
actors say and how they frame critical arguments. As Majone reminds us,
'policy is made of words' (1989, p2). He continues by suggesting that debate
and argument are key components of the way that participants in the policy
process learn and change. In this view, a key issue in policy reform is that of
facilitating real, two-way debate, in which participants not only put forward
their own views and interests, but adjust the views they hold as a result of
the process of debate. In terms of the poverty reduction arena, this raises
the question of how to ensure that real debate takes place within the structures
of power and policy that exist in particular social and political contexts.

Many commentators, accepting the notion that policy and discourse
are closely related if not analogous, have focused on the linguistic devices
employed in the policy process, and the mechanisms through which
discourses change. These discussions offer important departures from the way
that policy change – and the role of knowledge in it – is conceptualized in
the mainstream model of development. In place of a version of policy in
which expert-based knowledge is provided to rational decision-makers,
policy discourse analysis suggests that biases, practices and narratives are as
influential in decision-making as 'information' (Apthorpe, 1997).

Many alternative perspectives on policy emphasize the importance of
power in understanding how policy changes. Some critiques have focused
on political power relationships between different interests in a policy process
(Clay and Schaffer, 1984). Others have pointed to the ways in which power
is used to exclude people and issues from the policy agenda (Davies, 1994;
Gledhill, 1994; Gaventa and Cornwall, 2000). Others still have suggested that
the relationship between power and knowledge is an integral part of policy
processes, as it is in all social relations (Shore and Wright, 1997). Understanding the mechanisms through which certain versions of 'reality' are
filtered becomes critical in this version of policy.

In the context of these diverse views on the policy process, what does a
critical perspective on the relationship between participation and poverty
reduction policy imply? Firstly, it suggests the necessity of situating ourselves
as producers of knowledge in policy processes, and reflecting on the structure
of those processes. Secondly, it suggests the need to understand what power
relationships are at play around the production of knowledge within the

policy process. Thirdly, it demands contextualized understandings of how policy changes.

These issues are central to understanding how participatory research can and does influence policy, and for increasing the possibility that new spaces will be opened within processes of formulating and influencing policy in which relatively powerless groups can articulate their interests. Surrounding such processes are the dynamics of power and powerlessness, of personal and institutional learning and understanding, of the social and political context surrounding policy change, and of the creation of information and knowledge. It is dynamics such as these which are addressed by the case studies in this collection.

DILEMMAS AND TRADE-OFFS: KNOWLEDGE, ACTION AND CONSCIOUSNESS

It is our hope that policy-makers will come to understand that what is being scaled up is much more than a 'technique'. Participation is a way of viewing the world and acting in it. It is about a commitment to help create the conditions which can lead to a significant empowerment of those who at present have little control over the forces that condition their lives. (Blackburn and Holland, 1998, p3)

The claim of participatory research to further an empowerment agenda rests on its focus on knowledge, action and consciousness, and their role in catalysing processes of social change and challenges to dominant relations of power (Gaventa and Cornwall, 2000). What has been the fate of these claims in the practice of carrying out participatory research for policy influence? The notion of participation – an 'infinitely malleable concept' (Cornwall, 2000, p6) – has been transformed through its adoption by powerful development actors, and the nature of that transformation has resulted in a version of participation which is heavily weighted towards knowledge production, to the detriment of action and consciousness.

Such shifts have been accompanied, unsurprisingly, by ethical dilemmas, methodological innovation to meet emerging demands, and by debates on research quality and validity. Is it possible to apply participatory research techniques to produce policy messages that are relevant at the national and supra-national level? How do the data emerging from 'contextual' participatory research compare with those generated by 'non-contextual' methods such as household surveys, in terms of their relevance to policy-makers and their validity as the basis for policy formulation?[7] As participatory poverty research and the framing of these questions about it has developed, its very roots have also been under attack. The methods and practice of PRA have been subjected to accusations of hubris (Cooke and Kothari, 2001), doubts as to how participatory it is in practice (Mosse, 1995; Guijt and Shah, 1998), and claims that rapidity, instead of being an asset, can diminish quality (Booth, 1995; McGee, 1998; Chambers, 1995).[8] Thus, the participatory school of poverty research at present confronts both the full range of epistemological questions to which all social research should be subjected, and a series of additional questions relating to its specific characteristics: its participatory quality, its earlier claims of rapidity, and its own foundational epistemological critique of conventional poverty research methods.

Seeing participation in terms of three interlocked, co-evolving components – knowledge, action and consciousness – offers a useful framework for introducing some of the dilemmas raised by these diverse perspectives, and outlining some of the trade-offs between different aspects of participation which we have encountered in practice.

Knowledge: A resource that affects decisions?

Participatory research advocates a more open and democratic process of knowledge production than conventional social science research, through recognising local people's expertise and allowing categories based on local knowledge to be framed and given voice. These views form the basis of action or decision-making.

Participatory research for policy, in contrast with much earlier experience, has sought to influence decision-makers at a centre of power removed from the local arena, whether in a state or national capital or in Washington. This has two important implications for practice.

Firstly, there has been a demand for participatory research to establish methodological credibility among policy-makers who are used to relying on different kinds of research. Participatory research methods have been accepted in dominant institutions as a poverty assessment method, and thus their interface with existing poverty assessment methods has come sharply into focus. This has opened up a technical domain for reflection about participatory methods in the context of debates about validity, representation and applicability. This domain is the focus of Chapter 2. Shaffer examines the contributions and limitations of participatory poverty research for policy. He looks at the limitations of orthodox poverty measurement methods, which arise from relying on stylized accounts of poverty, and argues that the strength of the participatory tools used in the Myanmar PPA lay in their focus on social change and the forces and processes behind it. Using examples from the PPA, he highlights key dilemmas that arise when drawing policy conclusions from local studies, discussing issues of comparability, reliability, the extent to which the issues can be generalized and causal weighting.

Secondly, the process of decontextualizing 'local people's knowledge' has brought questions of representation and distortion to the forefront. Questions about whose voices are raised and whose are excluded as local knowledge is filtered and transposed are addressed in two chapters. Rademacher and Patel examine the process of abstracting local voices to produce a 'global' story about poverty in the analysis of PPAs carried out for the Voices of the Poor study. They identify an important trade-off in the process, whereby the broader analytic relevance of a global narrative of poverty masks important local specificities. They argue that 'acknowledging this trade-off places the researcher and her choices at the centre of the knowledge creation process'.

Similar issues are addressed by Chambers in his contribution, which focuses on the dilemmas and choices he faced as a researcher analysing findings from the Voices of the Poor fieldwork. These choices centre on methodological, epistemological and ethical dilemmas. He argues, as do Rademacher and Patel, for the necessity of reflexivity: the process of reflecting critically on the part one plays as a researcher in the formation, framing and construction of knowledge.

Action: Contexts and possibilities

In participatory research, knowledge is not produced for its own sake, but is seen as being embedded in processes of social change or problem solving, inseparable from the idea of action. Participatory poverty research tends, often implicitly rather than explicitly, to emphasize policy change as the result of an episode of knowledge production. Although this does not preclude the possibility of local action — as illustrated by the activities of local communities in Brazil and Somaliland described in Chapter 4 by Adan and colleagues — it shifts the broad focus for action away from local arenas. This means that developing an understanding of policy contexts is critical to situating action, and understanding what might limit that action.

Yates and Okello's account of the Uganda Participatory Poverty Assessment Project (UPPAP) provides a detailed picture of the process itself and its policy context. As a second-generation PPA, UPPAP was one of the first PPAs to take policy influence into account in the initial design of the process. The dilemmas raised in implementation include trade-offs between different domains of action and limited resources. UPPAP aimed to have an impact not only on the elaboration of national poverty policy, but also on the dynamics of policy implementation at the district level, and on action planning at the village level. At each of these levels, enabling and constraining factors that shaped impacts on policy are discussed.

Adan and colleagues' contribution focuses on the impact of the Consultations with the Poor research in five of the countries in which fieldwork was carried out. While recognizing that the principle objective of the study was to influence the World Development Report 2000, the researchers found that there had been a wide variety of other impacts, which ranged from local-level action to influencing the formation of national poverty strategies. Institutional, social and political features of local contexts are the critical factors in creating enabling environments for action. Among the key constraints identified is the challenge of changing the attitudes of policy-makers and the institutional biases of key poverty policy actors.

Consciousness: How the construction of knowledge produces change

The participatory tradition conceptualizes research as a process of reflection, learning and action, producing the development of a critical consciousness. Consciousness is seen as an important component in challenging existing power relations, and includes the social learning that can take place among those involved in a participatory research process. It is perhaps the most neglected element of participation as applied to poverty research.

This book addresses the issue from three different perspectives. Firstly, as already noted, there is a strong emphasis on researchers themselves developing a critical consciousness. The second perspective asks how policy-makers learn and change, and is the subject of McGee's chapter. She suggests that a little-explored avenue for policy influence is the experiential learning of policy-makers through direct exposure to situations of poverty. When such exposure is supported by an intentional and structured process of self-critical reflection, she argues, it can provoke changes in vision and practice. The chapter draws on reflective writings from fieldwork in Colombia and a process of exper-iential learning in India, and makes suggestions for building experiential learning into the design of participatory poverty research.

Thirdly, Chapter 4 provides a local perspective on consciousness. In Somal-iland, the Consultations with the Poor research was carried out by local residents who were members of community-based development organiz-ations. They situate the research process as part of an ongoing process of participatory reflection and action for local development planning. Local people saw the research as providing them with a 'neutral' space in which to discuss poverty-related issues that were considered contentious in other fora. This was particularly true of the relationship between poverty and gender. The opportunity for reflection offered by the research was seen to have had an impact on subsequent discussions and action planning.

The related issues of knowledge, action and consciousness provide a convenient map to some of the issues under discussion in this book. They also imply a forward agenda: how to move towards practice in participatory research which finds a balance between all three, in order to maximize and occupy spaces in the policy process for poor people's perspectives?

The pursuit of such an agenda implies awareness of a fourth important dimension. This is the question of scale. Case studies for this book are drawn from a very wide range of contexts, from the local to the multinational. The scale of a research episode is an important factor in defining the balance between different elements of participatory practice, and is one of the major determinants of outcome.

The voices and perspectives represented by these six chapters are diverse and mixed. The authors all work at different interfaces of participatory practice and the policy process; we all take different positions in our work and our practice, and the reflections we put forward are not without their contradictions. Our reflections identify and question a multifarious range of channels for influencing policy with participatory research. Collectively, they emphasize the range of entry points which are available to us as actors in policy processes, to engage in knowledge-based relationships with other actors. Broadly, they suggest that improvements in practice might happen as a result of greater attention to balancing knowledge, action and consciousness through a combination of critical reflection, action to offset distortions arising from power relations, and methodological pluralism.

NOTES

1 Many thanks to Raj Patel for work on an earlier draft, and to Rosie McGee and Robert Chambers for their editorial comments.
2 For accounts of the spread of PPAs see Robb, 1999 and Norton et al, 2001.
3 Voices of the Poor consisted of two principal elements: the 'Consultations with the Poor' study, which undertook primary research using participatory methods in 23 countries (published as Narayan et al, 2000a); and reviews of existing PPA and other participatory research on poverty (published as Narayan et al, 2000b and Brock, 1999). The whole initiative was originally called 'Consultations with the Poor', but adopted the title 'Voices of the Poor' in late 1999.
4 The only process at a similar scale was a study supported by the Canadian International Development Agency (CIDA), also called 'Voices of the Poor', which was carried out in five Asian countries.
5 This is perhaps typified by Poverty Reduction Strategy Papers (PRSPs), the policy instrument introduced by the World Bank and the IMF to mainstream poverty reduction at the national level, and a key mechanism for asserting political conditionality over debt relief. Guidelines for implementing PRSPs rely heavily on civil society consultations throughout the policy process.
6 Making one's voice heard politically.
7 Contextual and non-contextual methods are discussed further by Booth et al, 1998 and Hentschel, 1999.
8 These attacks are being countered from within: for example, in PRA's latest incarnation, participatory learning and action (PLA), claims are not made for rapidity, nor are the benefits of rapid interaction extolled.

REFERENCES

Apthorpe, R (1997) 'Writing development policy and policy analysis plain and clear', in Shore, C and Wright, S (eds), *Anthropology and Policy: Critical Perspectives on Governance and Power*, London, Routledge, pp43–58

Blackburn, J and Holland, J (1998) 'General introduction', in Blackburn, J and Holland, J (eds), *Who Changes? Institutionalising Participation in Development*, London, Intermediate Technology Publications

Booth, D (1995) 'Bridging the macro-micro divide in policy-oriented research: Two African experiences', *Development in Practice*, Vol 5, No 4, pp294–304

Booth D, Holland J, Hentschel J, Lanjouw, P and Herbert, A (1998) *Participation and Combined Methods in African Poverty Assessment: Renewing the Agenda*, London, DFID Social Development Division/Africa Division, February

Brock, K (1999) 'It's not only wealth that matters, it's peace of mind too: A review of participatory work on poverty and illbeing', unpublished paper for Voices of the Poor workshop, Washington, DC, September

Clay, E and Schaffer, B (1984) 'Room for manoeuvre: The premise of public policy', in Clay, E and Schaffer, B (eds), *Room for Manoeuvre: An Exploration of Public Policy Planning in Agricultural and Rural Development*, London, Heinemann

Chambers, R (1995) 'Participatory rural appraisal (PRA): Challenges, potentials and paradigm', *World Development*, Vol 22, No 10, pp1437–1454

Cooke, B, and Kothari, U (2001) *Participation: The New Tyranny?*, London, Zed Books

Cornwall, A (2000) 'Beneficiary, consumer, citizen: Perspectives on participation for poverty reduction', *Sida Studies*, No 2, Stockholm, Sida

Davies, S (1994) 'Information, knowledge and power', *IDS Bulletin*, Vol 25, No 2 (Knowledge is Power? The Use and Abuse of Information in Development)

Gaventa, J and Cornwall, A (2000) 'Power and knowledge', in Reason, P and Bradbury, H (eds), *Handbook of Action Research: Participative Inquiry and Practice*, Thousand Oaks, CA, Sage Publications

Gledhill, J (1994) *Power and its Disguises: Anthropological Perspectives on Politics*, London, Pluto Press

Grindle, M and Thomas, J (1991) *Public Choices and Policy Change*, Baltimore, Johns Hopkins Press

Guijt, I and Shah, M K (eds) (1998) *The Myth of Community : Gender Issues in Participatory Development*, London, Intermediate Technology Publications

Hentschel, J (1999) 'Contextuality and data collection methods: A framework and application to health service utilisation', *Journal of Development Studies*, Vol 35, No 4, April, pp64–94

Keeley, J and Scoones, I (1999) *Understanding Environmental Policy Processes: A Review*, Working Paper 89, Brighton, Institute of Development Studies

Lipsky, M (1980) *Street-level Bureaucracy: Dilemmas of the Individual in Public Services*, New York, Russell Sage Foundation

Majone, G (1989) *Evidence, Argument and Persuasion in the Policy Process*, New Haven, Yale University Press

Mosse, D (1995) 'Authority, gender and knowledge: Theoretical reflections on participatory rural appraisal', *Economic and Political Weekly*, 18 March, pp569–578

McGee, R (1998) 'Looking at poverty from different points of view: A Colombia case study', unpublished PhD thesis, University of Manchester

McGee, R with Norton, A (1999) *Participation in Poverty Reduction Strategies: A Synthesis of Experience with Participatory Approaches to Policy Design, Implementation and Monitoring,* Working Paper 109, Brighton, Institute of Development Studies

McGee, R and Brock, K (2001) *From Poverty Assessment to Policy Change: Processes, Actors and Data,* Working Paper 133, Brighton, Institute of Development Studies

Narayan, D, Chambers, R, Shah, M and Petesch, P (2000a) *Voices of the Poor: Crying Out for Change,* Oxford, Oxford University Press

Narayan, D, Patel, R, Rademacher, A, Schafft, K and Koch-Schulte, S (2000b) *Voices of the Poor: Can Anyone Hear Us?,* Oxford, Oxford University Press

Norton, A, Bird, B, Brock, K, Kakande, M and Turk, C (2001) *A Rough Guide to PPAs: Participatory Poverty Assessment, An Introduction to Theory and Practice,* London, Overseas Development Institute

Robb, C (1999) *Can the Poor Influence Policy? Participatory Poverty Assessments in the Developing World,* Washington, DC, World Bank

Schaffer, B (1984) 'Towards responsibility: Public policy in concept and practices' in Clay, E and Schaffer, B (eds), *Room for Manoeuvre: An Exploration of Public Planning in Agriculture and Rural Development,* London, Heinemann

Shore, C and Wright, S (eds) (1997) *Anthropology of Policy: Critical Perspectives on Governance And Power,* London, Routledge

Thomas, J and Grindle, M (1990) 'After the decision: Implementing policy reforms in developing countries', *World Development,* Vol 18, No 8, pp1163–1181

CHAPTER 1

THE SELF IN PARTICIPATORY POVERTY RESEARCH

Rosemary McGee[1]

THIS CHAPTER EXPLORES one way in which the impact of participatory poverty research for policy might be enhanced. Examining the various avenues through which participatory poverty research can influence policy formulation and outcomes, it posits that a potentially important but little explored avenue is the experiential learning of policy-makers themselves through direct exposure to situations of poverty. As illustrated, drawing on reflective writings from the field, such exposure – coupled with a carefully structured process of self-aware, critical reflection – can provoke changes in inward and outward vision and in practice, which affect the policy impact of participatory poverty research. The social science literature on reflexivity and experiential learning, and exposure programmes currently being developed in NGOs and some donor agencies, offer useful theoretical and attitudinal models for building such learning into the design of participatory poverty research.

INTRODUCTION

A PPA team comprising NGO personnel, researchers and government officials arrives in a village. It explains its mission, sets up camp in the health centre, builds rapport, holds dynamic workshops using participatory rural appraisal (PRA) tools with different groups in the community, spends time with people in their homes and fields, joins in agricultural chores, triangulates all findings, and after a week moves on to the next research site. The researchers are experienced, the methods are sound, the villagers are compensated for their efforts by a small grant to support a community project of their choice and design. The findings from around the country are synthesized and disseminated; the PPA ends, the team disbands. Members return to their everyday activities and never think about the villagers again. Sometimes, when needing facts and illustrations about poverty at the micro-level, they consult the PPA reports.

An alternative scenario: the same PPA team arrives in a village. It goes through all the same steps, comes away with the same data, the same community project is funded. The findings from around the country are synthesized and disseminated, the PPA ends; the team disbands. Members return to their everyday activities. They each carry within them the people of the village, their personalities, their homes, their daily lives, their stories, and the experience of putting themselves into these people's hands as novices and outsiders. They use these experiences as reference points when taking decisions in their work. They tell others about them. They think about going back to the village one day, to tell the villagers about the impacts the PPA has had on national and sectoral policy, and on their outlooks.

This chapter is about the difference between these two scenarios. It argues that this difference can be a critical determinant of whether participatory poverty research succeeds in making policy more responsive to the needs of poor people. Its objective is to explore one way in which the impact of participatory poverty research, conducted so as to inform policy, might be enhanced. Drawing on case material from outsiders' experience of immersions in poor communities, it analyses the sort of process undergone by the researchers in the second scenario, and concludes by identifying lessons for enabling policy-makers to see things differently. The terms 'participatory' and 'research' are used loosely and do not refer only to exercises of academic enquiry which satisfy all the requirements of fully participatory research (Cornwall and Jewkes, 1995; Tandon, 1981), but also to research and knowledge-generating processes that employ participatory techniques in some form.

HOW DOES PARTICIPATORY POVERTY RESEARCH TAKE EFFECT?

Ideally, participatory poverty research has the effect of opening up policy processes, permitting the incorporation of poor people's perspectives. These perspectives can then inform policy design and decisions, making them more beneficial to poor people. In addition, the political 'voice' gained by relatively powerless groups in the process can increase their leverage for bringing about sustained improvements in their situations. Which conditions need to be in place for participatory poverty research, specifically, to be taken seriously and have some chance of influencing policy?[2]

In the first place, some clarification is needed of what we mean by 'policy'. As highlighted by Brock (this volume), traditional models of policy-making tend to obscure the extent to which policy is shaped by interactions on multiple levels as it is translated into action. Among other limitations, those models pay insufficient attention to how knowledge is created and applied in policy-making, by whom, and how these actors are positioned. While high-level commitment to poverty reduction is centrally important, it is not itself a guarantee of successful implementation, and neither is the availability of 'perfect' information. Rather, the policy process, and the role of knowledge in it, involve a complex configuration of interests and interactions between a range of differently positioned actors.[3]

By this definition, there are many more 'policy-makers' than those located in the cabinet or parliament, permanent secretaries of ministries or members of the political coteries surrounding national leaders. These additional actors are perhaps better described as 'policy shapers', after Cornwall and Gaventa (2000). For the purposes of this chapter, 'policy-maker' refers principally to the high-level actors formally vested with national decision-making authority, but does not exclude local government officials, who are charged with a similar role at lower levels of decentralized government. They are becoming increasingly influential as policy, planning and budgetary processes are decentralized in more and more countries.

Information is only one kind of input or influence on policy thus defined. The making and implementation of policy are portrayed as less technical, neutral and objective exercises than most approaches to policy analysis suggest. Nonetheless, information is one of the few influences on policy which is broadly legitimate, acknowledged and actively sought by policy-makers and implementers. To have an influence, participatory poverty research, still struggling to establish itself alongside conventional positivist research paradigms, first needs to overcome a general lack of familiarity with this approach in policy circles, and often scepticism and perceptions of inferior quality among policy-makers and technicians. The following conditions have been identified by commentators:

- There has to be a *demand* for participatory research in the policy community, and an *appreciation* of what it can contribute, at least in terms of new information, to get participatory research outputs onto the policy agenda (Bird and Kakande, 2000, p46).

- Participatory poverty research must stand up to *methodological scrutiny* by the non-participatory school concerned that participatory research is 'low-tech' (Kemmis and McTaggart, 2000, p591) and to *ethical scrutiny* by participatory practitioners concerned with safeguarding research ethics (see Narayan et al, 2000a, p16; Chambers, this volume).
- Relatedly, it must be considered *valid*. The validity criteria applied to conventional research have been adapted, with four alternative parallel criteria established for exploring the validity of qualitative and interpretative research: credibility (plausibility), transferability (context-embeddedness), dependability (stability) and confirmability (the degree of explicitness related to values) (Lincoln, 1995, p277; Pretty, 1995, p1255; Marshall and Rossman, 1995, p143).
- It needs to be conducted and presented in forms that are *acceptable and accessible to policy-makers* – that is, conducted over a limited time frame and written up concisely in a format resembling standard policy reports (Conlin, 1985; Rist, 2000).

While all these conditions are necessary, they all correspond to just one of the channels through which participatory poverty research can influence policy: the informational channel. At the most basic level, the new information made available fills lacunae in the mass of data at policy-makers' disposal. This can enable decision-makers and technicians to design, and implementers to implement, better policies and programmes which have a greater poverty-reducing effect (Booth et al, 1998; Norton and Francis, 1992; Robb, 1999, especially section 2.1). On another level, new information generated by participatory research does not only fill information gaps; it also challenges the descriptive categories and concepts used hitherto and demonstrates poor people's capacity to analyse and problematize their own experience.

A second important channel, increasingly discussed in assessments of the impact of PPAs, is the indirect route of stimulating local-level action. In this case, poor people in communities involved in participatory research are stimulated by the experience, or by what they have learned through it about their own and other contexts, to undertake advocacy and action to address their needs (see Adan et al, this volume). This results in the local solution of problems and/or a stronger and more effective response by the state and other agencies to those problems which cannot be solved locally.[4] The stimulation of local action by participatory research processes has been proposed as one among several criteria for assessing the authenticity of participatory and process-oriented inquiry, validity criteria being considered necessary but insufficient for judging this kind of interaction (Pretty, 1995, p1255).

A third channel, which has been emphasized in some analyses of the most recent PPAs such as those in Uganda and Viet Nam, is the impact participatory poverty research can have on the relationships between actors involved in poverty reduction issues (see Norton et al, 2001). This effect, which might be termed the broadening of the 'epistemic community'[5] concerned with poverty reduction, is political in nature. It consists of the formation of new relationships and the strengthening of existing ones between different kinds of actors concerned with poverty and pro-poor policy shifts, so that the policy dialogue is opened up to a larger group of stakeholders with more diverse perspectives and priorities.

It is mainly on these three channels – the informational route, the stimulation of local action and the broadening of the epistemic community – that Booth et al (1998) base their claim that 'PPAs have the potential both to give us a fuller understanding of poverty, and to make it more difficult for poverty to be ignored or side-lined by politicians and other decision-makers' (p5).

A fourth channel, closely connected to the third but little analysed in the literature on participatory poverty research so far, is a more direct impact on policy direction and process via the experiential learning of policy-makers. By this channel, policy-makers gain personal, first-hand knowledge of the 'policy problem' through contact with poor communities. This can engender empathy with poor people and a process of reflexive critical reflection, eventually leading to a heightened commitment among policy-makers to act in the interests of the poor. They may assume the role of 'champion of the poor', advocating for them and their interests through the means available to them. Many decision-makers in southern countries have, of course, had contact with poor communities, but rarely as part of a purposeful learning or 'immersion' in which they are facilitated to reflect on what they learn and to challenge their own preconceptions.

Naturally, given the range of more-or-less visible and legitimate influences and factors that come into play in policy processes, none of these four channels in isolation, nor any combination of them, are enough to guarantee the success of participatory research in influencing policy, nor of policies in reducing poverty. But unlike some of the determinants of success, these four channels can be built in and promoted through careful design and imple-mentation of participatory research. Given that the last avenue is relatively little recognized or explored, it is to this that we now turn.

EXPERIENTIAL KNOWING

The value of experiential knowing is strongly emphasized by the participatory action research, human inquiry and cooperative inquiry schools of social science research.

The basic coin in the realm of knowing is direct, intimate, experiential knowing. Everything else can be likened to banks and bankers, to accounting systems and checks and paper money, which are useless unless there is real wealth to exchange, to manipulate, to accumulate and to order. (Maslow, cited in Reason and Rowan, 1981, p87)

. . .when I interact directly with a person, I construe and encounter him or her as present more fully than when I observe a person interacting with someone else. And the more fully I interact the more fully I construe him or her as a presence. I construe a person more fully as a presence when we are in a very aware, committed, concerned, exploratory, inquiring relationship. Hence [. . .] the paradigm of cooperative inquiry. (Heron, in Reason and Rowan, 1981, p30)

While experiential knowledge is not sufficient in the absence of complementary conceptual knowledge, practitioners argue that it is *sine qua non* for understanding the world of human experience, whether of poverty or other phenomena. Learning experientially requires both a highly developed receptivity and an openness to challenge one's personal values and status:

To be able to listen – really, wholly, passively, self-effacingly listen – [. . .] is rare [. . .] The most important thing in all this [. . .] is an appropriate humility. The researcher should be willing and eager to learn. (Reason and Rowan, 1981, p87, citing Maslow)

A recent overview of education and social psychology literature on how people learn discusses various models of experiential and action learning (Merrifield, 2000).[6] The spiral model of learning suggested by Dewey (1938), the single-loop versus double-loop models proposed by Argyris (1992), the 'perspective transformation' process described by Mezirow (1990), and Freire's 'praxis' – the relationship between thought and action – differ in detail but share one central tenet. All recognize that when experience generates learning, the experience itself transforms the learner, so that subsequent learning will never start from quite the same point. The original vantage point will have been left behind as a result of questioning and reflecting on the assumptions that underpinned it. Such models are a warning against reifying 'experience': experience is partly the process of gaining it, and the past experiences of each individual shape their absorption and interpretation of current and future experiences.

Three caveats are in order. Firstly, 'the belief that all genuine education comes about through experience does not mean that all experiences are genuinely or equally educative' (Dewey, 1938). A range of factors and conditions need to be in place for learning to result, and various tools –

conceptual, procedural and material – have been developed to facilitate this. Secondly, the knowledge gained does not necessarily confer any power to change the status quo: 'knowledge is only power for those who can use it to change their conditions' (Shor, 1992, cited in Merryfield, 2000, p27), and many are constrained by their circumstances from doing so. Thirdly, while learning is undertaken by an individual, putting the learning into practice so as to change the status quo often depends on a larger structure (an organization or firm), full of imperatives and norms that resist the individual's efforts to apply new learning (Merrifield, 2000, citing various authors; Argyris, 1992; Mezirow and associates, 1990).

The transformation of experience or action into learning hinges on a process of critical reflection by the learner. Normal reflection might involve analysing how to do things. Critical reflection involves in addition analysing why, and with what consequences; questioning the validity of the presuppositions one has applied in previous learning. It cannot be done simultaneously with gaining the experience, but requires 'a hiatus' in which to stand back and reassess one's perspectives (Mezirow and associates, 1990). In the context of experiential learning, critical reflection is essentially reflexive – that is, directed towards oneself and one's own behaviour and frameworks of meaning. The resulting shift in personal paradigms can be a painful, even traumatic, process, involving 'the negation of values that have been very close to the centre of one's self-concept' (Mezirow and associates, 1990, p12), and the introduction of new ones based on the new reality one has experienced. The three-step metaphor used in some organizational change literature to conceptualize the change process is apposite: un-freezing, introducing new values and concepts, and re-freezing (Argyris, 1992, p10).

REFLEXIVITY

While reflection is a process for making sense of experience, reflexivity is an attitude, a state of mind. Described as 'a conscious experiencing of the self as both inquirer and respondent, as teacher and learner, as the one coming to know the self within the processes of research itself' (Lincoln and Guba, 2000, p283), reflexivity is an important concept and practice in qualitative research. It forces researchers to come to terms with their research problem and those with whom they engage, and to interrogate the multiple selves which they themselves adopt in the conduct of the research (Lincoln and Guba, 2000, p283–284). It also provides researchers with ways of demonstrating to others outside the research context

their [own] historical and geographical situatedness, their personal investments in the research, various biases they bring to the work, their surprises and 'undoings' in the process of the research endeavour, the ways in which their choices of literary tropes lend rhetorical force to the research report, and/or the ways in which they have avoided or suppressed certain points of view. (Gergen and Gergen, 2000, p1027)

Thus it has the double epistemological function of refining oneself, the human instrument, as the main research tool, and of laying bare one's biases to one's audiences: both with a view to increasing the quality and the validity of the research.

In participatory research literature, reflexivity occupies a role of growing importance. It is described as being 'open and willing to change. . . [it] requires a high degree of critical self-awareness, as well as a capacity for self-evaluation, ie the recognition of one's own limits and the willingness to embrace error' (Blackburn with Holland, 1998, p146). Thus defined, reflexivity has had two main functions in participatory research. The principle of self-awareness proposed by the ABC (attitude and behaviour change) of PRA, which seeks to develop among researchers non-judgemental attitudes and non-hierarchical behaviour towards their local co-researchers, is a form of reflexivity proposed essentially on ethical and moral grounds.[7] Another angle on reflexivity is the 'self-critical epistemological awareness' promoted by Chambers (1997, p32). This seeks to instil in researchers a self-critical monitoring of their application of methods, and has epistemological implications in that the uncritical use of participatory methods and inattention to process and context in interpreting outputs can diminish the quality and trustworthiness of the research.[8]

In this chapter, the arguments for reflexivity are taken a little further. Reflexivity is a means by which personal experience of or exposure to participatory research among people with power can lead to learning and change, so as to affect the impact of the research on policy and its outcomes.

REFLEXIVE CRITICAL REFLECTION ILLUSTRATED

My interest in reflexivity started when conducting ethnographic fieldwork in rural Colombia for my doctoral thesis. I was committed, in a theoretical way, to an experience of anthropological research and exposure to something unknown. My choice of subject – the nature and causes of poverty, how the state assesses poverty and responds to it – was driven partly by intellectual interest but partly by personal politics.

I arrived as a total outsider. I had never felt so conspicuous or alone. For the fieldwork venture to succeed, I was going to have to first narrow the vast gaps between 'me' and 'them'. Alarming though it was to have drawn a virtual blank when trying to find out in advance what an ethnographer was actually meant to do all day in the field, it was more alarming still that no-one had told me how to narrow these gaps.

No one could have: they were built on shifting sands. 'I', as such, would not last long; neither would 'they' as I then conceived of them. In my daily field log I recorded not only the details of what went on around me and the fruits of my data-gathering labours, but also my own internal commentary on 'me' and 'them'. 'They' changed rapidly at first and steadily thereafter, exposing the ignorance and narrow-mindedness that I had brought with me despite my worthy commitments and best intentions. 'I' changed and reverted, changed and reverted. Throughout the log, heartfelt diatribes against the injustices my neighbours suffered are interspersed with exasperated commentary on the sort of behaviour Scott describes as 'everyday peasant resistance' (Scott, 1985) and on the petty frictions and gossip of small community life. But after ten months of spending most of my time in the community, I tore myself away and left in tears, feeling that I was leaving part of myself behind. Writing up the thesis felt less like an exercise to gain a qualification than a labour of love for those who taught me so much and deserve so much better than the injustice of their daily lives. It was also a step forwards along a professional path to doing something about it.

The case material used here to illustrate reflexivity is drawn from two sources. The bulk of it comes from my field log. My research consisted of ten months' ethnographic research in one small, isolated, rural community, and rapid rural appraisal studies in two further communities, to compare the scope and usefulness of contrasting methodological approaches (ethnographic, rapid appraisal and survey questionnaire) to poverty assessment. My log is used here to illustrate a process of reflexive learning by an outsider through an experience of immersion in a poor community. The research was essentially extractive in function,[9] although the methods and approach were largely drawn from the participatory school. Thus, it is not an example of policy-focused research, nor research conducted by a policy-maker. I do not know of any policy-maker involved in participatory poverty research who has published their personal reflections on the process.

A second source drawn on here is a trip report by Ravi Kanbur (Kanbur, 1999), erstwhile leader of the World Bank team commissioned to write the *World Development Report 2000/2001: Attacking Poverty* (World Bank, 2000). This annual, high-profile development publication is influential in shaping development policy, globally and nationally, among both Southern governments and Northern and international donors (see Chambers, this volume). In preparation for drafting the report, some members of the team undertook an 'exposure and dialogue trip' to poor communities, where they were hosted by local people. The exposure was organized by the Exposure and Dialogue Programme of a German organization, the Association for North–South Dialogue (Osner and Krauss, 2000). The Association's starting point is the fact that decision-makers in the North, whose actions are critical in the fight against world poverty, have no personal experience of it. Its activities aim to provide this experience and fresh understandings to Northern and, more recently, Southern decision-makers through an immersion and learning process that leaves participants equipped to deploy their experiential learning in their daily work, to the benefit of people living in poverty.

Kanbur's exposure and dialogue trip was to a community in Gujarat, India, facilitated by the Self-Employed Women's Association (SEWA).[10] As leader of the World Development Report team, Kanbur had some scope to influence the orientation of the Report and its policy messages. On return, he circulated widely among World Bank colleagues and the interested public (via the World Bank web page) his personal reflections on the exposure trip and what he saw as implications for the Report.[11] His 'back-to-office report' is used here to illustrate the potential role of such experiences of immersion and reflection in shaping policy-makers' outlooks.

The excerpts from the sources were selected for the insights they offer into the development of a reflexive attitude, and the power of reflexivity to change outlooks.

REFLECTIONS FROM THE FIELD[12]

Excerpts from my own extensive fieldnotes and writings are grouped into sections here to illustrate particular dimensions and stages of the reflexive process. They were selected after a careful reading of all notes and associated materials written during the field period, and in one case written immediately after it but closely based on fieldnotes. Within each section the excerpts are presented chronologically, since there appears to be some relationship between their substance and the length of my residence in the community.

An early entry reveals the onset of my dilemmas about 'me' and 'them' and the gap between us:

17 June 1996: I have a feeling of guilt and treachery for having been there [at the country estate of wealthy friends] this weekend. As though I'm doing things I didn't come to Colombia to do [. . .], being a class enemy. [. . .] The problem is that [building rapport with these people] is expedient. It makes things happen more quickly, with less personal efforts, at less personal cost, requiring less energy, making less demand, than doing things the normal, troublesome way would. But the problem is that I've come here looking for a particular experience, and mustn't be seduced by ease, comfort, speed, when those I seek to understand have no access whatsoever to these commodities — the very thing which differentiates their lives from 'ours'. . .

Some early observations reflect my own nervousness at having to take up residence in the community. For as long as I felt a totally isolated outsider, some of my feelings towards 'them' verged on intolerance, even disgust:

26 July 1996: I think I've found the place! [. . .] Ugly, ugly scenery, as though the land's been bled for all it's worth. Pines, cabuya,[13] red sore slopes where the earth looks torn away. A storm was brewing, which added to the ugliness. [. . .] It's small but not too small, with an unused market building on the scrubby mess which I suppose does as the plaza, and lots of semi-dismantled market stalls all around it – today was market day [. . .]. There's a taverna[14] right there with crackly music blaring out at top volume, vallenatos[15] and stuff, plus two other sources of loud music nearby. There were a few drunks lying around near the taverna. The church is simple, modernish and ugly, with loudspeakers and bells, and looks very unused. A shop and a billiard hall are at the entrance to the village near where we left the car (couldn't hide it, unfortunately – we were in the village before we knew it and in any case had brought a woman and children who were hitching and they would have spilt the beans even if we hadn't). [. . .] The whole place just looks poor – nothing to embellish it in any way and the soil around looks tired and angry. [. . .] It's going to be very hard. The place is ugly and sad and socially deteriorated [. . .]. But the people we met were good people and have offered their help, and I can do it with their support. It's amazing how much easier I feel with campesinos[16] now than on arrival in Colombia.

6 September 1996: Don Marco Tulio has the worst feet I've ever seen. One dyed green, I presume from some herbal remedy he's had tightly strapped to it without removing it for days; all the knuckles lumpy and many with greenish dried sores; toenails not recognizable as such but thick, greeny-yellow crusty scabs. Well, they have been walking for 90 years. . .

23 October 1996: There's a repulsive smugness about evangelicals. Among the other topics [that an evangelical farmer talked about as I worked with him]: that some people with so much education think they know it all, and in fact they're shrouded in ignorance – men and women (was this aimed at me or am I getting paranoid?) – 'God has kept us in the dark a bit so that we wouldn't see so much rubbish' [. . .] They hate [the richest man in the village] and there was a lot of racist talk against indigenous people and blacks, portraying them as thick or lazy.

Steps in the process of integration, growing familiarity and mutual acceptance were recorded – including the occasional setback, which was devastating in the circumstances:

27 August 1996: I'm not at all desperate at the prospect of staying all day tomorrow here, nor even the next day as well. . .

17 September: Felt like coming home when I arrived today [after a fortnight away from the field]. Doña Floralba and Don José had missed me, and I them, especially her [. . .]. She said the youngest daughter of Mariela Fernández had asked after 'la gringa', and wanted to be informed when I arrived [. . .]

18 September: Floralba invited me in. Sitting on the beds, she told me in a whisper guerrilla stories. Understandable that everyone fears them more than liking them – they had a reign of terror here [. . .] There are informants in the village, who?

23 September: Feels more like coming home each time I arrive. . .

22 October 1996: [On being informed of a local rumour that I was in the village to steal babies for international adoptions] I was stunned, and immediately went back over all my actions, comments, less-than-welcoming receptions [. . .] Here I am trying to get into and understand a small, strange community, feeling chuffed at each success, and meanwhile such rumours endanger my whole being here, and also show some very sad things about how people think.

21 November 1996: Deiba talked about her sister's Argentinian husband who was 'very nice and so unpretentious, a lovely man, because he's got money and is from a good family and everything but when he came here he fitted in so well, made no fuss about anything, treated everyone as an equal'. And went on to say: 'It's like you. That's why my father is so fond of you, and me and my grandparents and my sister and everyone. My father says about you, she's so simple, you just don't feel any shame with her; she's not all superior about having studied and all that; she comes right into the house without pulling faces as if she's smelt a bad smell; she doesn't care what we're looking like or what state the house is in; she treats everyone just as decently as she treats everyone else'.

15 December 1996: Don Gregorio referred to me as a friend this morning. I went to say hello and he checked when I was returning so that he could get me some pineapples from a neighbour, from whom he'd say he wanted them 'para una amiga'. . .

18 December 1996: Floralba told me that Mariela's youngest, Dianey, said when I'd first been to their house, 'There's a gringa who lives up there at Floralba's house, but she isn't a bad gringa, she's a good gringa'. . .

Empathy for people was provoked sometimes by their circumstances alone, but more often on observing the treatment they received at the hands of the more powerful, in which cases the fieldnotes express outrage and anger:

6 September 1996: [On a survey team which had visited on behalf of the public utilities companies] They treat people like shit, these government functionaries[. . .] A team came today to measure some houses, without explaining themselves at all but sticking a sticker on the door saying 'SIAP, Municipality of El Tambo'.

19 September 1996: They behave so vilely, those with money. I've noted before how chiva[17] *drivers stop at every* fritanga *or* gaseosa *stand[18] on the way, only to prove (i) that they have money to eat and drink in every port and (ii) that they're in charge of this* chiva *and have the power to make all 60 people on board sit and wait while they stuff their fat guts. [. . .] They behave like small* caciques.[19] *When people here inch a few inches out of poverty and get somewhere in life, this is how they use it — to show others they've moved one step ahead of them, to swagger and show off and throw money around, to show who's who and what's what and keep people in awe by acting the big man. . .*

21 October 1996: The chiva *left town late [for the village] because several passengers,* cabuya *producers, had been paid in cheques (bastard traders) and were queuing in the bank to cash them [these were farmers whose sole income source,* cabuya *production, had dried up because of a crisis in the national market. Having given all their land over to a monoculture of* cabuya *when the government heavily promoted it years before, they no longer grew any food crops and had waited weeks for payment for their last sale of* cabuya*].*

27 November 1996: I returned from hearing Carlos and Rosa's life stories astonished, as always, at how hard people's lives are, how hard they've had to struggle, and in the case of Rosa, how terribly sad her early life [was]. . .

22 January 1997: The teacher took advantage of the situation to scold the community for ever suggesting they were un-collaborative: 'look at you, this is your committee, your public funds, and you've been called four times to meet and you haven't done so!' She talks to them like babies or imbeciles, really offensive. . .

February 1997: Not everyone can enjoy the dubious luxury of living among the poor to learn from them at first hand. It falls to those of us who can, to disseminate the realities we seek to share. From my experience in Colombia the two impressions I feel most compelled to disseminate are, firstly, that the promotion of 'participation' in development, viewed from below, looks more like a tactic deployed by those at the top to reduce costs, disguised in euphemism. Secondly, carefully drafted development plans whose implementation depends on existing social structures and institutions are, like these structures and institutions, impregnated with power and gender biases. [. . .] A woman whose husband does not allow her to act for the good of her community [by joining the school parents' committee]; a girl whose father would deny her the benefit of literacy; a woman with severe mental disabilities repeatedly raped by her neighbours — all need far more visibility, far more knowledge generated about their situation, and far more radical and transformative policies, if their poverty — not only their lack of income, but their lack of power, their social inferiority, their isolation, their vulnerability — is to be reduced. [. . .] Being a woman, British and committed to social and gender equality, I have sometimes had to face charges of ideological imperialism and arguments of cultural relativism which seek to defend and uphold the status quo in Colombia. [But] failure to denounce injustice is sometimes tantamount to complicity in it. . . (McGee, 1997, pp99–101).

The fieldnotes reveal that I started from a position of intellectual superiority, notwithstanding all my good intentions and careful self-coaching to dispel such distorting and blinkering preconceptions. Entries record how I gradually began to understand why people did the things they did and how distorted some of my early perceptions had been, and how I learnt to respect people's intelligence and rationality.

6 September: People are so inconsistent: only yesterday it was again reiterated to me that one never sees apples round here any more, and today I met an apple-buyer who comes every Friday [to the market] to buy the local apples. . .

19 September: Funny the way people take the piss out of those with money. They all mocked the chiva *driver when he wasn't strong enough to [change a wheel with a punctured tyre], and told a beggar woman who came along that he was the one with the money – he hotly denied this.*

6 October: The annual general meeting of the school's parent association was an opportunity to watch community relations and dynamics in action. The school hall was crowded with some five fathers and 60 others, some of whom had walked for an hour to come. [. . .] Teachers spent much of the meeting haranguing the parents for their lack of support in the struggle to get a secondary teacher for the village, blaming their passive attitude for the delay. [. . .] The teachers then consulted those present about dates for holding a workshop for setting out rules, regulations and grievance procedures for the school, which all parents were obliged to attend. Parents were not forthcoming about dates. The teachers berated them for their lack of interest in their children's education and their laziness in wanting the teachers to do everything. Eventually a mother spoke, saying that for her at least, it was very difficult to extricate herself from domestic and agricultural tasks for even one day, let alone the three demanded. Others murmured agreement. The teachers pressed further, stressing how much of their own time they gave to the community. The parents yielded; dates were set (McGee, 1998, pp177–178)

27 January 1997: [Commenting on the introduction of private health providers and demand-side subsidies for the poor, including many inhabitants of the village, so that they can exercise freedom of choice about which provider to use] Deiba said 'How are we going to choose between all these providers if we don't know anything about any of them? It's senseless. They should have registered all the inhabitants of the village with just one, to save all the confusion that's been caused by having several options and people registering with different ones. . .'

30 January 1997: I feel that the community closes ranks and presents a united front to intruders from outside, and that once these intruders' status starts changing through continued presence or increasing intimacy and trust, the cracks appear. People themselves are very aware of the superficial view which is collected and taken away by most survey enumerators, government or municipal functionaries and agricultural technicians, and are now quite open with me about their hostility, dislike and forms of resistance towards these intrusions. Notwithstanding the great warmth and kindness I have discovered in most people, it seems that their very vulnerability makes every approach towards them a threat until unequivocally proved otherwise.

Kanbur's exposure trip was brief (ten days including both exposure and dialogue components) and the trip report, written up after the event, is short. These factors preclude analysis of trends in his reactions and reflections. Excerpts are presented here as an uncategorized assortment, but some correspond to the categorizations made above.

I am glad that circumstances conspired to send me on this program — it has been one of the most educational and moving experiences of my life.

We experienced the daily routine of our host lady, worked with her, ate with her and her family, and slept and awoke in the same accommodation as her family. It is easy to be cynical about such experiences, since ultimately we get to come away and the host lady does not. But there is nothing like using the same toilet facilities to highlight the gap between what Moses Naim once referred to as our 'G-4 culture'[20] and the reality of the lives of the people we are ostensibly trying to help. There is nothing like walking three kilometres to fetch water and wood for cooking, to put into perspective the stress that all of us sometimes feel in our jobs here in Washington. And there is nothing quite so moving as the quiet dignity and resolve in the face of unimaginable adversity, to give motivation for our own work.

Since it was a weekday, we wondered if it would be possible to go and sit in on a class [at the village school]. Basrabai [the host lady] then informed us that the Master (the teacher) was not there, had not been there for a while, and in fact came once a month, if that. He seemed to be protected by the district level education officer, and could do pretty much what he wanted. In fact, the Master came the next day, because word had got to him that the village had visitors. He came into Basrabai's house, and a conversation started about the school and the children of the village. This was a shocking experience. Thinking the educated guests to be kindred spirits, he launched into a litany of his difficulties and the difficulties of teaching the village children. He referred to them as 'junglees' (from the jungles), a put-down instantly recognizable in India [. . .]. The [. . .] incident encapsulated for me the gap between macro-level strategies and ground-level realities in the poverty reduction discourse, a gap which was revealed again and again in the next few days.

[A man was gored in the face by a cow]. It was late at night, and the nearest doctor was in the next big settlement, 10 kilometres away. Without immediate treatment, the wound was bound to get infected. As it happened, our Jeep was here and [the man] was taken to the doctor and brought back. The fragility and vulnerability of rural life was brought home to me in this incident.

[On the 'dialogue' component that followed the 'exposure' experience] Back in Ahmedabad, all the participants tried to make sense of what they had experienced. Alongside the emotion of the experience (the quiet dignity of our host ladies, and the utter commitment of our SEWA facilitators, moved most of us to tears as we told our stories), we tried to analyse what we had seen and to relate it to the more conventional discourse on poverty reduction strategies.

For my part, I have promised Basrabai that I will return in a year's time to present the WDR to her and to the village.

WHAT GOES ON WITHIN

In each of these two cases, the experience of exposure to situations of poverty had a profound effect on the individual. This section first draws out some lessons about what is needed for the experience to be translated into new knowledge and new ways of applying it. For present purposes, the actors who need to apply these lessons are not researchers, as in my own case, but policy-makers. An effort is therefore made to adapt these lessons to the context of policy-makers responsible for formulating poverty reduction policy. Finally, the various threads of argument are pulled together in a set of practical propositions about how the impact of participatory poverty research can be enhanced via the exposure of policy-makers to situations of poverty.

What makes the experience 'work'?

In both case studies, there was an awareness from an early stage of the size of the gap between the outsider and those with whom s/he interacted. This consciousness led the protagonists to grapple deliberately with the dilemmas – ethical, personal, moral, methodological – posed by this gap. There was a predisposition in both cases to be affected by the experience. The degree of such disposition partly determines how long an exposure needs to be for it to take effect: Kanbur's case suggests that, entered into in the 'right' spirit, even a week can be enough. The experience being potentially turbulent on psychological and emotional levels, it is important that outlets exist for the personal upheaval generated: a bolt-hole for periodic withdrawal during long periods of exposure, as in my case, or the opportunity for sharing the experience with a peer with whom ongoing discussion can take place, as in Kanbur's case.

In addition to strategies for managing the personal impacts of the experience, tools for reflection are needed. Kanbur had a period of structured reflection in which the experience could be processed on leaving the field. The structured reflection experience, which North–South Dialogue builds into its Exposure and Dialogue Programme, provides exactly the 'hiatus' Mezirow and associates (1990) call for, and is discussed in more detail later. I kept a private journal which acted as a non-judgemental 'ear' and an organizer of my thoughts throughout. The functions of a field journal are multiple. As well as being a form of private outlet, it is a prompt for the continual, steady observation of 'me' as well as 'them'; it records the personally rewarding moments in a possibly difficult and destabilizing experience; it forces one to admit to and confront one's departures from intended behaviour and attitudes and makes these harder to paint out of the formal record of the experience; and it acts as a lasting testimony, allowing one to relive or share the experience later.

Can these lessons be adapted for policy-makers?

From my prolonged immersion in an alien community as an anthropological researcher, I would sum up the change process that I went through in terms of various components. One was a self-questioning process, in which I became increasingly uncomfortable with the privileged position I enjoyed in comparison to my hosts. Another was the growth of my respect and liking for the local people, which manifested itself in a gradual adoption of their perspective on things and empathy with them. Another was my ceasing to take my privileges for granted, and the emergence of a commitment to do what I could to narrow the gap.

While intrinsic value might be attached to all these stages, it would be unrealistic to base prescriptions to policy-makers upon such transformative, intimate and emotive foundations. Policy-makers need knowledge on which to base their decisions and actions. They can obtain this through the traditional route of printed and verbally transmitted information – statistical information, or commissioned studies based on conventional or less conventional research methods. But if they can complement this conceptual and metric knowledge with knowledge of the experiential kind, in which they construe poor people as human beings and acquaintances, they can undergo different reactions from those induced by printed and verbal stylized facts. Kanbur's report is a startling testimony to this re-construal of poor people and their human agency.

It is now increasingly accepted that good qualitative research, as well as meeting methodological criteria, should be judged by 'authenticity/ethical' criteria, which emphasize among other aspects 'the fostering, stimulation and enabling of social action' (Lincoln, 1995, p277). This criterion is particularly relevant to the branches of action research and participatory research, wherein the action is conceived as taken jointly by outsiders and local people as co-researchers. This 'new epistemology'[21] is not unproblematic, as it presupposes an ability to act, a freedom from the constraints which many actors – for example, poor people and functionaries who are cogs in bureaucratic machines – face in real life. But in principle, when policy-makers are among the outsiders co-researching alongside local people, the call to action embraces them as well. Policy knowledge ceases to be merely the generation and absorption of technical data and 'facts', and takes on a dimension of deepening ethical and professional commitment to act on the policy problem.

The need for different practical prescriptions for policy-makers as opposed to researchers relates to the different constraints on each kind of 'outsider', and also to the different image and status of social science researchers as compared to policy-makers in governments or donor agencies. Experiential learning, while not widely practised, is a relatively uncontroversial concept today in the world of social science. But how is it received in an institutional context where poverty knowledge is generated strictly for policy purposes, and only technocratic language tends to be taken seriously? The tools for reflection mentioned above are geared towards facilitating a productive processing of the experience by the individual. There is no guarantee that the individual who is a policy-maker, emerging from the immersion experience with changed insights and outlooks, can then transfer the personal impact of her/his experience to the institution or organization within which s/he works.

When policy-makers learn by interacting with their staff or reading policy briefings, they run no risk of stigma, humiliation or the undermining of the authority ascribed to them. Their adoption of the role of *experiential* learners, in contrast, carries all these risks. Kanbur's experiential learning took place at some of the most basic levels – using the sanitation facilities of a poor Indian village; sleeping and waking in the same space as an entire family of relative strangers. As my fieldnotes reveal, this can deeply challenge the self-image and sense of security of even a doctoral researcher, whose position is ascribed far less authority and respect than a government decision-maker's. But if the experience is approached with openness and an attempt to render the process palpable, conscious and progressive, the affirming personal experience can strengthen the individual's resolve and resourcefulness for applying it professionally.

Anthropologists wishing to be taken seriously as policy advisors (and even as academics among other social scientists) long ago developed the art of writing up their reflexive research in a range of diverse literary forms, some predominantly reflexive and introspective, others more tailored to the expectations of non-anthropologists or non-academics. This tactic helps, on the one hand, to solve the problems of the contrasting and apparently incompatible descriptive and analytical styles favoured by anthropologists and policy-makers and bemoaned by Conlin (1985, pp84–85). On the other hand, it also allows for field experience to be written up both in a reflexive, holistic way – thus helping to legitimize field immersion and reflexive practice – *and* in a way that meets the norms of policy reports and briefs – thus increasing the chance that the outputs of reflexive field experience will find their way into usage in a policy context. Publishing the former sort of document would be a new departure for government and donor bureaucrats[22] but the urge to record and sometimes to publicize such experience is often a part of the development of consciousness, and indeed is one way of acting on the 'knowledge' gained. The recent appearance of a few bold, pioneering examples[23] in the public domain may well encourage others to do likewise. Also, emerging frustration with the presentation of participatory research outputs in policy reports, typically over-reliant on tokenistic and marginal forms such as text boxes containing verbatim quotes, is prompting the development of more radical representational forms that might one day include self-critical reflection by outsider participants on the process and the meaning of the experience, rather than the transcription of substance alone.[24]

In defence of reflexive ethnography, Davies has argued that:

> *ethnographic methods may produce valid knowledge without complete participation and total acquisition of local knowledge by ethnographers so long as they honestly examine, and make visible in their analysis, the basis of their knowledge claims in reflexive experience.* (Davies, 1999, p92)

An analogous, though less categorical, argument can be developed about participatory poverty research on the basis of the foregoing discussion, along these lines: participatory poverty research can produce more valid 'knowledge' (in the extended sense outlined above, embracing action for change as well as facts absorbed) if it includes the exposure of influential actors to field realities, and if its outputs – whatever form these take – honestly examine and make visible the basis of these actors' knowledge claims in reflexive experience. Without these components, participatory poverty research can still be valid and useful, but it will be limited to working through only the first three of the four channels of impact mentioned earlier. In themselves these may be insufficient to overcome the obstacles that prevent new information and local-level action from gaining significant purchase.

The effectiveness of the fourth channel does, of course, depend largely on synergies between all channels. If policy-makers learn about poverty experientially, a stronger and more sustained demand for new and alternative poverty information, a more conducive environment for nurturing and responding to demands on policy-makers and deliverers arising from local-level mobilization, and a wider, more varied community of advocates of pro-poor policy are likely to result. The interactions between the different channels, stages of the process and actors involved can be represented diagrammatically (see Figure 1.1).[25]

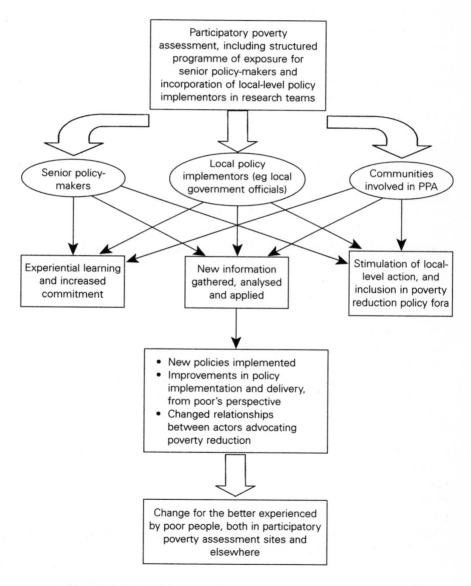

Figure 1.1 *Participatory poverty assessment, actors and impacts*

Practical propositions for enhancing the impact of participatory poverty research

What does the recommendation for 'participatory poverty assessment, including a structured programme of exposure for senior policy-makers, and incorporation of local government officials in research teams' actually mean in practice? Some PPAs have already included senior figures from government or the civil service in their teams, or at least ensured that they were given exposure to field situations during the design, preparatory and training stages of the exercise. Some have incorporated local government officials as key members of research teams and synthesis and follow-up activities.[26] In the Uganda PPA, for example, the high level of government ownership and involvement has led various senior officials to engage in more-or-less planned and sustained ways throughout (see Yates and Okello, this volume). However, no PPA to date has listed the experiential learning of senior decision-makers among its objectives, nor included a structured programme of exposure and dialogue for them among its activities.

The 'factors for success' in the case studies presented here were a mixture of logistical and attitudinal aspects. All of them could feasibly be built into the design of a PPA and some of them could be incorporated into an ongoing one, in the rare cases in which funding arrangements are sufficiently flexible.

Attitudinal preconditions include, first and foremost, a willingness by senior decision-makers to participate and, once they are participating, a predisposition fully to enter into the spirit of the immersion or exposure, and to be conscious of the personal, professional and ethical challenges implied. Superiors need to be prepared both to release their subordinates for the necessary time and to provide opportunities for them to apply the experience in their jobs afterwards, making it strategic to target senior persons before (or simultaneously with) their more junior staff members. These attitudinal preconditions will probably require preparatory work in the form of exchanges of experiences with countries or individuals more familiar with such approaches, and collaborative PPA planning workshops involving the senior officials in question, facilitated by the leaders or 'champions' of the PPA and with the aim of working towards designing practicable exposure programmes.

Logistical factors have already been well thought-through by the Association for the Promotion of North–South Dialogue, and are enshrined in its methods and guidelines.[27] While the exposure and dialogue and part of the reflection all happen within a ten-day period to accommodate the busy schedules of most participants, further follow-up and support is provided at a later point. The Association structures its exposure and dialogue programmes as follows:

- A 'meeting' (extensive personal interaction between guest participant and host), intended to provide the guest with a personal reference point for interpreting and remembering their experience.
- Reflection, which is encouraged by the use of journals and the writing of hosts' life-stories, happens throughout but also, in structured form, takes up a quarter of the programme's duration, coming after the exposure component.
- Dialogue with hosts and other participants, and with external resource people able to facilitate the process of generalizing and drawing transferable lessons from the experience.
- Exposure not only to situations of poverty but also to poor people engaging in self-help initiatives that work, so that participants are inspired to support and replicate such initiatives in their future work.
- Follow-up some months later, including structured group reflection on experiences and attempts to put them into practice, the publication of participants' experience reports and sustained networking among ex-participants.

A review of reports written by a range of participants in World Bank staff immersion programmes (Grassroots Immersion Programme (GRIP) and Village Immersion Programme (VIP))[28] suggests that, while these initiatives have had a profound effect on some participants as they stand, they could transform more participants' outlooks if closer attention were to be paid to the context in which the immersions are carried out, especially the provision of a carefully designed and sustained structure for optimal learning, critical reflection and reflexivity along the lines tried and tested by the Association for the Promotion of North–South Dialogue.

The Association is continually learning from each programme undertaken and revising its approach accordingly. Having been developed with influential decision-makers in mind, some aspects of the design address the special needs of participants who will be implementing their learning in the environment of a large institution. To date, the Association has focused more on individual transformation than on converting this experience into changed institutional attitudes and practices, but it is now turning its attention to the latter (Karl Osner, personal communication).

A further design consideration, relevant when the experience takes place in a research setting rather than an immersion programme, is the desirability of producing outputs in alternative formats. The now-familiar PPA report, of telephone-directory dimensions, would only become more unreadable and unwieldy if its bulk were swollen further with reflexive musings by deeply touched policy-makers. Some alternative formats that merit more serious treatment and offer greater potential impact include video, reflexive and/or creative writing for personal use and restricted circulation, experience-sharing events with counterparts in other countries or sectors where such approaches are still unheard of, and the use of more 'popular', media-based channels of communication.

In years to come, PPAs and similar approaches are likely to become monitoring and mobilizing vehicles in support of Poverty Reduction Strategies or the national equivalent. In this context, powerful stakeholders will be looking for demonstrable impacts from participation and pro-poor policies in the shortest time possible. The risk that PPAs will come to constitute a co-opting of participatory research (as cautioned against by Gaventa and Cornwall, 2000, cited above) is very real, especially given the limited or negligible experience of many governments in leading or engaging in participatory policy processes, and the power relations and disparities – global and national – embedded in the PRSP framework. But as the central promise of the PRSP is country ownership and leadership of the national poverty reduction process, participatory approaches – and especially experiential learning with national policy-makers taking a front seat and international donors trying to take a back seat – stand to make a vital contribution to the long-term goal.

CONCLUSIONS

On the theoretical level, three conclusions can be drawn. First, policy-makers' disposition for personal involvement with poor people in learning about poverty affects the soundness of the knowledge claims they can make. Second, the choice of knowledge-gathering approach can have profound implications for the personal attitudes and outlooks of influential actors in the poverty reduction project. Third, personal attitudes and epistemological soundness both have a bearing on how far participatory poverty research achieves higher audibility, credibility and leverage for poor people in policy development and delivery. Hence, the personal becomes epistemological, the epistemological becomes personal, and the promotion of personal experiential learning by the powerful, structured so as to maximize its transformative potential, is a promising strategy that needs to be more deliberately included in participatory poverty research design than has been the case hitherto. By borrowing theory from various social science literatures and building on incipient practical experiments in experiential learning for development policy-makers, we can construct a new channel for participatory poverty research to have an impact on policy: policy-makers knowing poverty through immersion in the unfamiliar terrain of daily deprivation and struggle for survival.

On a practical level, two major challenges are pending. One is to further build the case for such an approach by monitoring its early outcomes and identifying changes wrought by those who have benefited from exposure and learning experiences. So far there are few candidates, but each new initiative in this regard needs to incorporate a component of self-monitoring and self-evaluation so as to continuously refine the approach and help convince sceptics of its value. Another challenge is to develop solutions to the problems that policy-makers encounter on returning to their working environment after a transformative experiential learning episode. The solutions are likely to lie partly in equipping individuals with tools to withstand organizational environments hostile to challenges, and partly in integrating programmes for individuals' immersion and exposure with broader programmes of organizational transformation, in which a critical mass of 'insiders for change' is nurtured on several fronts simultaneously.

Other chapters of this book, and other publications on participatory poverty research, ask whether the poor can influence policy. This chapter has suggested that participatory poverty research as commonly practised provides opportunities for them to do so only very indirectly. The identity and agency of the participatory researchers (or other outsiders involved as intermediaries) are crucial factors in influencing policy, and then only under certain conditions. The poor can influence the information outputs that researchers put before the policy-makers; they can articulate their demands through actions of their own which might or might not succeed; they can influence the positions of policy-makers if enabled to participate in more open and diverse policy fora, but they can influence the policy-makers themselves if brought face-to-face, on their own ground, in a process of co-existence and outsider learning. Efforts to maximize the impact of poverty research now need to concentrate on exploiting these opportunities to the full.

NOTES

1 Comments on an earlier draft from Karen Brock, Robert Chambers, Juliet Merrifield, Andy Norton and Karl Osner are gratefully acknowledged.
2 A conducive policy environment, in terms of institutions, governance and economic stability, has been identified as a vital prerequisite for public action on poverty to occur, whether prompted by research or other stimuli. This was a finding of a six-country study in Africa by Greeley and Devereux (1999). The existence of this precondition has also been considered critical to the comparative success of the Uganda Participatory Poverty Assessment Project (UPPAP) in influencing policy, as analysed in detail by McClean (1999) and Bird and Kakande (2000). It is beyond the scope of this chapter to deal in detail with the broader environment: suffice it to note that, given a reasonably conducive political and institutional context, participatory poverty research can have more or less impact on policy, which is the issue of interest here. For the case of PPAs (as defined by the World

Bank, which is a wider definition than some would use), Robb (1999) has discussed the impact they have had on policy, and the means by which this influence occurs.

3 This discussion of policy owes much to conversations held in the context of research into poverty knowledge and policy processes being carried out by IDS's Participation Group and funded by DFID.

4 Attwood and May (1998) argue that the prime objective of PPAs should be to stimulate this sort of local empowerment and growing control over development processes. For some examples, see Yates, 2000 and Yates and Okello (this volume) on the Uganda PPA; Melo, 2000 on some sites involved in the Voices of the Poor exercise in Brazil; and Agyarko, 1997 on the Ghana PPA.

5 Haas (1992) defines epistemic communities as 'networks of knowledge-based experts'. Wright (1995, p79) uses the term 'policy communities', which she defines loosely as 'all the people and organizations involved' in a policy initiative, '[. . .] not a rhetorical but a political space'.

6 This section draws heavily on the paper, and on comments from Merrifield on an earlier draft of this chapter, which are gratefully acknowledged.

7 An offshoot of the recent focus by practitioners on ABC is that PRA has, in some contexts, come to mean 'participatory reflection and action' or 'participation, reflection and action': in Pakistan, for example, there is now a Participatory Reflection and Action Network (Robert Chambers, personal communication).

8 An example of self-critical epistemological awareness is found in the Bangladesh Human Development Report (UNDP, 1996), based on a participatory appraisal. The researchers kept field diaries recording their observations and impressions of the participant communities and research process, and some of these, reproduced in the final report, are important clues to interpreting findings and assessing the usefulness of the research outcomes.

9 Some findings were written up and published in Colombia in an attempt to inform social welfare policy and the poverty safety-net system, but my lack of personal influence and institutional backing, and the low credibility of qualitative and participatory research in Colombian policy circles meant that they had negligible impact.

10 SEWA is an organization of poor, self-employed women workers. Its aim is to organize women workers for full employment, with job security, income security and food security.

11 Two complex and contested questions that cannot be answered here are whether and how the exposure and dialogue programme had an impact on the *World Development Report*; and how and to what extent the WDR influences development globally.

12 Where the source is not given, the excerpt is from my field log. References for other sources are given in the bibliography.

13 *Cabuya* is henequen or *Agave Furcrae*, used for making sacking and rope. It has been the main cash crop grown and processed in this region since it was introduced and actively promoted by the government in the 1950s. Demand has recently collapsed as synthetic alternatives have taken over.

14 A bar.

15 A genre of Colombian music, typically played in bars and very popular in *campesino* communities. The lyrics are usually about unrequited love.

16 Peasants or country people.

17 The local form of transport connecting rural communities in the Andean region. A *chiva* is a vehicle with a truck cabin and an open back on which a wooden structure is built to accommodate people seated on wooden benches. Luggage, market produce, livestock and so on travel on the roof or on a platform at the rear.

18 *Fritanga* is fried food, often sold with *gaseosa* – fizzy drinks – at stalls by the sides of roads.

19 *Cacique:* chief, headman, local ruler; local party boss; despot (Collins Spanish–English/English–Spanish Dictionary).

20 G-4 is the type of visa required for entry to the US by those non-US citizens working in the international financial institutions. Naim, once an Executive Director at the World Bank, used the term 'G-4 culture' to sum up the vulnerable and sometimes compromising position in which non-US citizens working at the Bank find themselves vis-à-vis Bank management, given that their stable, affluent North American lifestyle could disappear overnight with the loss of the Bank job and the G-4 visa (Ravi Kanbur, personal communication).

21 Discussed in many of the contributions to Reason and Rowan, 1981, and also many contributions to Denzin and Lincoln, 2000.

22 As evinced by the dearth of case material I encountered when researching this chapter.

23 For example, the series of back-to-office reports by members of Bank staff taking part in the *World Development Report 2000/2001* Exposure and Dialogue Programme, and other Bank immersion experiments like the Grassroots Immersion Programme (GRIP) and the Village Immersion Programme (VIP), made public on the Bank website.

24 As mentioned above, the Bangladesh Human Development Report (UNDP, 1996) goes some way towards doing this, but the diary excerpts are restricted to impersonal observations of the process and discussions of the methodological implications of process issues.

25 Thanks to Robert Chambers for the beginnings of this diagram.

26 In the UPPAP, Ministry of Finance, Planning and Economic Development staff accompanied researchers through much of the training process, including field piloting of methods. Researchers were also visited during fieldwork by Ministry officials and donor staff. Each field research team included one member of the district government, who was expected subsequently to play a pivotal role in institutionalizing participatory approaches in district planning systems.

27 For further information, see the Association's website at www.exposure-nsd.de, or Osner (1999) and Osner and Krauss (2000).

28 See World Bank website, www.worldbank.org.

REFERENCES

Agyarko, R (1997) 'In Spite of the Rains, The Ground is Still Dry':The Ghana Participatory Poverty Assessment Studies – Impact, Implications and Lessons for the Future, abstract, Brighton, IDS

Argyris, C (1992) On Organizational Learning, Oxford, Blackwell

Ascher, W (1994) Scheming for the Poor: The Politics of Redistribution in Latin America, Harvard, Harvard University Press

Attwood, H and May, J (1998) 'Kicking down doors and lighting fires:The South African PPA' in Holland, J with Blackburn, J (eds) (1998) Whose Voice? Participatory Research and Policy Change, London, Intermediate Technology Publications

Baulch, B (1996a) 'Editorial – The new poverty agenda: A disputed consensus', IDS Bulletin, Vol 27, No 1, January, pp1–10

Baulch, B (1996b) 'Neglected trade-offs in poverty measurement', IDS Bulletin, Vol 27, No 1, pp36–42

Bird, B and Kakande, M (2000) 'The Uganda Participatory Poverty Assessment Process' in Norton, A et al (2001) A Rough Guide to PPAs: Participatory Poverty Assessments – An Introduction to Theory and Practice, London, DFID

Blackburn, J with Holland, J (eds) (1998) Who Changes? Institutionalizing Participation in Development, London, Intermediate Technology Publications

Booth, D (1995) 'Bridging the macro–micro divide in policy-oriented research: Two African experiences', Development in Practice, Vol 5, No 4, pp294–304

Booth, D, Holland, J, Hentschel, J, Lanjouw, P and Herbert, A (1998) Participation and Combined Methods in African Poverty Assessment: Renewing the Agenda, London, DFID Social Development Division/Africa Division

Brock, K (1999) 'It's not only wealth that matters, it's peace of mind too: A review of participatory work on poverty and illbeing', unpublished paper for 'Voices of the Poor' workshop, Washington, DC, World Bank

Brock, K, Cornwall, A and McGee, R (2000) 'Getting it right: Poverty knowledge and policy processes', project proposal submitted to Economic and Social Research Fund of DFID, London

Chambers, R (1995) 'Participatory rural appraisal (PRA): Challenges, potentials and paradigm', World Development, Vol 22, No 10, pp1437–1454

Chambers, R (1997) Whose Reality Counts? Putting the Last First, London, Intermediate Technology

Chambers, R (1998) 'Beyond Whose Reality Counts?: New methods we now need', Studies in Cults, Organizations and Societies, Vol 4, pp279–301

Conlin, S (1985) 'Anthropological advice in a government context' in Grillo, R and Rew, A (eds), Social Anthropology and Development Policy, ASA Monograph 23, London, Tavistock

Cooke, B and Kothari, U (eds) (2001) Participation: The New Tyranny?, London, Zed Books

Cornwall, A and Jewkes, R (1995) 'What is participatory research?', Social Science and Medicine, Vol 41, No 12, pp1667–1676

Cornwall, A and Gaventa, J (2000) 'From users and choosers to makers and shapers: Re-positioning participation in social policy', IDS Bulletin, Vol 31, No 4

Davies, C A (1999), Reflexive Ethnography, London, Routledge

Denzin, N and Lincoln, Y (eds) (2000) Handbook of Qualitative Research (second edition), London, Sage Publications

Dewey, J (1938) *Experience and Education*, New York, Collier Books/Macmillan

Ellen, R F (ed) (1984) *Ethnographic Research: A Guide to General Conduct*, London, Academic Press

Gaventa, J (1998) 'The scaling-up and institutionalization of PRS: Lessons and challenges' in Blackburn, J with Holland, J (eds) *Who Changes? Institutionalizing Participation in Development*, London, Intermediate Technology Publications

Gaventa, J and Cornwall, A (2000) 'Power and knowledge' in Reason, P and Bradbury, H (eds), *Handbook of Action Research: Participative Inquiry and Practice*, California, Sage

Gergen, M and Gergen, K (2000) 'Qualitative inquiry: Tensions and transformations' in Denzin, N and Lincoln, Y (eds) *Handbook of Qualitative Research* (second edition), London, Sage Publications

Greeley, M and Devereux, S (1999) 'Getting it right: Policy, process and poverty reduction – an overview of six SSA country studies', paper presented at second research workshop, Abidjan, African Development Bank, July

Grillo, R and Rew, A (eds) (1985) *Social Anthropology and Development Policy*, ASA Monographs 23, London, Tavistock Publications

Grindle, M and Hildebrand, M (1995) 'Building sustainable capacity in the public sector: What can be done?', *Public Administration and Development*, Vol 15, pp442–463

Grindle, M and Thomas, J (1991) *Public Choices and Policy Change*, Baltimore, Johns Hopkins Press

Guijt, I and Shah, M K (eds) (1998) *The Myth of Community: Gender Issues in Participatory Development*, London, Intermediate Technology Publications

Haas, P (1992) 'Introduction: Epistemic communities and international policy coordination', *International Organization*, Vol 46, No 1

Hentschel, J (1999) 'Contextuality and data collection methods: A framework and application to health service utilization', *Journal of Development Studies*, Vol 35, No 4, pp64–94

Holland, J with Blackburn, J (eds) (1998) *Whose Voice? Participatory Research and Policy Change*, London, Intermediate Technology Publications

IDS (1998) 'Participatory poverty assessments (PPA) topic pack', unpublished information pack, Brighton, IDS

IIED (1995a) *PLA Notes No 24: Critical Reflections from Practice*, London, IIED

IIED (1995b) *PLA Notes 22*, London, IIED

Kanbur, R (1999) 'Basrabai, Meeraiben, and the Master of Mohadi: Back-to-office report' (Annex 2), *Approach and Outline: World Development Report 2000/1, Attacking Poverty*, www.worldbank.org

Keeley, J and Scoones, I (1999) *Understanding Environmental Policy Processes: A Review*, Working Paper 89, Brighton, IDS

Kemmis, S and McTaggart, R (2000) 'Participatory action research' in Denzin, N and Lincoln, Y (eds) *Handbook of Qualitative Research* (second edition), London, Sage Publications

Lincoln, Y (1995) 'Emerging criteria for quality in qualitative and interpretive research', *Qualitative Inquiry*, Vol 1, No 3, pp275–289

Lincoln, Y and Guba, E (2000) 'Paradigmatic controversies, contradictions and emerging confluences' in Denzin, N and Lincoln, Y (eds) *Handbook of Qualitative Research* (second edition), London, Sage Publications

Lipsky, M (1980) *Street-level Bureaucracy: Dilemmas of the Individual in Public Service*, New York, Russell Sage Foundation

Long, N and Long, A (eds) (1992) *Battlefield of Knowledge: The Interlocking of Theory and Practice in Social Research and Development*, London, Routledge

Marshall, C and Rossman, G (1995) *Designing Qualitative Research* (second edition), London, Sage Publications

McClean, K (1999) 'Utilising PPA results to influence policy: Experience in Uganda', note prepared for Global Synthesis Workshop of Consultations with the Poor, World Bank, September

McGee, R (1998) 'Looking at poverty from different points of view: A Colombia case study', unpublished PhD thesis, University of Manchester

McGee, R (1997) 'La brecha de percepciones', *Ensayo y Error*, Vol 1, No 2, pp82–101

McGee, R (1996–97) fieldnotes

Melo, M (2000) 'The consultations with the poor process in Brazil', draft paper prepared for IDS, Brighton, June

Merrifield, J (2000) 'Learning citizenship', unpublished discussion paper prepared for IDS (Participation Group) and Society for Participatory Research in Asia (PRIA), Brighton, IDS, September

Mezirow, J and associates (1990) *Fostering Critical Reflection in Adulthood: A Guide to Transformative and Emancipatory Learning*, Jossey Bass, San Francisco

Mosse, D (1996) 'Authority, gender and knowledge: Theoretical reflections on participatory rural appraisal', *Economic and Political Weekly*, March 18, pp569–578

Narayan, D with Patel, R, Schafft, K, Rademacher, A and Koch-Schulte, S (2000a) *Voices of the Poor: Can Anyone Hear Us?* Washington, DC, World Bank/Oxford University Press

Narayan D, Chambers R, Shah, M and Petesch P (2000b) *Crying Out for Change*, World Bank, Washington, DC

Norton, A and Francis, P (1992) 'Participatory poverty assessment in Ghana: Discussion paper and proposal', draft proposal for the World Bank, Washington, DC

Norton, A, with Bird, B, Brock, K, Kakande, M and Turk, C (2001) *A Rough Guide to PPAs: Participatory Poverty Assessments – An Introduction to Theory and Practice*, London, DFID

Osner, K (1999) 'The exposure and dialogue programme 'Empowerment through Organizing': Brief report and initial evaluation', unpublished report, Bonn, Association for the Promotion of North–South Dialogue

Osner, K and Krauss, A (2000) 'Exposure and dialogue as a powerful instrument for shaping policy-making', presentation at the Second Annual Meeting of WIEGO (Women in the Informal Economy, Globalizing and Organizing), Cambridge, MA, May

Pretty, J (1995) 'Participatory learning for sustainable agriculture', *World Development*, Vol 23, No 8, pp1247–1263

Reason, P and Rowan, J (eds) (1981) *Human Inquiry: A Sourcebook of New Paradigm Research*, Chichester, John Wiley and Sons

Rist, R (2000) 'Influencing the policy process with qualitative research' in Denzin, N and Lincoln, Y (eds) *Handbook of Qualitative Research* (second edition), London, Sage Publications

Robb, C (1999) *Can the Poor Influence Policy? Participatory Poverty Assessments in the Developing World*, Washington, DC, World Bank

Scott, J (1985) *Weapons of the Weak: Everyday Forms of Peasant Resistance*, London, Yale University Press

Shaffer, P (1996) 'Beneath the poverty debate: Some issues', *IDS Bulletin*, Vol 27, No 1, pp23–35

Smith, C, with Bermejo Marcos, M and Chang Rodriguez, E (1971) *Collins Spanish– English/English–Spanish Dictionary,* London and Glasgow, Collins

Tandon, R (1981) 'Participatory research in the empowerment of people', *Convergence,* Vol XIV, No 3, pp20–29

Tendler, J and Freedheim, S (1994) 'Trust in a rent-seeking world: Health and government transformed in northeast Brazil', *World Development,* Vol 22, No 12

UNDP (1996) *UNDP's 1996 Report on Human Development in Bangladesh: A Pro-poor Agenda – Poor People's Perspectives,* Volume 3, Dhaka, UNDP

World Bank (2000) *World Development Report 2000/2001: Attacking Poverty,* New York, Oxford University Press

Wright, S (1995) 'Anthropology: Still the uncomfortable discipline?' in Shore, C and Ahmed, A (eds) *The Future of Anthropology,* London, Athlone Press

Wuyts, M, Mackintosh, M and Hewitt, T (eds) (1992) *Development Policy and Public Action,* Oxford, Oxford University Press

Yates, J (2000) 'Review of the process of implementation of the Uganda Participatory Poverty Assessment Project (the UPPAP)', unpublished report for Oxfam GB, Kampala, Oxfam GB

CHAPTER 2

PARTICIPATORY ANALYSES OF POVERTY DYNAMICS: REFLECTIONS ON THE MYANMAR PPA

Paul Shaffer[1]

Economics is mainly about outcomes. . . [not] about processes. Economists, of course, have models of perfect competition, or bargaining to reach a Nash equilibrium, or surplus extraction and use by the dominant class. But economists' tests show only whether a modelled process is consistent with the measured outcomes. . . Only seldom does the economist empirically explore the processes themselves. (Lipton, 1992, p1541)

INTRODUCTION

THE DYNAMICS OF poverty are complex. There are many variables that may explain why people enter into, escape from, or remain in poverty over the short, medium and long term. Further, these variables interact in ways that are hard to understand and predict. The inherent complexity of processes of poverty-relevant social change would seem to call for detailed empirical studies of actual processes of change with a view to a better understanding of their underlying dynamics. Typically, this is not how the analysis of poverty dynamics proceeds in economics.

The analysis that follows reviews some of the ways that poverty processes are analysed in economics. It argues that a major limitation of these sorts of analyses is the highly stylized account of poverty processes which informs them. In this context, PRA-type or participatory analyses of poverty processes have a central role to play in examining actual processes of social change and the forces that constrain or impel them. There are a number of special problems that arise, however, when attempting to draw policy conclusions from PRA-type analyses of poverty dynamics. A recently conducted PPA in the Union of Myanmar provides a concrete illustration of many of these issues.

The format is as follows: the first section examines the scope and limitations of participatory analyses of poverty dynamics. The second section examines the scope and limitations of economic analyses of poverty dynamics. The third section illustrates some of the issues discussed in the preceding section drawing on the Myanmar PPA. The final section concludes.

Before proceeding, two preliminary points are relevant. First, it is necessary to explain how the term 'poverty dynamics' is being used in the present chapter. For the present purposes, 'poverty dynamics' is defined broadly as processes of social change that increase, reduce or perpetuate poverty. There are at least three points about this definition that are relevant to note. First, poverty dynamics include the longer-term processes contributing to chronic poverty as well as shorter-term processes generating transitory poverty. Second, poverty dynamics are primarily concerned with the causes of (transitory and chronic) poverty and not simply with tracking changes in it, or movements or people into and out of it. Third, poverty does not necessarily refer to low levels of income or consumption expenditure. In economic analyses it tends to be defined this way but not elsewhere, as in the Myanmar PPA. It should be clear that the term 'poverty dynamics' is being used in a different sense from its usage in the recent literature in economics, which tends to focus on transitory poverty and its determinants, though in a way that seems closer to its usage in everyday language.

Second, it is relevant to note my own role in the Myanmar study as well as my own biases and predilections. I was contracted by the United Nations Department of Economic and Social Affairs (UNDESA) to serve as team leader for an integrated study of 'social deprivation' in Myanmar as part of UNDP's Human Development Initiative. UNDP operates under a unique mandate in Myanmar, which places heavy restrictions on direct contacts with government and which aims to reduce poverty through a range of local-level initiatives. The full study included statistical analysis of household survey data as well as the PPA. For the PPA, I was responsible for formulation of the methodology, training and coordinating/participating in the report

drafting process. My approach to the study, which is consistent with my disciplinary background in development studies, was to draw on as many different sources of data and methodological tools as possible, subject to the resources constraints that we faced. Further, a major goal of the study was to rely heavily on local partners for data collection and analysis, and limit my own function to oversight and review.

PARTICIPATORY ANALYSES OF POVERTY DYNAMICS: SCOPE AND LIMITATIONS

How are the dynamics of poverty analysed in the PRA tradition? Typically, a range of techniques, many borrowed from anthropology, are used to understand why people become better or worse off, and/or how their livelihoods change. Examples include focus group discussions, semi-structured interviews, oral histories and time lines. The third section of this paper will review how these techniques were used in the Myanmar PPA to come to an understanding of poverty dynamics.

The great strength of participatory analyses of poverty dynamics is to focus attention squarely on actual, empirically informed processes of social change and the mechanisms that generate them, as articulated by people experiencing them. The small-scale and local nature of the data generated by most such analyses raises immediate questions about its applicability for drawing policy conclusions over a broader area. This poses problems when attempting to draw policy-relevant conclusions. But what do we mean here by 'policy-relevant'?

For the present purposes, 'policy-relevant' refers to a number of characteristics of data, or the data-gathering process, which qualify them as inputs to policy formulation at national or regional levels. Four such conditions relate respectively to issues of comparability, reliability, generalizability and causal weighting. It should be emphatically stated that these types of issues, although often regarded as purely technical, are both ideological (in the broadest sense) and political. They are ideological in that they reflect epistemological positions concerning validity criteria for adjudicating between knowledge claims. They are political in that the way they are handled affects the credibility afforded to research results in political processes.

Comparability issues here relate to whether or not the chosen conception of wellbeing, or poverty, is represented in a common unit across the domain of the comparison. As discussed above, economic analyses satisfy this requirement by using indicators like income, consumption and nutrition. A common feature of PPA-type analyses, on the other hand, is to base analysis on local conceptions of poverty culled through focus group discussions or wellbeing ranking exercises. Two problems immediately arise.

A first problem occurs even in the extremely unlikely event that the 'basket' of deprivation, and weighting of its constituent elements, is identical across communities. The lack of a common unit of measurement precludes inter-personal comparisons of wellbeing across communities because there is no way to distinguish between *levels* of deprivation across communities. The problem for the analysis of poverty dynamics is that locally relevant processes of change can apply to relatively better-off groups (though locally poor) who would not be deemed as 'poor' when using a common standard over a broader population (Shaffer, 1998).

Second, when conceptions of poverty differ across groups, then the under-lying processes of change within each group will be referring to different things. While in principle it is possible to develop finer categories of processes linked with finer conceptions of poverty, in practice it may be difficult because local conceptions of poverty often comprise overlapping dimensions whose relative weighting is extremely hard to ascertain.

The second minimal condition of policy relevance relates to data reliability. Specifically, there must be reason to believe that research results are not investigator-specific but may be replicable if conducted by others in similar circumstances. Some argue that this requirement foists positivist trustworth-iness criteria onto a fundamentally non-positivist research programme (Lincoln and Guba, 1985; Brock, this volume). In fact, it is more likely to draw on the regulative ideal of an 'idealized speech community' than on the notion of a detached, disengaged subject of inquiry (Shaffer, 1999b). In any event, it is unclear how results that are mainly driven by the predilections or prejudices of particular researchers could qualify as policy relevant unless there is some criteria for establishing their validity.

Problems of data reliability affect both economic and PPA-type analyses of poverty dynamics, though they have often not received enough attention in the former case. At the level of data collection, however, there is reason to believe that this problem is more severe, *in principle*, for PPA analyses. The reason is that the process of data collection is much more standardized in economic analyses that rely on fixed-response household surveys.[2] The data-collection aspect of PPA is purposefully less standardized as it seeks to grasp the complexities of local realities using, where possible, local categories and definitions and to enable the unexpected to emerge. Research techniques are modified as the circumstances dictate. Further, the dynamics of focus group discussions make it much more difficult to ensure that the personal predilections of the PPA facilitator are not driving results. This latter point applies equally to the process of filtering information generated during group discussions in the field and, later, when drafting research results (see Chambers, this volume). As a consequence, it is likely to be more difficult to ensure the reliability of PPA-type results and generalize across them.

The third condition relates to generalizing research results from a limited number of local studies across a broader spatial area. By definition, public policy must do this to a greater or lesser extent. Economic analyses do not face this same type of problem because their underlying database is usually representative of a broader geographical area. Generalizing results from case studies, however, requires a judgement about the typicality of findings in the population about which a generalization is made (Hammersley, 1992). The crux of the issues lies in determining 'typicality'. In practice it is very hard to do this, especially given the claim of many PPA practitioners that results are highly contextual and may defy generalization.

Finally, there is the problem of causal weighting. Among the many variables that explain why people enter into, escape from or remain in poverty, which are the most important? As discussed, economic analyses use econometric techniques to address this question. In principle, case studies could approximate this approach by carefully selecting cases that are similar in all characteristics but one, and examining differential outcomes across cases (Martin, 1989). In practice it is extremely hard to find such cases, and it would require an enormous resource commitment to find enough of them to make meaningful statements across many variables. Another approach would be to try to garner people's sense of the importance of different variables in determining outcomes, which could result in a partial ordinal ranking of more-or-less important causes. PPAs do attempt to do this in wellbeing or priority rankings, in which people are asked to rank the relative importance of different variables in explaining relative wellbeing. However, problems arise here if there is wide disagreement about the relative importance of causes and/or if people's perspectives diverge widely.

The weaknesses of participatory analyses of poverty dynamics are the strengths of economic analyses, and vice versa. The following section turns to economic analyses of poverty dynamics and reviews their strengths and limitations.

ECONOMIC ANALYSES OF POVERTY DYNAMICS: SCOPE AND LIMITATIONS

How are the dynamics of poverty analysed in economics? The next section presents a typology of explanatory models used in economics, while the subsequent section discusses the scope and limitations of these analyses.

The dynamics of poverty have been analysed in different ways in economics. It is possible to categorize many such analyses on the basis of the type of data available as well as the amount of 'structure' that is put in the explanatory model. Having 'structure' here refers to being premised on an

Table 2.1 *Typology of economic analyses of poverty dynamics*

	Structure		
Data	Less ⟵		⟶ More
One-off	* Household welfare/poverty status regressions[4]	* SAMs[5]	* Agricultural household models[6]
Time series	* First difference regressions[7] * Growth decompositions[8]		
Panel	* First difference regressions[9] * Poverty status regressions[10] * Duration/hazard models[11]		

A Social Accounting Matrix (SAM) depicts the flow of income and expenditure within an economy between production activities, factors of production (land, labour, capital), institutions (households, firms and governments), capital acounts (investment and saving) and external transactions

explicit explanation of the processes generating observed outcomes. The relevant data distinction depends on whether the explanatory model relies on:

1 data at one point in time (one-off data);
2 data at two or more points in time (time-series data); and
3 data on the same households at more than one point in time (panel data).

Table 2.1 situates a number of economic models within this framework. We arrange the analyses along a spectrum according to whether they have more or less structure. It should be stated that this discussion is meant to be illustrative, rather than an exhaustive account of economic modelling on poverty.[3]

The above models differ in many important ways. For the present purposes, however, their common features are more important. Three seem particularly germane. First, all make use of regression techniques to ascribe numerical values to parameters in the models. Second, the causal processes or pathways through which variables are supposed to influence one another are almost always based on some tenet of economic theory. Third, the central causal mechanism at the individual level, or the force driving causal processes, is almost always based on assumptions of rationality, ie maximizing behaviour, at the individual level.[12]

There are at least three properties of the models presented above which facilitate their use in providing policy-relevant information. Specifically:

1 the wellbeing measures they use facilitate consistent interpersonal comparisons (though assumptions are required);
2 their results may be deemed statistically representative of a given geographical area; and

3 they allow for an estimate of the relative explanatory importance of different variables, which can give a sense of the likely poverty impacts of different policy choices.[13]

First, the wellbeing measures used in the above models facilitate consistent interpersonal comparisons of wellbeing because they are represented in a common unit, which is applied across the domain of the comparison. A common unit implies a common standard with which to gauge the wellbeing status of individuals or households. A common standard is necessary to make consistent interpersonal comparisons of wellbeing in the sense that one's wellbeing status should not depend on village or community-specific standards but to standards common across the domain of the comparison. Likewise, for purposes of national or regional comparisons, it is necessary to identify the poor and derive their characteristics in a consistent way.

Second, findings can stake a claim to being representative of large geographical areas. In most models, this claim is based on the fact that the underlying data are culled from nationally or regionally representative household surveys. In the case of the Social Accounting Matricies (SAMs), the claim is based on its reliance on national accounts data as well.

Third, in principle, the multiple regression framework facilitates an estimation of the relative explanatory importance of the different variables contributing to poverty, though there are important caveats when comparing regression coefficients across variables.[14]

There are many critiques of the above models and their underlying assumptions as tools for explaining complex social phenomena (Gleick, 1987; Lawson, 1997; Hodgson, 1998).[15] The present discussion focuses on their highly stylized and often empirically unexamined accounts of both the *causal* processes through which poverty changes and the *causal mechanisms* driving change. Otherwise put, there is very little *empirical* attention devoted to an understanding of *how* explanatory variables produce their estimated effects. For example, the models with least structure, such as the poverty status or household welfare regressions, end up with large lists of 'determinants' of poverty (such as household size, level of education and region) but very little explanation of the pathways and mechanisms by which these 'determinants' determine.

In many of the models with least structure, such as the poverty status regressions, there is explicit recognition of this fact. The underlying structural equations (which are not included) are held to represent many of the causal processes in question. Two problems emerge. First, it is unclear in what sense regressors may be referred to as 'determinants' rather than 'correlates'. Without an explicit understanding of the causal mechanisms at work, it is unclear why the association between variables is deemed to be causal rather than correlational.[16]

Second, as more structure is added, an evermore stylized depiction of social change emerges. This depiction owes much more to tenets of economic theory than to a detailed empirical understanding of what is going on. An example is provided by the agricultural household model tradition, which is exemplary in its attempt to explain real-world micro-phenomena in an empirically grounded fashion.[17] Even here, however, we begin with a world of rational agents whose underlying problem is to maximize a household utility function subject to budgetary and resource constraints.[18] For the analyst, explaining social change amounts to solving this maximization problem using standard maximization techniques (deriving and solving first-order conditions).[19]

While the model may incorporate many features of real-world economies – such as imperfect information, missing markets, risk and uncertainty – its basic structure is highly stylized and analytically restrictive. What is missing in all of this is an empirically grounded understanding of processes and mechanisms of change. We want to know *how* institutions and social arrangements differentially affect poverty, and not simply whether highly stylized models of maximizing agents (even in the presence of imperfectly functioning markets) are good predictors of observed poverty outcomes.

THE MYANMAR PPA

Overview

A concrete illustration of many of the issues broached in the preceding sections is provided by examining results of the Studies in Social Deprivation (SSD) project.[20] The SSD project was a follow-up to a major fixed-response household questionnaire survey, the Human Development Initiative Baseline Survey (HDIBS), conducted in 1995–96. Results from this survey were presented in tabular form, which facilitated comparisons of household characteristics associated with low levels of many of the included variables (Evans, 1997).

Results from the HDIBS were presented at a workshop organized by UNDP in October 1996, attended mainly by UNDP staff and project personnel.[21] Workshop participants noted that the HDIBS provided scant information on the dynamics of poverty/social deprivation. Specifically, they suggested supplementary analysis on 'the dynamics of poverty, coping strategies and household behavioural response'. These recommendations are translated into the first objective of the SSD project document: 'to identify the causes of poverty and coping strategies at the household level'. It is worth pointing out that the critique outlined by seminar participants is virtually identical to the critique of economic analyses of poverty dynamics outlined above.

It should be noted that the link between the SSD project and UNDP programming was never particularly close. SSD results were supposed to provide inputs to the next cycle of UNDP's Human Development Initiative, but the mechanisms through which this was to occur (ie the exact programming-relevant questions that SSD results were supposed to address) were never clearly specified. It must be said that more thought was given to remedying knowledge gaps on poverty than to linking research closely to programming. This is one reason why the impact of this study on UNDP programming has been quite limited.[22]

Understanding poverty dynamics entailed the analysis of actual processes of impoverishment, perpetuation of poverty or escape from poverty. The conceptual framework used in the PPA to address this question is presented in Figure 2.1. It distinguishes between coping and enabling strategies. The former are responses to downward pressures (stresses and shocks). The latter are responses to upward pressures (opportunities). Coping strategies might be successful, fending off downward pressures, or unsuccessful, precipitating entry into poverty/social deprivation (or descent into greater poverty/social deprivation). Likewise, enabling strategies might be successful, precipitating escape from poverty/social deprivation, and/or unsuccessful, culminating in a steady state of poverty/social deprivation. The ability to take advantage of opportunities and/or fend off stresses and shocks depends on the forms of capital[23] with which communities and individuals are endowed. The four forms of capital of particular importance for the present study were: economic capital (land, labour, physical capital, credit, assets); social/political capital (social networks, organizations and social relations); environmental capital (the natural resource base and its management); and physiological capital.

In addition to general concerns of social change and seasonality, there were two thematic entry points for the analysis: gender and the environment. Specifically, attention focused on the gendered effects of social change processes. The environmental dimension focused on environmental stresses and shocks as well as local strategies of natural resource management.

Methodology

This conceptual framework is operationalized *primarily* by means of a range of PRA techniques collectively grouped under the rubric of a PPA.[24] The main PRA techniques used to understand the dynamics of poverty were focus group discussions and semi-structured interviews. Particular emphasis was placed on village and life histories with a view to understanding major reasons for changes in wellbeing over time. These were supplemented with an assortment of ranking, mapping and diagramming techniques including social maps, natural resources maps, time lines and Venn diagrams. Figure

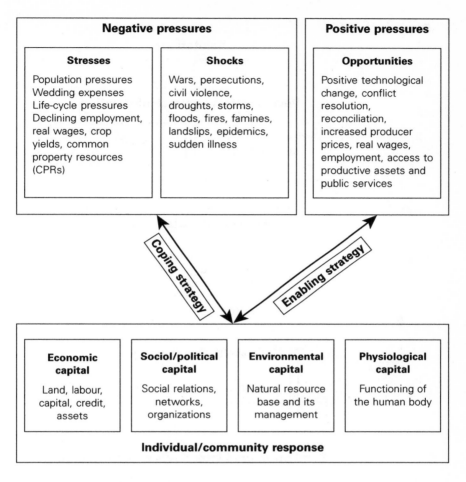

Figure 2.1 *The dynamics of social deprivation*

2.2 presents a typical village work plan, which shows the sequencing of these techniques.

The PPA was conducted in 12 villages in four different regions of Myanmar (Northern Rakhine State, Shan State, Delta Region and the Dry Zone). Two study teams comprising four to six people each visited six villages over a span of approximately two months. Team members included PRA specialists, agricultural specialists and economists. Research teams stayed in each village for approximately one week. Both teams comprised members who had lived for extended periods in the regions covered and were familiar with local practices in some, though not all, of the sites visited.

Three components of the methodology of the village studies dealt specifically with issues related to social change and seasonality: the history/social change focus group discussion (day 2), semi-structured interviews

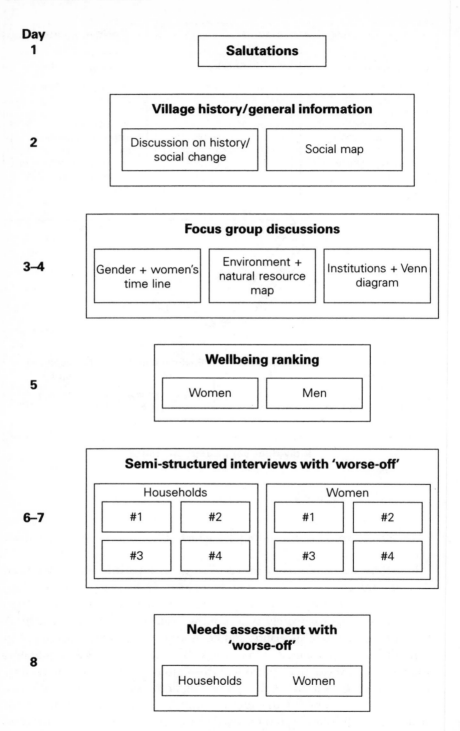

Figure 2.2 *A typical village work plan*

with 'worse-off' households (days 6–7) and the priority ranking with 'worse-off' households (day 8). These exercises sought answers to the following questions:

- What are the major events (positive and negative) in village history and how has life changed?
- Has the village and/or worse-off households become better-off or worse-off, and why?
- Do villagers and/or worse-off households become better-off or worse-off over the course of a year and why (seasonality)?
- What are the major problems of the village and/or worse-off households?
- What are the major needs of the village and/or worse-off households?

Three components of the methodology of the village studies dealt specifically with issues related to gender: the gender focus group discussion (days 3–4), semi-structured interviews with worse-off women (days 6–7) and the priority ranking with worse-off women (day 8).[25] These exercises sought information on the following issues:

- the present state of, and changes in, specific aspects of social deprivation of potential relevance to women and girls (time burden; control of household finances; decision-making authority; intra-household distribution of consumption (especially nutritional intake); access to education; domestic violence);
- major external (downward and upward pressures) and internal (coping and enabling strategies) factors contributing to any such changes;
- institutions and organizations of particular importance to women; and
- major problems facing women and proposed solutions.

Three components of the methodology of the village studies dealt specifically with issues related to the environment: the environment focus group discussion (days 3–4), semi-structured interviews with worse-off households (days 6–7) and the priority ranking with worse-off households (day 8). These exercises sought answers to the following questions:

- What are the most important environmental pressures facing the village and/or worse-off households?
- What are the coping or enabling strategies people use in response to these pressures (in particular, successful coping strategies?)
- What do villagers need to enable them to respond better to these pressures?

This methodology allows for comparison of views of better-off households/women, who presumably dominated the focus group discussions, and households/women identified as worse-off in the wellbeing ranking, who participated in the semi-structured interviews and the priority rankings.

Main policy-relevant findings

The main operational implications of the Myanmar PPA are presented below. Only some of these will be discussed in subsequent sections but including them all gives an idea of the sort of policy conclusions drawn from the village studies. It should be noted that some of the findings could very well have come from household survey data. It might be useful, therefore, to explain how some results differ and to clarify the relationship between data collection and analysis.

First, the preceding critique of economic analyses of poverty dynamics applied to a limited group of analyses whose database usually consists of fixed-response questionnaires. The point was to highlight the limitations of the analytical framework, ie reducing social change to a constrained maximization problem, rather than to criticize the database.

Second, there is the issue of data contextuality. National household surveys are tailored to reflect country-specific characteristics but not community-specific characteristics. Thus, it is likely that certain locality-specific characteristics will be missed in national questionnaires, even after a good pre-test. One example is information on local coping strategies in the face of environmental stresses (below). This could be captured if open-ended questions were included in questionnaires, but, as mentioned, the vast majority of household surveys that measure living standards are fixed-response.

Third, there is the issue of contextuality in analytical categories. In economics, variables that figure in models include land, labour, consumption and household characteristics. The choice of these variables is usually based on theoretical assumptions about their importance in explaining outcomes, assumptions which are not restricted by local or national boundaries. The problem here is that important country- or locality-specific variables tend to receive short shrift. For example, in rural Myanmar, the understanding of social change (or its absence) is predicated on an understanding of the role of the monastery and Buddhist culture in village life.[26] Of course, it is possible to include a 'monastery' variable in a regression, but this is almost never done. More importantly, the critical issue is to understand *how* Buddhist culture influences even economic decisions, such as those relating to savings and labour supply. This issue would be missed even if the 'monastery' variable were included.

Fourth, there is the issue of the sources of information on poverty processes. In economics, when explicit accounts of processes appear they almost always come from some tenet of economic theory. For example, in some versions of the agricultural household model tradition, a household's production decisions are driven by profit-maximization considerations and are a function of land and labour inputs and prices. If assumptions about market structure change, then a different model is required.[27] Sometimes these assumptions are reasonable approximations of production decisions, but at other times they are not. For example, the production decisions of Bengali women in parts of Northern Rakhine State (below) are hardly guided by profit maximization considerations, but by oppressive social norms that impose severe mobility and occupational restrictions, actively devaluing female work contributions and instilling notions of female inferiority. In this context, the understanding of processes drawn from economic theory hardly seems relevant.

Social change and seasonality

The coping and enabling strategies used by worse-off households are highly variegated and extremely diversified. One common theme, often repeated in the semi-structured interviews, is that villagers cope with illness, death, crop failure and drought by selling off assets such as livestock and land. This provides support for income-generating activities, which also create assets such as livestock breeding. There are important seasonal dimensions to the (downward and upward) pressures that households face. It might be prudent to tailor project intervention to respond to the most pressing stresses that households face at particular times in a year. Thus, for example, credit provision to make up for seasonal shortfalls of income (for consumption or productive purposes) might be appropriate. In over half of the villages, population pressures were cited as major forms of downward pressures. This finding attaches urgency to the imperative of increasing factor productivity in agriculture, and/or non/off-farm activities, to forestall increased rates of rural–urban migration. Concerning methodology, there are systematic differences between better-off and worse-off households in their perception of pressing problems and needs. This finding strongly suggests that the results of 'participatory' meetings or assemblies with better-off village representatives should be treated with caution if the objective is to get the views of worse-off villagers.

Gender

Life-cycle pressures associated with the childbearing years, coupled with high fertility rates, are probably the most frequently cited factor precipitating a deterioration in living standards of worse-off women. This underscores the need for an effective population policy that does not exclude worse-off women. In a significant number of villages, processes leading to female headship (eg death, separation, abandonment or illness of a spouse) were instrumental in precipitating a decline in living standards. It appears likely that there are sub-groups of female-headed households that face severe social deprivation and might be good candidates for targeting. There are important seasonal dimensions to social deprivation with gendered implications. Project intervention should be timed to coincide with periods of relative labour abundance to avoid placing demands on women's labour time in periods of stress. Furthermore, activities that do not require year-round commitments but can be conducted seasonally (petty manufacturing, handicrafts) might be particularly beneficial.

Many women face mobility restrictions due to domestic and childcare responsibilities and security considerations. In the light of this, some home-based income-earning activities (such as livestock breeding) and improvement of transportation links (in particular, the construction of all-weather roads) might be particularly appropriate (livestock breeding ranked highly in many priority rankings for worse-off women). The situation of Muslim women in those parts of Northern Rakhine State in which *purdah* norms are strictly enforced requires special attention. Here, the *sine qua non* of any positive change is educating, organizing and mobilizing (ie empowering) women. The work of Bangladeshi NGOs with experience in this area, such as Nijeri Kori, might be particularly relevant.

Environment

The village studies provide evidence from different regions that worse-off households degrade natural resources, as do better-off households. In almost all cases, villagers are well aware of what is going on, though unaware of obvious solutions. This is one area in which further research is required to identify successful local strategies of natural resource management that can be replicated elsewhere (as discussed below). In some, but not all, situations, villagers have adopted strategies to deal with various environmental stresses, including thatch cultivation in denuded forests, reforestation of mango and rain trees on individual plots, use of traditional water-conservation methods such as checkdams and gully plugs, and use of substitute fuels (pigeon pea, coconut frond and toddy palm leaf). Supplying inputs in support of existing best practices should be examined with a view to determining whether this is more cost-effective than embarking upon new programmes. It is note-worthy that all the successful cases of reforestation uncovered in the village studies involved planting on individual plots of land. This finding provides some support for the view that one way of regenerating fuelwood resources is to confer title or long-term use-rights to individuals or households for common (state) lands. It also implies that further research is required on successful examples of collective action to manage fuelwood extraction with implications, say, for the design of community forestry projects.

Water shortages disproportionately affect worse-off households, and in almost all cases, worse-off women, who have the primary responsibility for water collection. Improving village access to drinking water is one type of intervention that is likely to fare well on both equity and gender-equity grounds.

Problems of policy relevance

The Myanmar PPA provided a host of extremely interesting material about processes of social change with operational implications. In light of the above discussion of the scope and limitations of participatory analyses, it is important to review how issues of comparability, reliability, generalizability and causal weighting were addressed.

Comparability

The two problems of comparability identified earlier related to the difficulties of making interpersonal comparisons of wellbeing consistent across very different communities because of the absence of a common unit across the domain of the comparison, and the prevalence of different conceptions of wellbeing associated with different processes of change across individuals or communities.

The first problem is inherent in the PPA approach and cannot be addressed unless a common unit is selected. This implies that the 'poverty' in 'poverty dynamics' refers to poverty relative to living standards in select villages. This problem was addressed in two ways. First, discussion focused on specific processes themselves and not the associated conception of wellbeing/poverty. For example, the focus group discussions and semi-structured interviews that dealt with environmental issues inquired into important environmental stresses and shocks as well as individual/community responses. Discussion focused on floods, typhoons and deforestation and on local strategies of coping and adaptation. The explicit discussion of underlying conceptions of wellbeing/poverty, for example security of livelihoods or basic consumption fulfilments, was not essential for the inquiry at hand. So, inter-site differences in this underlying conception did not impinge on inter-site comparisons between these specific processes.

Addressing the second problem involved teasing out effects of particular processes that correspond closely to particular dimensions of wellbeing/poverty. Thus, the gender discussion enquired about differences between males and females across a number of dimensions of wellbeing/poverty (health, education, decision-making authority, wealth, status/esteem and food consumption) and the reasons for any identified differences. In this way, particular dimensions of poverty were mapped onto particular processes.

In general, problems of comparability were not as intractable in the analysis of poverty dynamics as they often are when trying to make consistent interpersonal comparisons of wellbeing across very different groups.

Reliability

Reliability issues were addressed in three different ways. First, a training manual with detailed questions was drafted to guide the focus group discussions and semi-structured interviews. The guidelines provided structure for the group discussions and interviews without restricting inquiry to the topics covered. As such, they attempted to enhance reliability by standardizing the types of questions posed by different facilitators in different settings. In training sessions prior to field research, the questions were tested and practised in simulated discussion groups and interviews. This of course limits the open-endedness of the inquiry and the possibilities of discerning and exploring anything unanticipated. However, given the purpose of the SSD, it was felt that a more closed-ended but (conventionally speaking) reliable approach was suitable. Second, interviews and group discussions always involved two or more team members, all of whom actively participated. This was one way to attempt to mute the excessive influence of any one team member on research outcomes. Third, at the report drafting stage, each team member was responsible for at least one village report. All of the individual reports were presented, critiqued and revised accordingly by all team members. This form of quality control served to catch remaining errors of interpretation and build a consensus among team members that report results accurately reflected field-study findings.

It should be emphasized that it is unclear how effective these measures were in improving reliability of results. Revisiting the villages using the same methodology with different facilitators would be one way to find out.

Generalizability

As discussed above, generalizing research results requires a judgement about the typicality of findings across different populations. The Myanmar PPA used a four-stage process to establish typicality, which required:

1 specifying the population characteristics;
2 identifying indicators of those characteristics;
3 selecting broad regions or areas that are *predominantly* characterized by these characteristics; and
4 selecting a limited number of villages that are typical of these broad areas.

More concretely, the primary focus of the study was on coping and enabling strategies of the poor. Variation in coping/enabling strategies is closely related to variation in livelihood strategies (point 1). The selected indicators must be those which *best* differentiate between major livelihood types in a given region (point 2). The actual indicators selected include land-use type (Northern Rakhine State), access to water (Dry Zone), elevation and access to water (Shan State) and water type and land use (Delta Region) (point 3). The selection of particular villages within different land-use categories requires knowledge about whether the village is typical of the broader category to which it belongs (point 4).

There were two secondary criteria used in the selection process: Human Development Initiative (HDI) project area and ethnicity. A percentage of the chosen sites receive HDI project support and are composed primarily of ethnic populations (Bengali, Danu and Karen). These additional criteria, which were specified in the project document, respond to the objective of capturing variation in coping/enabling strategies related to one or both of these variables.

The selection process used in Northern Rakine State (NRS) provides an example. The initial stage of village selection was based on information contained in the economic and financial survey of the townships of Maungdaw and Buthidaung conducted in 1996 by the French NGO, GRET (Groupe de Recherche et d'Echanges Technologiques). The document identified the following five geographical areas and the corresponding land-use patterns:

The above typology did not include the township of Rathedaung, which figures in the present study. Discussions with resources experts familiar with NRS, however, suggested that no significant land-use patterns in Rathedaung were omitted by the above categorization.

The next stage entailed choosing villages that were deemed 'typical' of the different land-use patterns. Two information sources were used: a detailed United Nations High Commission for Refugees (UNHCR) map of the three townships specifying individual village tracts and villages in the three townships, and a discussion with resource persons in Yangon (UNDP project personnel) and NRS (radioed transmission) concerning particular villages to select. Following this process, a preliminary list of villages was drawn up.

The last stage involved final modification of the said list by village team-members in the field. This followed discussion with UNDP project field-staff concerning the accuracy of the above land-use typology, as well as the

Table 2.2 *Geographical areas and land-use patterns*

	Area	Land use
1	Sea and Naaf river	Fishing
2	Salty coastal area	Prawn growing, salt making
3	Lowlands (eventually flooded)	Large/medium paddy cultivation, vegetable gardens
4	Hilly areas	Medium/short paddy, mustard, potato, groundnut, betel leaf cultivation
5	Mountainous areas	Bamboo cutting, cane cutting, wood cutting, thatch cutting

Source: GRET, 1997, p8

typicality and size of selected villages. Village size was relevant because the wealth ranking exercise becomes difficult in very large villages. As a result of the discussion, two modifications were made to the above land-use categorization. First, the 'mountainous area' category was omitted, because there are no real 'villages' in the mountains, just a small number of dwellings occupied by ethnic groups. Second, the sea/Naaf river category was not sharply demarcated from the lowland category, because it was concluded that most fishing villages also engaged in agriculture.

There are a number of limitations of this type of analysis. First, if properly done, results may only be deemed representative or typical of a *limited number* of coping–enabling strategies/livelihood types (proxied by the above indicators). As a consequence, they cannot stake a claim to national represent-ativeness unless the selected livelihood/coping–enabling strategy types cover all those found nationally (the present study clearly does not satisfy this requirement).

Second, the *primary* reliance on one variable per region as an indicator of livelihood/coping–enabling strategy assumes that these variables do not vary widely within a given region. If this assumption is violated, then the chosen indicators will be too broad. They will have to be further disaggregated by other variables that account for the variation in question (eg access to markets/roads, irrigated or rain-fed cultivation, access to modern inputs and extension services).

There are many unanswered questions about the strategy of village selection pursued in the villages studies, including the number of categories and villages required to establish typicality.[28] The provision of answers requires an informed judgement about the many causal variables that are likely to affect poverty outcomes, drawing on different data sources. Here, the regression results on the determinants of poverty, of the sort presented in Section 3, might form the basis for the development of detailed typologies for village selection (and further inquiry on the actual causal mechanisms at work). In any event, the construction of detailed real-world typologies as the basis for the generalization of village-based studies has been under-utilized in poverty analysis and is a promising area for future research.[29]

Causal weighting
Assessing the relative causal importance of the many variables that increase, reduce or perpetuate poverty was the most difficult and least satisfactory part of the Myanmar PPA. There is obviously no basis for assigning a cardinal value to the different variables. The construction of a partial ordinal ranking among them (based on greater or lesser degrees of importance) was based on the frequency with which particular processes were mentioned, as well as the subjective sense of researchers as to their importance. This method is obviously subject to many criticisms and should not be pursued too far.

Nevertheless, it can provide insights when there is general agreement about big differences in causal importance among variables. For example, major one-off or infrequent events, such as cyclones, floods or the construction of a school, have enormous impacts on wellbeing/poverty, often with cumulative effects. Furthermore, life-cycle pressures associated with the early child-bearing years were cited again and again by women as major factors precipitating downward spirals in living standards. Here again, it would be instructive to construct detailed typologies of the sorts discussed above to determine whether a partial ranking of causally important variables could be developed.

One important general lesson from the Myanmar PPA is that concerns of comparability, reliability, generalizability and causal weighting are much more likely to be addressed in a more satisfactory way if the scope of the inquiry is narrow. The dynamics of poverty comprise an extremely broad subject area, which covers a wide range of issues. As the subject area is narrowed to, say, the relationship between environment and poverty, much more precise questions can be formulated and posed, and much more meaningful policy-relevant answers generated. Comparability is likely to be greater as specific aspects of wellbeing/poverty are distilled. Reliability might be enhanced because it might be possible to add greater structure to the content of focus group discussions or semi-structured interviews. Generalizability might be enhanced as it will be easier to develop typologies based on a more limited number of causal variables. Finally, causal weighting might become more tractable, because the scope for controlled comparisons increases as the number of causal variables diminishes.

CONCLUSION

Participatory analyses help to fill an important gap in the analysis of the dynamics of poverty by examining actual processes of social changes and the forces that impel or constrain them. As such, their analytical focus is precisely that area which receives inadequate treatment in standard economics analyses of poverty dynamics.

The highly contextual, village-based nature of the inquiry, however, raises questions about the relevance of any ensuing data for policy formulation. The present chapter has drawn attention to a number of problems in PPA-type analyses, which relate to issues of comparability, reliability, generalizability and causal weighting. Results from the Myanmar PPA provide a concrete illustration of how these issues have been addressed.

Specifically, issues of comparability were addressed by acknowledging the impossibility of making interpersonal comparisons of wellbeing and by clearly linking specific aspects of poverty with specific processes of change. Issues of reliability were addressed by attempting to minimize the investigator effect by developing a training manual with guidelines for focus group discussion, by conducting semi-structured interviews in pairs, and by requiring all team members to draft village reports that were subsequently critiqued by the group and revised. Issues of generalizability were addressed by attempting to base site selection on region-specific typologies of conditions that have important bearings on livelihood patterns. Finally, issues of causal weighting were addressed more subjectively based on the respondent's sense of the frequency and relative importance of different forces of change in their lives.

Taking these issues seriously has important political consequences, in that results are less likely to be dismissed off-hand. In the follow-up dissemination seminar, the fact that we acknowledged the limitations of the study and specified the differences between, say, a generalization and an interpersonal comparison of wellbeing, or between statistical inference and empirical generalization, clearly enhanced the credibility of the study results. At the very least, the ability to respond to these criticisms in public fora strengthens one's hand against those who are eager to dismiss results for other reasons.

There is no doubt that participatory analyses of poverty dynamics have real limitations, but all research programmes do. Rather than eulogizing or decrying them out of hand, it might be useful to profit from their insights without attempting to over-extend their reach. The present chapter and the Myanmar PPA have attempted to do just this.

NOTES

1 I am deeply grateful to my fellow team members in Myanmar – Khin Khin Aye, Hiroki Kajifusa, Ohmar Lwin, Tun Aung Prue, Yee Yee Than, Wah Wah Thein, Win Tun, Ronald Wai and Tin Win – and to Rosemary McGee, Karen Brock and Neil McCulloch, whose comments significantly improved this chapter.

2 For example, a recent guide to the surveys of the World Bank's Living Standards Measurement Study (LSMS) (a major poverty assessment initiative for measuring poverty in developing countries) attempts to reduce the investigator effect through processes of standardization: 'several features of the questionnaire help to minimize interviewer error. . . requiring virtually no decision-making by the interviewer. All of the questions are written out exactly as they are to be asked. Moreover, suggested questions for further probing are printed on the questionnaire. . . together these features reduce the conceptual skills required of the interviewers and the potential for variation among them.' (Grosh and Glewwe, 1995, p6)

3 The notable omissions are multisector models, such as computer general equilibrium (CGE) models.

4 Examples include Glewwe (1991), Kyereme and Thorbecke (1991) and Coulombe and McKay (1996).

5 Examples include Pyatt and Round (1979), Thorbecke and Jung (1996) and Khan (1999).
6 Examples include Singh et al (1986) and Bardhan and Udry (1999).
7 Examples include Wodon (1999) and Glewwe et al (2000).
8 Examples include Datt and Ravallion (1992) and Ravallion and Datt (1996).
9 Examples include Glewwe and Hall (1998), Glewwe et al (2000) and Grootaert et al (1997).
10 Examples include McCulloch and Baulch (2000) and Jalan and Ravallion (2000).
11 Examples include Bane and Ellwood (1986) and Baulch and McCulloch (1998).
12 In economics, 'rationality' usually refers to personal-wellbeing-maximizing behaviour, which entails a correspondence between knowing, preferring and choosing what is in one's own best interests. Rational behaviour, in this sense, may include other-regarding preferences, but precludes situations where one acts against one's own best interests. There are other definitions of rationality used in economics, such as behavioural consistency and strategic choices in game theory, but these are not the standard ones used in applied economics. Good accessible reviews of many of these issues include Hollis (1987) and Sen (1987).
13 Assumptions must be made about projectability over time (observed patterns will repeat) and space (fallacies of aggregation will not occur). A fallacy of aggregation occurs when something that works individually or in small numbers does not work in the aggregate.
14 For example, where variables are highly co-linear, regression coefficients might be individually insignificant and small, yet jointly significant and large. Though there are ways of dealing with multi-colinearity, such as incorporating extraneous information or dropping variables, at times there is no obvious fix. In practice, multi-colinearity is often ignored, as it does not lead to bias (only high variance) of the estimator. A good intuitive discussion of this issue, and econometrics generally, is in Kennedy (1998).
15 The introduction to Bardhan and Udry (1999) provides a concise overview of different objections and shows that proponents of economic modelling are not unaware of their limitations. However, the authors feel that they contribute to an understanding of social phenomena.
16 On the necessity of understanding the mechanisms for explaining causality, see Simon (1979) and Elster (1989).
17 An outstanding application of the model exists in the economic theory of rural organization, which attempts to explain such real-world phenomena as share-cropping, credit-market functioning and interlinkages between factor markets (Hoff et al, 1993).
18 The basic model posits a unitary household that maximizes utility (consumption and leisure) subject to a 'full-income' constraint. The full-income constraint includes a budget constraint (consumption cannot exceed revenue) as well as a number of resource constraints related to labour, land and time. Agricultural household models have been used to explain household decisions related to production and consumption activities, including labour supply and demand and consumer demand. Modified versions of the model have been used to explain a range of human capital outcomes including fertility, education, health and nutrition (Strauss and Thomas, 1995).

19 The basic process is as follows. The first step entails specifying the maximization problem subject to a number of constraints. The second step entails solving this problem by setting the first-order partial derivatives of the original equation to zero and solving simultaneously (this is often facilitated by transforming the original function into a Lagrangian function and solving). The first derivative is set to zero because this represents a maximum or minimum point of a function (the rate of change is neither increasing nor decreasing). The underlying point is that explaining social change is reduced to a constrained maximization problem, which can be solved mathematically and estimated econometrically.

20 The study was undertaken in the Union of Myanmar by UNDESA and UNDP in 1998–99 (Shaffer, 1999a).

21 UNDP/UNDESA, 1997.

22 Issues of lack of credibility or poor quality of results have never been raised as major critiques of the study. On the contrary, the results were well received at a dissemination workshop, which contributed to the decision by UNDESA and UNDP to publish and distribute the study results more widely.

23 'Capital' is used here in a non-technical sense to denote assets or resources that can be drawn upon to meet social objectives, however defined.

24 There is much debate about the meaning of 'participation' and the minimal conditions required if research is to qualify as participatory. The Myanmar study is participatory in the sense that it relied on local definitions of poverty and their causes, and actively involved villagers in research activities. This is, admittedly, a limited definition of 'participatory' in that the research agenda was not set by communities, research results were not drafted by communities and the research project did not entail follow-up action to directly benefit communities. Of course, this type of research raises ethical questions, despite the fact that the research objectives were made clear to all the communities on the first day. In my view, this type of research is ethically defensible if researchers are non-obtrusive, courteous and respectful of the time and resource constraints that people face.

25 Worse-off households were identified in the wellbeing ranking of day 5. Worse-off women were identified in a special wellbeing ranking where individual men and individual women were ranked against each other.

26 The role of institutions, including monasteries, was addressed in the village studies and included in the village-specific reports.

27 Specifically, if markets for land and labour work 'well' then a separation or recursive property holds, which simply means that production decisions are independent of a household's time and land endowments and consumer preferences. Concretely, if households can bring in or hire out land and labour, then household endowments shouldn't matter in production decisions. When these markets function poorly, and/or when insurance markets function poorly in risky environments, household endowments and preferences matter and a new model is required. The point is that the understanding of the processes driving outcomes comes from economic theory and assumptions about market structure, and not from an empirically informed understanding of what is going on.

28 For discussion, see Lipton and Moore (1972).

29 For discussion, see Diesing (1971) and Wilber (1978).

REFERENCES

Bane, M and Ellwood, D (1986) 'Slipping into and out of poverty: The dynamics of spells', *Journal of Human Resources*, Vol 11, No 1

Bardhan, P and Udry, C (1999) *Development Microeconomics,* Oxford, Oxford University Press

Baulch, B and Hoddinott, J (2000) 'Economic mobility and poverty dynamics in developing countries', *Journal of Development Studies*, Vol 36, No 6

Baulch, B and McCulloch, N (1998) 'Being poor and becoming poor: Poverty status and poverty transitions in rural Pakistan', IDS Working Paper No 79, Brighton, IDS

Coulombe, H and McKay, A (1996) 'Modelling determinants of poverty in Mauritania', *World Development,* Vol 24, No 6

Datt, G and Ravallion, M (1992) 'Growth and redistribution components of changes in poverty measures', *Journal of Development Economics,* Vol 38

Deaton, A (1997) *The Analysis of Household Surveys,* Baltimore and London, Johns Hopkins University Press

Diesing, P (1971) *Patterns of Discovery in the Social Sciences,* Chicago, Atherton

Elster, J (1989) *Nuts and Bolts for the Social Sciences,* Cambridge, Cambridge University Press

Evans, A (1997) *Human Development Initiative Baseline Survey,* Yangon, Myanmar, MOA/SLRD/UNDP

Gleick, J (1987) *Chaos: Making a New Science,* New York, Penguin

Glewwe, P (1991) 'Investigating the determinants of household welfare in Côte d'Ivoire', *Journal of Development Economics,* Vol 35

Glewwe, P and Hall, G (1998) 'Are some groups more vulnerable to macroeconomic shocks than others? Hypothesis tests based on panel data from Peru', *Journal of Development Economics,* Vol 56

Glewwe, P et al (2000) *Who Gained From Vietnam's Boom in the 1990s? An Analysis of Poverty and Inequality Trends,* PRE Working Paper No 2275, Washington, DC, World Bank

GRET (1997) 'Rural area of Maungdaw and Buthidang townships. Economic and financial survey', *Discussion Paper,* No 1, January, Maungdaw, Myanmar, Groupe de Recherche et d'Echanges Technologiques

Grootaert, C et al (1997) 'The dynamics of welfare gains and losses: An African case study', *Journal of Development Studies,* Vol 33, No 5

Grosh, M and Glewwe, P (1995) *A Guide to Living Standard Measurement Studies and their Data Sets,* LSMS Working Paper No 120, Washington, DC, World Bank

Hammersley, M (1992) *What's Wrong with Ethnography? Methodological Explorations,* London and New York, Routledge

Hodgson, G (1998) 'The approach of institutional economics', *Journal of Economic Literature,* Vol XXXVI, March

Hoff et al (1993) *The Economics of Rural Organisation: Theory, Practice and Policy,* Oxford, Oxford University Press

Hollis, M (1987) *The Cunning of Reason,* Cambridge, Cambridge University Press

Jalan, J and Ravallion, M (2000) 'Is transient poverty different? Evidence for rural China', *Journal of Development Studies,* Vol 36, No 6

Kennedy, P (1998) *A Guide to Econometrics* (fourth edition), Cambridge, Mass, MIT Press

Khan, H (1999) 'Sectoral growth and poverty alleviation: A multiplier decomposition technique applied to South Africa', *World Development*, Vol 2, No 3

Kyereme, S and Thorbecke, E (1991) 'Factors affecting food poverty in Ghana', *Journal of Development Studies*, Vol 28, No 1

Lawson, T (1997) *Economics and Reality*, New York, Routledge

Lincoln, Y and Guba, E (1985) *Naturalist Inquiry*, Beverly Hills, Sage

Lipton, M (1992) 'Economics and anthropology: Grounding models in relationships', *World Development*, Vol 20, No 10

Lipton, M and Moore, M (1972) *The Methodology of Village Studies in Less Developed Countries*, IDS Discussion Paper No 10, Brighton, IDS

McCulloch, N and Baulch, B (2000) 'Simulating the impact of policy upon chronic and transitory poverty in rural Pakistan', *Journal of Development Studies*, Vol 36, No 6

Martin, R (1989) *The Past Within Us*, Princeton, Princeton University Press

Pyatt, G and Round, J (1979) 'Social accounting matrices for development planning', *Review of Income and Wealth*, Vol 23, No 4

Ravallion, M and Datt, G (1996) 'How important to India's poor is the sectoral composition of economic growth', *World Bank Economic Review*, Vol 10, No 1

Sen, A (1987) *On Ethics and Economics*, Oxford, Basil Blackwell

Shaffer, P (1998) 'Gender, poverty and deprivation: Evidence from the Republic of Guinea', *World Development*, Vol 26, No 12

Shaffer, P (1999a) *Studies in Social Deprivation in Myanmar: Final Consolidated Report*, New York, UNDESA/UNDP

Shaffer, P (1999b) 'The poverty debate with application to the Republic of Guinea', unpublished DPhil thesis, Brighton, IDS, University of Sussex

Simon, H (1979) 'The meaning of causal ordering' in Merton, R et al (eds) *Qualitative and Quantitative Social Research*, New York, Free Press

Singh et al (1986) *Agricultural Household Models: Extensions, Applications and Policy*, Baltimore, Johns Hopkins University Press

Strauss, J and Thomas, D (1995) 'Human resources: Empirical modelling of household and family decisions' in Behrman, J and Srinivasan, T N (eds) *Handbook of Development Economics* (volume IIIA), Amsterdam, Elsevier Science

Thorbecke, E and Jung, H (1996) 'A multiplier decomposition method to analyse poverty alleviation', *Journal of Development Economics*, Vol 48

UNDP/UNDESA (1997) 'Final report', presented to the workshop on the Human Development Initiative Baseline Survey, Yangon, October 9–10

Wilber, C (1978) 'The methodological basis of institutional economics: Pattern model, storytelling and holism', *Journal of Economic Issues*, Vol XII, No 1

Wodon, Q (1999) 'Microdeterminants of consumption, poverty, growth and inequality in Bangladesh', *Working Paper*, No 2076, Washington, DC, Poverty Reduction and Economic Management Sector Unit, World Bank

Learning from Uganda's efforts to learn from the poor: Reflections and lessons from the Uganda Participatory Poverty Assessment Project

Jenny Yates and Leonard Okello[1]

THE UGANDA PARTICIPATORY Poverty Assessment Project (UPPAP) is a project run by the Government of Uganda, and implemented on its behalf over four years by Oxfam GB, in partnership with a range of other NGOs and academic institutions. It is a 'second-generation' PPA, the design of which includes both participatory research and processes for feeding the findings into policy processes and seeks to maximize national ownership. The project's overall aim is 'to bring the perspective of the poor into national and district planning for poverty reduction' (MFPED, 1997, p2). The favourable policy context in which UPPAP is being implemented has been critical in its success in influencing national policy. A detailed examination of its design and implementation to date reveals how certain features have been key to the attainment of a range of impacts. Others have presented challenges of various kinds. This chapter examines the many and diverse outcomes of UPPAP, the range of factors that have contributed to them, and attempts to draw some lessons for contexts outside Uganda.

INTRODUCTION

Designed to last three years, UPPAP got under way in mid-1998. The first year's activities involved a PPA in nine districts of Uganda. The second year focused on using the information obtained for influencing policy, the dissemination of findings at national and international levels, and consultations with district authorities on their capacity for poverty-focused planning. In 2000, dissemination and follow-up took place in districts and communities, and further participatory research was conducted in 2001/2002.

This chapter aims to provide a critical reflection on the UPPAP process and outcomes to date. It draws on material gathered for a process review of the project carried out between April and June 2000 (Yates, 2000).[2] This review included interviews with key stakeholders at the national level: staff of UPPAP and Oxfam, officials in the Ministry of Finance, Planning and Economic Development (MFPED), donors, researchers and directors from seven of the nine institutions that implemented the PPAs in 1998–99. Visits were made to two districts where the PPA was conducted,[3] interviews were carried out with district officials, and group discussions were facilitated in four communities. One co-author of this chapter (Yates) conducted the process review as a freelance consultant. The other co-author (Okello) is an Oxfam employee who has been seconded to UPPAP as project manager since its inception. Thus, both have close links to the UPPAP process and have been intensively involved with it in different capacities.

POLICY CONTEXT AND ORIGIN OF UPPAP

An overview of the contemporary policy context in Uganda is helpful in understanding the conception and realization of UPPAP. The Ugandan economy has been growing at an average of about 6 per cent per annum since 1987. However, from the early 1990s, concerns grew that the benefits of economic growth were not trickling down to the poor. These concerns led, from the mid-1990s onwards, to formidable efforts by the Government of Uganda (GoU) to identify key areas for poverty reduction through consultations with academics, civil society, policy analysts and the public; to direct government resources to these areas; and to try to monitor and ensure that resources are used as intended. UPPAP represented an attempt to make these consultations more comprehensive by including the poor themselves. The GoU's efforts to ensure that resources are used for poverty reduction are summarized below.

Box 3.1 *Ongoing efforts by the GoU to use its resources to reduce poverty*

The Poverty Eradication Action Plan (PEAP) is the Government of Uganda's national planning framework, formulated between 1995 and 1997 with inputs from a variety of actors at the national level, such as employers' and workers' organizations, NGOs and academics. It is envisaged that the PEAP will be revised every three years, in order to ensure that it accurately reflects government's priorities at any one time. The first revision took place in 1999–2000, motivated largely by a desire within the MFPED to include information from and responses to UPPAP. An explicit goal in the PEAP's formulation was to identify strategic areas in which increasing budget allocations would lead to poverty reduction, and since its inception the PEAP has been the major guide to the allocation of resources. Its major areas of focus include:

- creating a framework for economic growth and transformation (measures to maintain macro-economic stability and encourage private-sector investment);
- measures to improve the ability of the poor to increase their incomes (support to infrastructure development, financial services for the poor, agricultural advisory services, etc);
- measures to improve the quality of life of the poor (support to health and education provision, provision of clean water, etc); and
- measures to improve governance and accountability.

When the World Bank and IMF announced in 1999 that eligibility for future debt relief under the Highly Indebted Poor Countries (HIPC) II Initiative would depend on countries producing and implementing a national poverty reduction strategy, Uganda's revised PEAP (2000) was presented and accepted as its poverty reduction strategy paper.

To ensure that government priorities as set out in the PEAP are translated into resource allocations, the GoU introduced the Medium-Term Expenditure Framework (MTEF). The MTEF spells out a three-year programme for the utilization of resources across and within sectors.

Sector investment plans were then needed. Kuteesa (2000) writes: 'Given the MTEF process and the need to focus on PEAP, it became imperative that each sector develop a strategic overall plan concerning the allocation of recurrent and development resources within the identified priorities for a specified period.' Education, health and agriculture have already developed their sector investment plans, while 'other plans which are under preparation include law and order, roads, accountability and water'. The plans show how the various sectors will allocate their resources (as determined by the MTEF) to priority areas within the sectors to maximize the impact on poverty reduction. The UPPAP findings have influenced the focus of some sector plans, particularly the plan for agriculture. Of course the sector investment plans also follow from the gradual move among bilateral donors away from project support to more general budget support.

To further improve transparency and accountability in the allocation of resources, the GoU has also opened up the budget process. During the 1998–99 budget preparation, sector working groups were formed with members from the line ministries, the private sector, NGOs and donors to recommend priority areas for resource allocations to reduce poverty. To ensure the integration of the UPPAP findings in the 2000–01 budget consultation process, the Poverty Eradication Working Group was also established to review each sector's working-group paper for poverty. Budget documents are made public: before final approval of the budget by cabinet, an abbreviated version is published; the 'Background to the Budget', a cabinet policy document giving background on expenditure priorities, is made available; and the MTEF is made available. Efforts are also being made to help the districts to improve their budgeting and planning processes: they are being required and supported to develop their own MTEFs, sector priorities and work plans. At the same time, efforts are being made to ensure transparency and accountability at the local level. For example, announcements are made in the press indicating the amounts disbursed to each district by sector. In the education sector, budget allocations for each school are placed on school notice boards.

The MFPED also established the Poverty Action Fund (PAF) in 1998–99, to channel additional resources from debt relief under the HIPC initiative to priority areas for poverty reduction, as determined overall by the PEAP priorities and as determined in more detail by the sector plans and budget consultation process. The PAF has also received additional bilateral donor support. PAF resources disbursed to line ministries and districts to fund the established priorities cannot be reallocated to other areas. The major beneficiaries under the PAF are: water and sanitation, primary education (projected to increase by more than 25 per cent on 1999–2000 levels) and primary healthcare, projected to increase by more than 80 per cent. Civil society and government officials are involved in monitoring the PAF outlays, with quarterly meetings to discuss delivery against budget allocations.

Monitoring of the impact of the government's efforts on poverty reduction also takes place through the Poverty Monitoring Unit of the MFPED. This collates 'quantitative and participatory data on poverty from both government and non-government sources for the purposes of feeding it into policy formulation. UPPAP is situated within the same department of MFPED as the Poverty Monitoring Unit and the links are strong' (Norton et al, 2001).

As noted by Brock (this volume), from the early 1990s onwards the World Bank promoted the implementation of PPAs in borrower countries. At the same time, a wide range of NGOs in Uganda had been using participatory methodologies in the design of their work and in policy analysis. Concern and protest about the perceived failure of economic growth to deliver poverty reduction in Uganda, combined with this spread of methodologies, meant that 'the ground was ripe in Uganda for a PPA'.[4]

Experience of participatory consultations in poor communities in two districts, carried out in 1997 to inform the World Bank's country assistance strategy, convinced some influential government officials that a large-scale PPA in Uganda would further the development and monitoring of the GoU's poverty policy. Supported by World Bank and DFID staff, they began to develop the idea and lobby for a PPA within the GoU.

Planning, design and implementation

The formulation of the proposal of UPPAP and the establishment of its objectives was undertaken by a small number of committed individuals from the MFPED,[5] DFID and the World Bank. UNDP and the NGOs Oxfam GB and Community Development Resource Network (CDRN) also became involved. A number of activities were undertaken in an attempt to get others on board and to develop the objectives and strategy.

Firstly, attempts were made to learn from the PPAs already carried out in Ghana, Zambia, South Africa, Kenya and Tanzania. This review of past experience showed that while previous PPAs had generated valuable lessons for policy and its implementation, limited use had often been made of the findings. Therefore, the decision was taken that UPPAP should not be a one-off exercise, but a three-year process designed to link findings to policy through GoU ownership and the involvement of key policy-makers at national and district levels. Commenting on a study tour to Tanzania undertaken by stakeholders during the preparation of UPPAP, an official in the MFPED noted 'we identified that the missing link in Tanzania was the involvement of policy-makers. We saw that if UPPAP were to influence policy, government needed to be at its centre'.

Meetings and a workshop were held in the MFPED to which senior officials were invited, including those on the PEAP task force and from line ministries. However, many senior government officials remained sceptical about the utility of conducting a PPA, due to doubts about the reliability of 'qualitative' data.[6] Indeed, some key individuals in the MFPED did not come on board until as late as mid-1999, when the initial results of the research started to come out and were seen to be useful.

Oxfam was then approached to be the implementing agency, due to the feeling that community-level work would be best undertaken by an NGO with experience of participatory techniques. At this time in Uganda, relationships between government and NGOs were not as developed as they are today – indeed, UPPAP has played an important role in breaking down suspicions and creating links. However, Oxfam was acceptable to the MFPED thanks to its work on debt relief, through which it had formed a collaborative relationship with government (Oxfam, 1998). Oxfam raised reservations about its involvement on the basis that this would not lead to the creation of ongoing capacity for participatory policy analysis within Uganda. Ultimately, the key stakeholders involved in the design of UPPAP decided that a number of institutions should be invited to carry out the research in order to avoid depending on any one organization, and nine were selected: five NGOs with experience of participatory and/or socio-economic research, three social-policy research institutions, and the Uganda Bureau of Statistics, which was selected so that links could be built between UPPAP and the Uganda national household survey.

On the basis of these consultations, the objectives of UPPAP were defined and a proposal was developed. Four specific objectives were formulated to:

1 enhance knowledge about the nature and causes of poverty and to generate and apply strategies for poverty reduction;
2 enhance district government capacity to plan and implement poverty reduction strategies using participatory methods;
3 develop systems for participatory and qualitative poverty monitoring; and
4 establish capacity for participatory policy research in Uganda (MFPED, 1997, p4).

In terms of the relative importance attached to the objectives by key stake-holders, when interviewed for the process review about what they hoped to achieve or gain from UPPAP donors noted that their primary interest was in getting a better understanding of the nature and dimensions of poverty to inform their strategies and the PEAP. Government officials stressed their interest in finding out what the poor think government should be doing. Hence the major interest of key stakeholders has been in obtaining inform-ation for national-level policy, not in district capacity-building, and certainly not in community-level action. The activities of UPPAP to date reflect these priorities.

The UPPAP design and proposal deliberately established strategic direct-ions rather than the detail of anticipated activities. 'It was understood from the beginning that the course of UPPAP was likely to be unpredictable and would be influenced by and respond to the rapidly changing policy environ-ment and institutional context in which it was situated' (Bird and Kakande, 2001, p45). Those involved in the project design who were interviewed for the process review stressed these points, noting that 'UPPAP has been a learning process for those involved', and 'we are not through with designing it'. Figure 3.1 shows the process and component activities of UPPAP.[7]

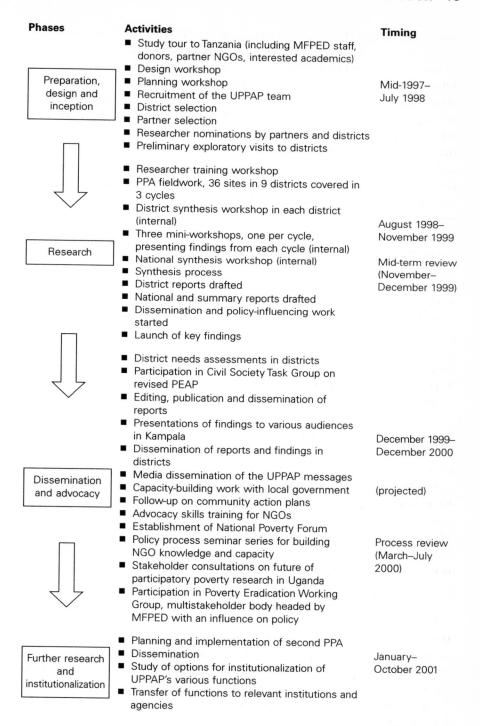

Phases

Activities

Timing

Preparation, design and inception
- Study tour to Tanzania (including MFPED staff, donors, partner NGOs, interested academics)
- Design workshop
- Planning workshop
- Recruitment of the UPPAP team
- District selection
- Partner selection
- Researcher nominations by partners and districts
- Preliminary exploratory visits to districts

Mid-1997–July 1998

Research
- Researcher training workshop
- PPA fieldwork, 36 sites in 9 districts covered in 3 cycles
- District synthesis workshop in each district (internal)
- Three mini-workshops, one per cycle, presenting findings from each cycle (internal)
- National synthesis workshop (internal)
- Synthesis process
- District reports drafted
- National and summary reports drafted
- Dissemination and policy-influencing work started
- Launch of key findings

August 1998–November 1999

Mid-term review (November–December 1999)

Dissemination and advocacy
- District needs assessments in districts
- Participation in Civil Society Task Group on revised PEAP
- Editing, publication and dissemination of reports
- Presentations of findings to various audiences in Kampala
- Dissemination of reports and findings in districts
- Media dissemination of the UPPAP messages
- Capacity-building work with local government
- Follow-up on community action plans
- Advocacy skills training for NGOs
- Establishment of National Poverty Forum
- Policy process seminar series for building NGO knowledge and capacity
- Stakeholder consultations on future of participatory poverty research in Uganda
- Participation in Poverty Eradication Working Group, multistakeholder body headed by MFPED with an influence on policy

December 1999–December 2000

(projected)

Process review (March–July 2000)

Further research and institutionalization
- Planning and implementation of second PPA
- Dissemination
- Study of options for institutionalization of UPPAP's various functions
- Transfer of functions to relevant institutions and agencies

January–October 2001

Figure 3.1 *Process and component activities of UPPAP*

During 1998 and 1999, a PPA was conducted in 24 rural and 12 urban communities in 9 of the 45 districts of Uganda. Sampling for the PPA was purposive, informed by UPPAP's objective of understanding the nature and causes of poverty. The district that ranked lowest on a range of criteria (such as the Human Development Index, exposure to natural calamities and degree of civil strife) was selected from each of Uganda's seven agroecological zones. Two districts were then added to the seven that had been purposively sampled: Kampala, as the national capital and a location of urban poverty; and Bushenyi, a district in which considerable socio-economic progress has been made and findings might be expected to shed light on how households and communities have moved out of poverty. Within each district, four sub-counties were selected to reflect the diversity of conditions within the district, and from these the poorest village or community was chosen as the PPA research site. A community within the main district town was deliberately selected in every case (McGee, 2000).[8]

The research agenda covered the areas explored in many PPAs: local concepts of poverty, vulnerability and relative wellbeing; perceptions of the causes of poverty and vulnerability; livelihood and coping strategies; what people see as the most important problems in their lives at present and how these have changed over the last ten years; views on access to, quality and relevance of government services; and areas that the poor see as being the most effective for actions for poverty reduction. More innovatively, and reflecting the agendas of certain influential stakeholders, the PPA also collected people's opinions on local governance structures, suggestions for improving their accountability, awareness of particular government policies, views on the relevance and impact of these policies and recommendations for their revision.[9]

The PPA was carried out by a core team of researchers, consisting of one researcher seconded from each of the nine implementing partner institutions working in collaboration with five officials from each district authority. Prior to going to the field, the researchers participated in a training workshop, a great strength of which was that it included practical fieldwork. Small groups of researchers made several visits to 'practice' communities and carried out participatory exercises. Difficulties in implementing the exercises were then discussed in the training, and practice reports were prepared from each site.

The research took place in three cycles over a seven-month period, with district report preparation and workshops to promote learning and analyse findings between each cycle. On average, the research teams spent seven to ten days in each community, staying on-site where insecurity did not preclude this. At the end of the research in each site, the researchers helped participants to formulate a community action plan (CAP), using a format developed at the training workshop. Participants were asked to rank the problems in the community that they had identified during the research, and then to make a plan to solve one of these problems, usually the one thought to be most critical. Many CAPs covered improving water supply and school construction, while a number covered road, latrine and health post-construction. Due to a shortage of time at the training workshop, a clear position was not formulated at that stage on whether UPPAP would assist with the implementation of the CAPs. Some communities were told by researchers that it would, providing that the community made a start; others were told that they should seek assistance from the district administration or from NGOs.

In using the findings of the PPA, emphasis was first placed on influencing policy within national government, conducting follow-up work using research findings from the districts and communities in which the PPA took place, and raising public interest in poverty issues in Uganda. The publication of national and district PPA reports was delayed until June 2000, more than a year after the research was completed, due to difficulties in synthesizing the huge volume of data generated and bureaucratic delays within the MFPED. This delay did not stop the results being used to influence policy processes, but did hinder timely dissemination to the districts. A strategic decision led to the concentration of UPPAP's limited human and financial resources on using findings for policy influencing as opportunities arose. The involvement of so many stakeholders ensured that findings were widely shared and used in numerous ways at both national and international levels as soon as they became available. As the director of one of the implementing partners commented: 'Lots of tentacular networks were being activated at the same time, by a number of donors and a number of the implementing partners and, most important, in its location within government.'

The findings soon started to feed into government policy processes. Some opportunities presented themselves while others were created by UPPAP staff, government officials and donors. Inputs were made to the 2000–01 GoU budget formulation process and to the development of the plan for the modernization of agriculture, while some findings were widely disseminated through their inclusion in the high-profile Uganda Poverty Status Report, published by the MFPED in mid-1999 (MFPED, 1999). This brought together findings from the Uganda National Household Survey, UPPAP and other studies 'to assess progress against the original objectives of the PEAP and to identify key challenges facing government in tackling poverty' (Bird and Kakande, 2001, p46). The publication of the report brought UPPAP to the attention of senior policy-makers and helped to establish its credibility, allowing it to become central to the updating and revision of the PEAP, which commenced in late 1999. The task force formed for revising the PEAP consisted of officials from the MFPED, line ministries and civil society organizations, members of the UPPAP team, donors and allies.

A video on the PPA was produced in January 2000, featuring people in communities speaking strongly on challenging issues such as corruption, exploitation, gender discrimination and ineffective service delivery, combined with senior government officials responding to these issues. This has been shown on Ugandan television on several occasions and at numerous government meetings and workshops, often sparking heated debate.

As well as the multistranded strategy adopted, dissemination was aided by the fact that it happened in the year leading up to presidential and parliamentary elections. Policy-makers and candidates, anxious to be seen to take the poor's concerns seriously, requested reports, studied them and in some cases held public debates about their contents.

The UPPAP findings have also been disseminated and used by civil society organizations (CSOs), principally the implementing partners. They were utilized by the Civil Society Task Force set up in January 2000 at the invitation of the government to provide inputs to the revision of the PEAP, so that – rather ironically – the findings of a government project have been used to lobby government. Oxfam's UK-based policy department, in lobbying the World Bank and IMF, has used UPPAP as an example of how PPAs can be deployed in the design and monitoring of Poverty Reduction Strategy Papers (PRSPs). An advocacy-skills training programme organized by UPPAP has helped Ugandan CSOs to advocate pro-poor policies more effectively at national and district levels. The reasoning behind this was that UPPAP realized it could not advocate thoroughly across all the important issues raised in the course of its research. As a result, it sought to impart information and skills to CSOs that it saw as as its natural allies in pro-poor advocacy.

The dissemination of the UPPAP findings at the international level has been carried out by the government officials, donors and academics involved. The findings have been presented by government officials in a number of international forms and shared widely by DFID and the IDS in the UK.[10] The far-reaching and diverse impacts of UPPAP are illustrated by the reaction of a member of the UK Poverty Commission, a voluntary body that publicizes and lobbies government on poverty issues in the UK. A commissioner declared herself impressed by the accessibility of the language used, comparing it favourably with the language used in UK efforts to lobby on poverty issues, and expressed her intention to learn from UPPAP's dissemination style (John Gaventa, personal communication).

Dissemination and follow-up to the PPA in districts and communities have been delayed by the lengthy process of publishing reports and by the priority accorded to influencing policy at the national level in the months following the PPA fieldwork. It has also been slowed down by debate among the main stakeholders about how UPPAP can best meet its second objective of enhancing district capacity to plan and implement poverty reduction strategies using participatory methods, and on UPPAP's role in follow-up to the CAPs developed during the PPA.

District needs assessments, carried out by UPPAP's implementing partners in late 1999, revealed the range of resource, training and capacity building required in the districts to improve planning processes, and contributed to the realization that district capacity building is a huge undertaking, requiring a budget and mandate that UPPAP lacks. Thus, in March 2000, it was decided that UPPAP's role should be to support the Ministry of Local Government (MoLG) in developing a strategy to assist the districts to undertake participatory and poverty focused planning. UPPAP has been working closely with the MoLG on this ever since. The direct involvement of UPPAP at the district level is limited to workshops in district centres and sub-counties in which the research took place, to feed back findings and provide information about how the PPA has influenced national policy.

Regarding the CAPs, it was eventually decided that UPPAP has an ethical obligation to assist communities to implement them. This assistance was therefore provided by UPPAP's implementing partners, with the project contributing up to 3 million Ugandan shillings (about US$1800) for each CAP, or for an alternative small project if the cost of the CAP is much greater than this and no additional funds are forthcoming.

With the publication and distribution of the national and district PPA reports to all line ministries, district authorities and main NGO networks, a concerted effort has been made by UPPAP to arouse public interest in poverty in Uganda. Short messages on the key causes of poverty identified in the PPA (such as insecurity, alcoholism, AIDS and a lack of market access) have been broadcast repeatedly on all the main national and regional radio stations in Uganda. Dramas on key issues have been broadcast, followed by phone-ins for listeners to discuss the issues raised. UPPAP staff have participated in a number of radio and TV chat shows on poverty issues.[11] All the PPA reports and many other UPPAP documents have been made available on the project website. A series of thematic papers, drawing together the PPA findings on decentralization, taxation, health, insecurity and governance,[12] have been produced and presented at a national poverty forum attended by politicians, GoU officials, academics and members of the public.

This dissemination effort has led to numerous demands on the UPPAP team from government departments, NGOs, churches and even the private sector to provide input to various plans and strategies, and for advice on participatory methods, planning and policy advocacy. The small secretariat has struggled to respond.

The third phase of UPPAP has now been planned. This will involve further participatory research in 12 more districts, some of which present particular livelihood and poverty issues not highlighted by the first round of research. In this second PPA the focus of attention will change from generating new information to using the insights from research to inform resource allocation and resolve policy implementation bottlenecks, especially at the district and lower government levels (Appleton and Booth, 2001; Booth, 2001). This has been characterized as a shift from hearing the poor's voices to hearing the implementors' voices and trying to respond to their information needs as regards planning, resource allocation and gaps in their capacity (Richard Ssewakiryanga, personal communication). The potential for integrating the next PPA with the National Household Survey, carried out annually by the Bureau of Statistics, has been explored. The conclusion was that merging the two methodological approaches was neither feasible, due to features of their design, nor desirable, as it would dilute each approach's comparative advantage (Appleton and Booth, 2001). Instead, plans have been developed for each to enrich the other.

As the second PPA gets under way, deliberations are ongoing in government and among UPPAP partners about how and where to institutionalize UPPAP's functions and the lessons it has generated, so as to make these sustainable and ensure that Uganda creates and maintains sufficient capacity in participatory poverty research and planning to respond to the great interest that UPPAP has aroused. These deliberations have taken the form of a study conducted by UPPAP which documents a wide range of stakeholders' positions on the best way forwards for policy-oriented participatory research (Ehrhart et al, 2000).

INFLUENCE AND IMPACT AT NATIONAL, DISTRICT, COMMUNITY AND INTERNATIONAL LEVELS

The findings from the PPA and the process of implementing UPPAP have had significant positive impacts at the national level. Impacts at the district and community levels have been much less pronounced. Below, the impacts at the different levels of project implementation (national, district and community) are discussed. Brief reference is also made to possible influences at the international level.

At the national level, UPPAP has had an impact on the understanding within the GoU of the nature and causes of poverty, and this has influenced a number of specific government policies. The process of implementing UPPAP has also built relationships between government, CSOs and donors. Taken together, these impacts have increased the consensus at the national level in Uganda about the necessary policies for poverty reduction, as well as support for reforms.

Robb notes that '[i]t is rarely possible to establish clear causality between the PPA and policy change because policy-making is part of a wider social process.' (Robb, 1999, p26) However, key stakeholders in UPPAP perceive that PPA findings have had a clear influence on the GoU's overall policy framework, the PEAP, as well as on a number of other government policies and actions as summarized in Box 3.2. One senior official in the MFPED noted during the process review that 'there are dramatic changes in PEAP II. It emphasizes improving governance and service delivery, and improving information flow and monitoring, really as a result of UPPAP'. However, it is important to note that in many cases, PPA findings 'confirmed what has been suspected or enhanced the focus on issues that have been highlighted in other studies or surveys' (Bird and Kakande, 2001, p49). Policy responses thus cannot be attributed entirely to UPPAP.

Box 3.2 *UPPAP findings and policy responses*

Findings

Poverty varies across the country. It is not uniform, and the responses to tackling poverty must reflect this.

Policy responses

Senior policy-makers have been struck by PPA findings that districts do not always use the resources allocated to them for particular activities because these activities are irrelevant to their needs. An example of inappropriate conditions attached to central government grants, highlighted by UPPAP, is the allocation of resources to Kalangala district to construct roads. Kalangala is a collection of tiny islands and needs money to improve boat transport, not roads. In response, the MFPED has organized a series of consultation seminars with district leaders on the conditions of various grants and introduced more flexibility. In the 2000–01 budget, funds were also allocated for the first time to non-sectoral conditional grants to districts. These grants are to be made directly to the sub-county level of the district administrations to meet needs identified by communities.

This finding has also influenced the proposed implementation framework of the new Plan for the Modernization of Agriculture (PMA). Plans to devolve decisions about how to use the resources to implement the plan right down to the village level are being discussed. An expansion of non-sectoral conditional grants for PMA implementation is likely.

The need for a safe water supply is a priority of the poor.

Funds allocated to improving water supply in the districts in the 2000–01 budget increased by 368 per cent compared to the 1999–2000 allocation.

The people are outraged by the level of corruption in the country, and the ineffectiveness of government in delivering basic services.

The revised PEAP highlights governance and accountability issues, although measures to turn this focus into action are still under discussion.

People lack information about government policies and resource flows, and about how they are meant to benefit from services and government programmes.

Discussions within government for a public information strategy have not yet been taken forward, in part due to the absence of a GoU body with clear responsibility for such a function. However, this finding influenced the MFPED to include a much greater focus in its own communications strategy on outputs that are accessible to ordinary people, producing, for example, a citizen's guide to the Uganda budget process (MFPED, 2000) in mid-2000.

Powerlessness is a key dimension of poverty, defined in terms of women who lack voice and are subject to domestic violence; an inability to call government to account; a lack of information; and factors beyond the control of individuals or communities, ie crop disease, disasters, insecurity.

The need for an increase in GoU spending on adult literacy, with a particular focus on women, has been recognized, with one billion shillings (approximately US$600,000) allocated to this by the Ministry of Gender, Labour and Social Development in the 2000–01 budget (the previous year's budget allocation was negligible).

Insecurity (due to war, insurgency and cattle rustling) is a fundamental factor that stops the poor from moving out of poverty. Insecurity also encompasses theft and domestic violence.

This finding raised the issue of insecurity as a key cause of poverty on the political agenda. The Ministry of Internal Affairs and Justice and law and order agencies are, for the first time, discussing their roles in poverty reduction and considering how to make their sectoral plans poverty-focused.

Government is seen by the people as being very distant; village leaders, however, are generally appreciated.

A proposal to strengthen the role of elected village councils in monitoring the performance of public-service delivery is included in the new PEAP, although no actions have been taken as yet.

Local people face great frustrations in their attempts to improve their livelihoods to achieve food security and higher incomes.	These findings led to the PMA being refocused on the needs of small, poor farmers, although concerns are still expressed by CSOs about the extent of the plan's poverty focus. As noted above, the PPA findings have also influenced the proposed implementation framework of the PMA.
Poor communities appreciated being consulted about poverty, policy and their priorities, and expressed a desire that government should continue to consult them on policy development, as well as monitoring the implementation of policy at the community level in order to ensure that programmes destined for the poor are delivered as intended.	It is intended that participatory monitoring of the implementation of the PEAP should be integrated into government's poverty monitoring framework. The mechanisms are still being discussed.

Adapted from Norton et al, 2001

As Box 3.2 shows, most policy responses so far to the PPA findings have come from within the MFPED. While there is interest within some line ministries, there is as yet little demonstrable impact on policy in these quarters. One explanation for MFPED officials' interest in UPPAP and ongoing poverty monitoring is that these give the officials information about the quality of service delivery which they can use in dialogue with the line ministries. The MFPED has a role in ensuring that the line ministries' policies are pro-poor, and wields considerable influence over them because the MFPED stipulates the use of line-ministry budgets. One former sceptic noted that the government's difficulty in addressing poverty stems not from a lack of information about the causes of poverty, but from a lack of information about whether policies are actually being implemented and, if they are implemented, whether they are achieving the intended results. Therefore, UPPAP, as a collection of information about what people know and think of government policies, is very interesting to the Ministry of Finance.

The experience of working with NGOs in UPPAP has boosted the MFPED's acceptance of engaging with civil society. According to one key stakeholder, it has created 'an environment in which CSOs can challenge government – those who have something to say. And this includes organiz-ations outside the UPPAP partnership.' According to a senior official in the MFPED, prior to UPPAP 'NGOs were seen as monsters, as a bunch of lions!' Suspicions of government within the NGO community are also seen to have decreased. Relations between NGOs and various government ministries have in fact been improving for a number of years: for example, the Ministry of Health has for some time been allocating funds to NGO health units, while NGOs have been working with the GoU on water supply and emergency relief. However, these relationships were built around NGOs fulfilling a service-delivery function. UPPAP appears to have improved NGO access to the MFPED, and helped to give NGOs some legitimacy and credibility in the area of policy analysis and policy advocacy.

Most of the government officials, at both national and district levels, and many others interviewed for the process review, stressed that they learned from the PPA that poverty 'is not just a material issue', 'not just about cash', but also about isolation, hopelessness, powerlessness and discrimination against women. In the revised PEAP, this multidimensional nature of poverty is clearly recognized.

Government officials interviewed for the process review noted that the PPA findings broadened their understanding of the causes of poverty, so that they now appreciate better the effects of poor governance, corruption and the lack of information. A recognition of the multidimensional nature of poverty, acknowledgement of causal factors such as corruption in government, and the strengthening of dialogue between government and CSOs, is seen by an official in the MFPED to have 'widened the consensus on where we want to go on poverty reduction'. This is seen to be critical for support for ongoing reforms in Uganda, because 'we have done the easy reforms. We are entering a phase of difficult reforms and these need a lot of consultation.' A recent demonstration of the significant support for government policies for poverty reduction among CSOs bears out these points. The Uganda Debt Network published an open letter in the country's main pro-government newspaper to the country director of the World Bank and the EU delegate, criticizing recent moves by bilateral donors to postpone debt relief for Uganda. The letter points out that 'CSOs carried out extensive consultations to prepare the PEAP', and that 'postponement of debt relief will delay its implementation'.[13]

At the international level, some claim that the Ugandan government's efforts to make its policies pro-poor have influenced current thinking at the IMF and the World Bank. For example, in the development of PRSPs, countries are recommended to commit to the adoption of a medium-term expenditure framework (MTEF) and to the creation of strong links between this and the PRSP. They are also asked to carry out participatory consultations with poor people in order to improve the quality of poverty analysis in the PRSP and to build ownership of the strategy. UPPAP is seen by some officials in the Bank and IMF to have persuaded the institutions to include this latter recommendation, by demonstrating, to a greater extent than previous PPAs, how PPA findings can be used to inform government policy. Uganda's

Permanent Secretary for Finance stated on a BBC World Service programme in October 2000 that the World Bank should pay Uganda for developing the idea of the PRSP, which it then took up and presented as its own.

At the district level, it appears that the impact of the UPPAP process and findings has been limited. The involvement of district officials in the 1998–99 PPA has created a basis of understanding and commitment to participatory methods, which the Ministry of Local Government (MoLG) can build on. Some have taken the initiative in attempting to apply what they have learned. For example, in at least two districts, district planners who participated in the PPA have broadened the process of producing the three-year district development plan to include consultations with the lower tiers of the local government structure. However, while alliances with planners have proved strategic, UPPAP was less successful in engaging with more senior district officials and politicians. In consequence, there is only limited commitment within district administrations to absorbing and acting on the information collected during the PPA or the district needs assessments.

The impact at the community level was also limited until the recent efforts by UPPAP's implementing partners to follow up the action plans made during the PPA. A presumption existed that communities would go on to implement their CAPs, most likely with assistance from district administrations. In fact, while just over half of the 35 communities in which CAPs had been formulated made some attempts to implement the plans, only one had fully succeeded a year later. In two cases the district administration implemented the CAPs (both for borehole construction), but most districts have been unwilling to provide assistance.[14] At the same time, the CAPs led to confusion about UPPAP's objectives and disappointment when assistance with implementation was not initially forthcoming.

However, it is interesting to note that in all four of the communities on which detailed information was gathered for the process review, there have been some positive outcomes of the PPA.[15] Local participants in the PPA have learned from the participatory exercises to which they contributed, or have successfully applied solutions to local problems that were suggested to them by researchers. Women in one community explained that they learned from a wealth-ranking exercise[16] how people move down from the top to the bottom wealth category. Since then, they have tried harder not to move down by holding on to their assets instead of selling them off in times of hardship, and by starting small businesses. In three communities in which discussions of local problems prompted researchers to suggest that people should join savings clubs, start small businesses, terrace fields to control soil erosion and construct latrines, these suggestions have been taken up. Many people commented that the suggested solutions were not new to them, but that more people were encouraged to take them up after discussion during the PPA.

ISSUES FOR REFLECTION

Certain features of UPPAP have been key to the attainment of a range of impacts, while others have presented challenges of various kinds. These characteristics merit detailed analysis, as they illustrate the distinctive nature of this participatory poverty assessment process, and lessons for other similar processes. They include the design of the process, management and staffing, issues of partnership and ownership, and perceptions of UPPAP.

Design

Many of the policy actors involved in UPPAP have shown considerable flexibility and willingness to learn. Donors, especially DFID, have allowed the process to unfold and have protected it from some of the rigidities normally associated with donor project-management and bureaucratic requirements. UPPAP staff have demonstrated a remarkable willingness to learn, and have tolerated long-term overwork and the management difficulties associated with an unpredictable and evolving process. Central government has shown itself to be ready to learn and keen to take up UPPAP's outputs, despite an initial lack of familiarity with its approach and notwithstanding the many structural obstacles to flexibility and changes in practice which exist in large bureaucracies.

While this generally flexible attitude to UPPAP's design has been a strength in many respects, two further aspects of design deserve further discussion: the design of the first PPA research, and how capacity building was dealt with in the design.

The design for the first PPA had strengths and weaknesses in terms of the research agenda to which it gave rise. The adoption of a broad agenda led to the collection of a huge range of interesting and important information. Giving the researchers the freedom to explore different thematic areas with a range of methods encouraged the participants' own priorities to emerge. However, certain aspects of this freedom were problematic. Broad and some-times contested terms like 'gender inequalities' and 'livelihoods' were included on the research agenda without ensuring that researchers shared a common understanding of the terms and of what they were looking for.[17] A range of different methods were used to investigate some critically important and politically sensitive issues – for example, poverty trends – which led to problems of inconsistency at the synthesis and reporting stage. The PPA therefore demonstrated the importance of clarifying at the outset the meaning of the terms used, what exactly the PPA is trying to find out, which data need to be comparable across PPA sites and with other sources of data, and also the potential benefits of standardizing tools or systematizing analysis across sites in relation to certain topics.

The strengthening of the capacity of researchers and partner organizations, while accorded importance throughout, was perhaps not adequately built in to the design. The production of national and district reports was slower and more tortuous than anticipated. In retrospect, it is clear that researchers needed more training in report writing, and that the tight timetable of the first PPA was not altogether realistic. Difficulties in synthesizing the data and a sudden wealth of opportunities to feed still-unpublished results into various national-level policy processes meant that the completion of district reports was delayed. In turn, this made the production of the national report very difficult. It should be noted, however, that difficulties with reporting did not stop UPPAP from using the results to influence policy. Moreover, one technical adviser commented that 'The analysis and synthesis of UPPAP were certainly difficult and the outputs are not perfect. . . But on reflection, given the size of the challenge, these are pretty good outputs really. It's easy to forget it, but no-one, anywhere, and least of all in Uganda, had any experience of a PPA on this scale at the time this work was done.'

Difficulties in securing suitable and sufficient technical support and supervision for the researchers in advance led to some inadequacies and gaps in the research data collected in the PPA. However, compared to other PPAs, the UPPAP researchers spent a relatively long time in each field site, which was critical to their ability to establish a good rapport with participants and thereby gather a huge amount of information about poverty and government policy.[18] The length of time spent in the field meant that considerable demands were expressed for technical back-up, but it also afforded researchers experiential learning and better local rapport, which probably helped to compensate for technical imperfections.

Management and staffing arrangements

As noted above, the project design established the vision and strategic direction of the project, but did not lay down a detailed implementation plan. This has been a strength, in that it has enabled UPPAP to be a flexible, evolving and learning process, able to respond to events in the policy process. That the initial design was so open-ended in this regard was – at least partly – a deliberate move to promote national ownership and a 'process' approach. However, at the same time the responsibility for decision-making in UPPAP – a complex, multistakeholder partnership – was not clarified, nor was a forum for this purpose established until a year after implementation got under way. In the absence of a clear management structure from the outset, some significant decisions were taken without adequate consideration of the consequences, or by default rather than by design. An example is the inclusion of the formulation of CAPs in the first PPA. No-one in the small secretariat had prior experience of implementing a PPA which they could bring to bear on all the problems and dilemmas arising throughout the process, and it has proved difficult to secure consistent technical support to supplement the team's experience.

UPPAP has always lacked adequate numbers of staff, leading to great pressure on the team, logistical problems and an inability to use all the available opportunities for influencing policy. A very small team was responsible for organizing the first PPA (a huge and complicated logistical exercise) and disseminating the findings. As a result, activities have been delayed and opportunities missed. The secretariat, with staff from Oxfam, has been based in the MFPED, but a lack of staff members seconded from within the MFPED (as envisaged in the project design) meant that the secretariat was weak in its understanding of government procedures and protocols, generating low confidence in the team about how to interface with the government system.

Partnership

UPPAP has gained from the comparative strengths of its range of implementing partners in government, donor agencies, Oxfam and other NGOs. The involvement of government officials has lent the process authority and credibility, as well as linking it to key opportunities for influencing the unfolding policy process. Its implementation by Oxfam has brought the commitment and dynamism of an NGO culture. The involvement of the donors in the actual implementation has led to funding flexibility in response to evolving needs. The donors have also helped to draw in technical advice and support and to relate UPPAP to the wider policy context, raising its profile internationally. In turn this has been helpful in winning or maintaining donor support for the GoU and, ultimately, securing for it more donor resources with which to implement pro-poor policies.

A key stakeholder from a donor agency noted that in the UPPAP design process, 'donors and government managed to come together as a partnership. This is unique – usually the donors go with their own objectives and programmes but here we were working for a common cause.' This partnership between government and donors, which has grown and been strengthened during the implementation of UPPAP, is also a key factor in its success in influencing government policy. Clearly, the attempt to learn from other PPAs was critical, as this led to the decision to locate UPPAP within government and the determination of key players that this PPA would have strong links to the policy process.

The involvement of so many implementing partners in the first PPA can be seen to have both helped and hindered the achievement of objectives. UPPAP's fourth objective is to establish capacity for participatory policy research in Uganda. Involving nine institutions has meant that only limited capacity building has taken place in any one institution, and this has caused tensions over ownership of the process and 'huge management complexities'.[19] On the other hand, the involvement of a number of diverse institutions has had many significant benefits for the UPPAP process. In the words of those involved, it has 'led to cross-fertilization, learning and networks',[20] 'built the profile of UPPAP'[21] and 'created a dialogue between civil society and government'.[22]

The building of partnerships with districts has proved to be a hard task, pursued with limited success. When attempting to engage the nine PPA districts and draw their staff into the research teams, UPPAP encountered several obstacles. Some of these were related to the low levels of human resources and capacity suffered by poor districts, which limited their ability to contribute staff to a long-term process, participate in research teams and serve as district 'multipliers' for participatory approaches. Some newer districts have not matured to the point that they can offer well-developed structures and systems for a process like UPPAP to relate to.[23] In addition, corruption and nepotism adversely affected the quality of some of the researchers seconded from the district administrations to participate in the PPA. Some districts demonstrated little commitment to UPPAP, which might be taken to indicate low understanding of its potential value to them and their populations, or cynicism at yet another extractive process coming from the centre, offering little but demanding time and scarce resources at the district level.

One party left out of the UPPAP design process was the MoLG. The failure to involve it at an early stage is regarded by many as having limited UPPAP's ability to make headway towards its objective of strengthening district capacity in planning for poverty reduction using participatory methods. It has been noted that if there had been a greater degree of 'thinking through' and investigation, there would have been more anticipation of the logistical and capacity problems that UPPAP would encounter in the districts, and more realism about the contribution that UPPAP could make to building capacity at district and lower levels of government.

As would be expected in a process based on such complex and multiple partnerships, different actors have had different agendas and priorities, which have ascended and descended in prominence over time since UPPAP began. This is perhaps most manifest in the range of views about UPPAP's obligations vis-à-vis the communities covered in the PPA. There are longstanding debates among PPA practitioners and commentators about whether PPAs are inherently extractive exercises, or can be vehicles for empowerment (see Norton and Stephens, 1995; Holland and Munro, 1997). A related question is whether they should include mechanisms to assist people in the communities in which the research takes place to address problems identified during the PPA, as a means of compensating for the extraction of information, consolidating a sense of purpose arising from the research, and giving some impetus to local poverty reduction.

From the outset, some UPPAP stakeholders – not the most influential – were keen that UPPAP should endeavour to promote community-level empowerment. This was not written into the project design or objectives. There was some brief discussion before the implementation of the PPA of the need to follow up with communities the problems identified in the research, but there was no serious consideration of the feasibility of this, and no conclusions were reached. Other actors have seen UPPAP as a project that will benefit the poor indirectly through the reform of government policies in their interests.[24] The playing out of various partners' more or less strong 'bids' to determine – and hence impose certain limits on – the UPPAP agenda, and the lack of clarity about these limits, caused confusion and led to disappointment, frustration and resentment in the communities in which the research was carried out. At the end of the research, UPPAP's national-level objectives took precedence, leaving the CAPs in limbo for well over a year.

Two points can be drawn from this discussion of UPPAP's partnership model. Firstly, a partnership model raises the likelihood of competing priorities among the different parties involved, and introduces the possibility that outcomes will partly reflect power differences between partners. Secondly, the more pluralist the partnership in a venture like UPPAP, the less control can be maintained over partners' competencies, actions and quality of outputs. The appropriate degree of pluralism for UPPAP thus needed to be decided with reference to all its objectives, and the ensuing trade-offs – for example, between capacity-building and ownership objectives on the one hand, and the production of credible outputs in useable forms on the other – needed to be faced squarely and explicitly.

Ownership

Lessons from other PPAs strongly influenced the manner in which ownership has been dealt with in UPPAP. Decisions to locate UPPAP in government and to establish strong links between it and the policy process have been critical in ensuring ownership by central government, with donors playing a supportive role. The issue of UPPAP ownership is closely related to the kind of partnership model adopted. The involvement of senior government officials has helped UPPAP in its attempts to influence government policy and win broader acceptance within government for consultation and partic- ipation in policy processes. The key officials involved have acted as internal advocates for the UPPAP findings within the MFPED, providing strategies for feeding the findings into government processes. In turn, feeding in the findings has helped to convince other senior officials, who were initially inclined to be sceptical but who now recognize the value of consulting poor people on what government should be doing and how well government policies are actually being implemented. UPPAP is undoubtedly unique among PPAs in its degree of central government ownership, which – although present at the start – has grown considerably as the process advanced.

At the district level, the very limited involvement of district authorities in UPPAP's planning stage militated against a stronger sense of ownership of UPPAP at that level. However, working harder to generate district ownership at that stage would have been very time-consuming, conflicting with the need to get the PPA under way in time to feed results into various policy initiatives (for example, the preparation of the poverty status report). In due course, a reasonable degree of involvement by district officials in PPA implementation was attained, and was instrumental in giving the findings credibility among some district authorities, while establishing a basis of understanding and commitment to participatory methods.[25] The MoLG can build on this as it seeks to help the districts to broaden consultations in their planning processes and improve the poverty focus of their plans.

Perceptions of UPPAP

Information that was gathered after the PPA about perceptions of UPPAP at the community level suggests that the researchers had difficulty in communicating clearly what UPPAP was about. In the communities that were visited for a mid-term review, people seem to have perceived UPPAP as some kind of NGO. The review notes that in both Moyo and Kampala, the communities 'recognize the need for "an organization like UPPAP" to be a facilitator that would assist them in the formulation of their plans and serve as an intermediary between them and the local authorities' (MFPED/ Oxfam, 2000, p16). In the community group discussions held during the process review, it appeared that in at least three out of six groups, people had very little idea about what UPPAP is or why the researchers came. Comments made by women in Sisimach village (Kapchorwa district) included the following: 'They said they came from Kampala but they didn't say who sent them'; 'They said they wanted to find out about poverty. They didn't say why.' A man in Bugarama village (Bushenyi district) commented: 'They came to build capacity and share knowledge and show us how to solve problems so that afterwards we could look after ourselves better and solve problems as a community.' The sentiments expressed here could cast doubt on the participatory nature of the process, or at least on the researchers' success in explaining the UPPAP process and what it could and could not offer. On the other hand, they must be interpreted in context: poor and, in some cases, isolated groups were responding to questions from a rare white visitor about other visitors, whose purpose was unfamiliar and from whom they might have expected certain benefits, no matter what disclaimers the visitors had made.

The mid-term review reports that the two communities in Kampala visited by the team 'were disillusioned' because nothing had come of their CAPs (MFPED/Oxfam, 2000, p16). In the seven group discussions held in four communities for the process review, the lack of follow-up regarding their CAPs was raised by all groups. Two out of the four communities visited had been told by the PPA researchers that they would receive external support, but in all four communities people echoed the sentiment expressed by one local leader: 'We didn't know who would fund our plan, but because we did a plan, we thought we would get help, and because it was UPPAP that did the research, we thought it would be the first to help us.' Pictures drawn by the groups in response to the question 'What picture best represents UPPAP?' reflect their perception of it as something that had failed to deliver expected benefits. One depicts a mud and wattle house with no mud on the walls, and no thatch on the roof and no door, just a skeleton of sticks. Another shows a maize plant that has tasselled but produced no cobs. A further drawing shows UPPAP as a tree without leaves and just two fruits. The leaves have withered and died due to a lack of fertilizer. The fruits represent the savings groups formed by women in the community, after the PPA researchers suggested they should come together to resolve problems. A fourth image used was a man hunting with a dog. The man catches an animal and walks away, leaving the dog with nothing. UPPAP is the man, the dog the community and the animal represents the information provided by the community.

Explaining the positive national-level outcomes of UPPAP proved virtually impossible in the two remote communities visited for the process review, as participants in discussions had little concept of central government and how it functions. However, in one more accessible and wealthy community, in a lengthy discussion of whether it is wrong for UPPAP to do research if it cannot provide funds and help for CAPs, the participants concluded that research can still be done because there will be indirect benefits for communities.

Concerns over raised expectations in communities, and the districts' unwillingness or inability to respond to the problems identified, led UPPAP to undertake a major, if tardy, effort through its implementing partners to provide funds and technical assistance to communities to implement the CAPs, over a year after the field research had concluded. Latrines are being built, roads repaired and loans provided for micro-enterprises. It seems unlikely that these community activities will lead to ongoing structures to tackle community problems, but they certainly mean that in the final analysis UPPAP has not been a purely extractive process for the communities involved.

CONCLUSIONS

Notwithstanding the exceptionally favourable circumstances in which UPPAP is being carried out, what useful lessons can other countries undertaking PPAs learn from the Uganda case? UPPAP has attempted to go far beyond the remit of other PPAs. It has not only attempted to gather and use information from poor people to influence national policy, but within this process it has also tried to enhance the capacity for participatory planning at the district level. In addition, it has attempted to respond to the expectations of assistance that the participatory data-gathering exercises raised at the community level. With such breadth of scope, UPPAP's successes and failures have much to say about both the potential and limits of PPAs, while the complex structure of the project points to lessons about PPA design and management.

At the national level, UPPAP has certainly achieved its objective of enhancing knowledge about the nature and causes of poverty and generating and applying strategies for poverty reduction. The favourable policy environment has been a key factor in this success. However, the influence of UPPAP also demonstrates the power of PPA-type information – power to communicate to and motivate a range of audiences by providing a vivid human picture of poverty that people can relate to, and by highlighting the terrible problems for real people of poor public-service provision, insecurity, geographical isolation, poor governance and discrimination against women. Perhaps, therefore, UPPAP indicates the potential value of a PPA in other less favourable contexts, and use of results by civil society, donors, politicians and government to promote policy change, even when the government as a whole is less committed to poverty eradication than is the GoU.

It is also worth stressing that UPPAP started with just a few key champions within government, but their support and the way they have used the PPA findings has gradually led to broader support for the process within the GoU and to greater credibility for the data collected using participatory methods. For those seeking to stimulate a UPPAP-type process elsewhere, this experience shows that a useful strategy could be to identify a few sympathetic individuals in senior positions within influential government institutions and to work with them. It is also worth remembering that in Uganda, the interest of officials was sparked when they actually participated in some participatory consultations on government policy in communities (see McGee, this volume).

At the district level, UPPAP has so far been less successful. While there have been some positive attempts to collaborate with district authorities, in general UPPAP has not been well understood or taken very seriously. It has shown that, at least in Uganda, convincing district officials of the utility of consulting poor people, and sitting down with them to work out how to do this, will be long-term processes. The tight timetable of the PPA, imposed by national-level requirements, was not well suited to protracted planning at the district level, which might have increased district ownership of the findings.

At the community level, the experience of UPPAP highlights the ethical dilemmas of PPAs. Is it fair to take up poor people's time and raise their hopes of assistance when the impact of the information they provide may very well be limited and, even if it is fed back to them, difficult for them to understand? In discussing these issues, Chambers writes that two points are widely agreed upon. First, 'facilitators should make it clear from the start who they are, what they are doing and why, and what can and cannot be expected' (Chambers, 1998, pxvii). The experience of UPPAP shows just how difficult it is to explain what a PPA is about. It raises the question of whether it is really possible to explain this quickly in communities that are new to the researchers and in which people have very little understanding of the workings of government. Though the training received by UPPAP staff made it very clear that transparency of purpose was a key element of facilitating the PPA research, even facilitators who are well versed in not raising expectations cannot always counter the dynamic that arises when outside researchers appear in isolated, seldom-visited communities.

Second, Chambers (1998) notes that 'communities and groups can be chosen where responsible follow-up may be possible through an ongoing programme'. UPPAP experience adds weight to the view that this is the only ethical approach to site selection in a PPA. It demonstrates that quick-fix solutions to concerns about the extractive nature of the research are hard to come by. Quickly helping people to make an action plan and then expecting them to implement it without support proved to be unrealistic. UPPAP also provides information, which is lacking in so many PPAs, about how far expectations are raised by a PPA, at least for some participants, and how disappointed they are by the absence of follow-up action.

In terms of design and management, UPPAP highlights the importance of considering the benefits (broad ownership, ideas, dissemination networks) of involving a large number of stakeholders in the process, versus the problems (limited capacity building for ongoing participatory policy work in any one institution, management difficulties) that this entails. It emphasizes that clear terms of reference and defined opportunities for partners to make an input to the process are essential, together with a clear and workable management structure.

This chapter has shown that a process like UPPAP, which was designed to introduce poor people's perspectives on poverty into policy-making, is continually presented with a wide range of potential activities and strategies. Inevitably, designing and implementing such a process involves trade-offs between different paths. The UPPAP experience, for example, demonstrates that it is not possible to work at the local, district and national levels simultaneously, and that a focus on national-level influence at a critical point in the process resulted in the relative neglect of other areas. Some of the lessons that UPPAP has to offer warn of spreading finite resources and capacity too thinly.

In terms of the five areas on which we have reflected in detail, the decisions made about each had implications for the others. In different PPAs there have been a range of experiences of ownership, from total or near-total ownership by donors, to strong national ownership that was vested in one government ministry or across several. Ownership can be broad-based, involving civil society actors, or not. The ownership of the UPPAP, vested mainly in one central government ministry and shared to some degree with civil-society partners, has necessitated the acceptance by all parties of a flexible approach to design, which, for donors especially, conflicts with their normal practices. It also requires an inclusive partnership model, but while a multiplicity of partners has enhanced the effectiveness and increased the prospects of sustainability, it has sometimes destabilized ownership by introducing confusions or tensions over multiple objectives. The management and staffing approach has had to be compatible with strong government leadership, which has obliged donors to accept less control than they are accustomed to. It has also sometimes led to other partners and the public perceiving the UPPAP as excessively governmental, and has hindered the achievement of technical excellence because of the shortage of nationals with PPA experience. Approaches to PPA design have ranged from the tightly specified and technocratic at one end of the spectrum to the loose, iterative UPPAP approach at the other. While the tight approach affords predictability, compatibility with standard donor procedures and a relative ease of management, it militates against national ownership and strong, sustained, in-country partnerships, which in turn has implications for sustained commitment and impact.

On balance, the trade-offs made in the UPPAP process on issues of design, management, partnership and ownership have, at least, ensured a deep commitment to the UPPAP and its poverty reduction objectives in government, and a growing body of civil society actors and the public, both during and after the three-year project. In these terms, they outweigh the potential and actual drawbacks of the model.

There are, of course, some questions that remain unresolved for PPA practitioners, despite the light shed on them by the UPPAP process. Can PPAs be better implemented and coordinated with other initiatives so as to respond more effectively to the needs and conditions of those increasingly important agents of poverty reduction located at decentralized levels of government? Can they do better at achieving an ethically defensible contract with the poor people who participate? It is on these matters that future PPAs will be judged.

NOTES

1 This chapter draws on the process review of UPPAP carried out in 2000 (Yates, 2000). We would therefore like to thank the all those who contributed to the process review. We would also like to thank Rosemary McGee and Karen Brock for their comments on and editing of the chapter.

2 This document can be found on the UPPAP website, www.uppap.org.ug

3 Kapchorwa and Bushenyi.

4 In the words of a director of an NGO that participated in UPPAP.

5 This ministry was created through the merger in early 1998 of the Ministry of Economic Planning and Development with the Ministry of Finance.

6 The idea that participatory methods generate qualitative data is very common, although in fact they can be used to collect quantitative information.

7 At the time of the process review on which this chapter draws (Yates, 2000), only the first phase – the initial PPA – had been completed, and dissemination activities and planning for Phase II were under way.

8 This document can be found on the UPPAP website, www.uppap.org.ug

9 Government policies discussed with participating communities included several of those prioritized in the PEAP, including: universal primary education, decentralization, modernization of agriculture and civil service reform.

10 The Institute of Development Studies (IDS) at the University of Sussex has provided technical support for UPPAP at various stages in its process so far.

11 In the week following one popular show, UPPAP received so many expressions of interest that it ran out of copies of the district reports.

12 Topics covered up to the time of writing.

13 *New Vision*, 25 May 2000.

14 Information on the status of the CAPs is given in UPPAP (2000), available at www.uppap.org.ug

15 See the process review (Yates, 2000) for a full report on the outcomes of the PPA in these communities.

16 Wealth ranking is a PRA technique, commonly used to explore local concepts of wealth, levels of wellbeing and determinants of change in wellbeing or wealth. For further reference, see IIED, 1997 and Grandin, 1988.

17 For example, it was difficult to report on livelihoods in the final report as the data revealed several different ideas of what is meant by 'livelihood'. There were tensions between the need to describe people's livelihoods and the need to analyse the barriers they experience in the process of gaining a livelihood.

18 Robb (1999, p10) notes: 'PPA teams have spent from one day to one week in a given community.' As noted earlier in the chapter, the UPPAP teams spent between seven to ten days in each community, staying in the communities so long as security considerations did not preclude this.

19 Director of an implementing partner.

20 UPPAP researcher.

21 Director of a partner NGO.

22 MFPED official.

23 The decentralization of functions to the districts was introduced very rapidly in Uganda. Although the functions of the districts are clearly established in the Local Government Act, for example producing three-yearly development plans through a consultative process, in reality the districts vary considerably in the development of their systems and in their capacity. Some 16 districts were created in the 1950s; another batch was created in the late 1970s; yet another batch in the 1980s and 1990s; and a further eight in 2000/1. Competencies and capacity tend to differ markedly between 'old' and 'new' districts.

24 This difference of opinion is not between CSOs and government/donors. On the contrary, some people working for the implementing partners with the most experience of community development programmes see community-level empowerment as 'a totally unrealistic goal for UPPAP'.

25 The involvement of local government officials in the PPA was not unproblematic, however. As well as the poor commitment to UPPAP encountered in some districts, the involvement of local officials seems to have made some communities suspicious of providing information and to have raised expectations of action to resolve problems identified during the research.

REFERENCES

Appleton, S and Booth, D (2001) 'Combining participatory and survey-based approaches to poverty monitoring and analysis', background paper for the workshop in Entebbe, Uganda, 30 May–1 June

Bird, B and Kakande, M (2001) 'The Uganda Participatory Poverty Assessment Process' in Norton et al, *A Rough Guide to PPAs: Participatory Poverty Assessments – An Introduction to Theory and Practice*, London, DFID

Booth, D (2001) 'Combining participatory and survey-based approaches to poverty monitoring and analysis: Workshop report', report on the workshop at Kampala, 30 May–1 June

Chambers, R (1998) 'Foreword' in Holland, J and Blackburn, J (eds), *Whose Voice? Participatory Research and Policy Change*, London, Intermediate Technology

Ehrhart, C, Nabbumba, R and Bugumbe, J (2000) 'Summary of interviews', reference resource for the UPPAP report *Participatory Research for Pro-poor Policy: Envisioning the Future*, Uganda, MFPED

Grandin, B (1988) *Wealth Ranking in Smallholder Communities: A Field Manual*, Nottingham, Intermediate Technology

Holland, J and Blackburn, J (eds) (1998) *Whose Voice? Participatory Research and Policy Change*, London, Intermediate Technology

Holland, J and Munro, M (1997) 'Profiling the purposive: Some thoughts on the site selection process in PPAs', unpublished note on the Egypt PPA, London, DFID

IIED (1997) *PLA Notes 28: Methodological Complementarity*, London, IIED

Kuteesa, F (2000) 'Pro-poor budgeting and public expenditure management', paper presented at Public Expenditure and Poverty Reduction Workshop, Ranch on the Lake, 27–31 March

McGee, R (2000) 'Analysis of participatory poverty assessment (PPA) and household survey findings on poverty trends in Uganda', unpublished mission report, Brighton, IDS

Norton, A and Stephens, T (1995) *Participation in Poverty Assessments*, Social Policy and Resettlement Division Discussion Paper, Washington, D.C., World Bank

Norton, A, with Bird, B, Brock, K, Kakande, M and Turk, C (2001) *A Rough Guide to PPAs: Participatory Poverty Assessments – An Introduction to Theory and Practice*, London, DFID

MFPED (1997) *Uganda Participatory Poverty Assessment*, Kampala, MFPED

MFPED (1999) *Uganda Poverty Status Report, 1999*, Kampala, MFPED

MFPED (2000) *A Citizen's Guide to the Uganda Budget Process*, Kampala, MFPED

MFPED (2000a) *Learning From the Poor: Uganda Participatory Poverty Assessment Report*, Kampala, MFPED

MFPED/Oxfam (2000) 'Mid-term review report part II: Main report: UPPAP', unpublished report, Kampala, MFPED/Oxfam.

Norton, A, Bird, B, Brock, K, Kakande, M and Turk, C (2001) *A Rough Guide to PPAs: Participatory Poverty Assessment – A Guide to Theory and Practice,* London, DFID

Oxfam (1998) 'Oxfam GB in Uganda: A proposal to be the implementing agency for the Uganda Participatory Poverty Assessment Project (the UPPAP) 1998–2000', internal Oxfam document, Kampala, Oxfam

Robb, C (1999) *Can the Poor Influence Policy? Participatory Poverty Assessments in the Developing World*, Washington, DC, World Bank

UPPAP (1998a) *UPPAP Field Guide*, Kampala, UPPAP

UPPAP (1998b) *Report on the Training Workshop*, Kampala, UPPAP

UPPAP (2000) *Phase II First Learning Workshop, September 25–26*, Kampala, UPPAP

Yates, J (2000) 'Review of the process of implementation of the Uganda Participatory Poverty Assessment Project (the UPPAP)', unpublished report for Oxfam GB, Kampala, Oxfam GB

CHAPTER 4

WHO IS LISTENING? THE IMPACT OF PARTICIPATORY POVERTY RESEARCH ON POLICY

*Ahmed Adan, Karen Brock,
Petia Kabakcheiva, Aklilu Kidanu,
Marcus Melo, Carrie Turk and
Haroon Yusuf*[1]

INTRODUCTION

THIS CHAPTER EXAMINES the outcomes of the World Bank's 'Consultations with the Poor'[2] study in five countries: Brazil, Bulgaria, Ethiopia, Somaliland and Viet Nam. It identifies a range of factors related to the social, political and institutional context that affected the impact of the study on policy at the national level and on action at the local level.

The 'Consultations with the Poor' process involved research teams from 23 countries in a qualitative research exercise, which used consultative and participatory research tools. Unlike any other PPA-type exercises to date, the study was designed to be broadly comparable across countries, and the policy-makers it primarily aimed to influence sat in Washington rather than in the capital cities of the South. The analysis of findings across countries, published as *Voices of the Poor: Crying Out for Change* (Narayan et al, 2000b), is the subject of Robert Chambers's chapter in this volume.

Although influencing national policy-makers was never the guiding objective of the exercise, the methodology guide states that 'the report will be available to local public, private and civil society leaders after the study reports are complete, who could use it for other ongoing activities and projects or for developing new ones.' (World Bank, 1999, p47). In addition to this, wherever possible studies were linked to existing projects and studies from the outset, as a principal mechanism for ensuring that study findings would feed into action. An extremely wide network of development and policy actors, in addition to the World Bank, was involved at different stages and levels of process.

This chapter documents the follow-up work of five of the research teams who were involved in carrying out national fieldwork. The follow-up work examined the impact of the process on policy within the teams' own countries one year after the original field research. Using 'the country' as a frame for the follow-up risks excluding the influence of changes in international discourses of poverty reduction in triggering policy change. In Bulgaria, for example, the team identified broad changes in policy-makers' attitudes to qualitative research, which were in part attributed to the national Consultations study, but in part to the influence of those international institutions which currently favour such approaches to poverty reduction policy. Through focusing on the influence of the Consultations at different moments and spaces in the national policy process, however, we are able to examine the responses of a range of policy actors to the 'new' knowledge that the study offered.

The research teams who worked on the study came from different kinds of organizations, ranging from a partnership between CBOs and an international NGO in Somaliland and academics in Brazil, Bulgaria and Ethiopia, to a multistakeholder partnership managed by the World Bank Country Office in Viet Nam. The follow-up research was commissioned by the Participation Group at the IDS,[3] with the aim of learning about the impact of the Consultations process in which some of us had played a supporting role. As co-authors of this chapter, it is important to recognize that the identity and objectives of our respective organizations and backgrounds have been a key factor in structuring the way the Consultations process was carried out and the influence that the study had in various arenas. Similarly, our own priorities for learning have shaped the content of this chapter.

One year after the original study fieldwork, the five teams undertook interviews with policy actors, reflected on the process as participants and returned to the research sites to discuss the local impacts. These enquiries had the aim of understanding whether and how our work had contributed to

Table 4.1 *Methodological approaches to the follow-up study*

	Brazil	Bulgaria	Ethiopia	Somaliland	Viet Nam
Semi-structured interviews with national government and international policy actors	✓	✓		✓	
Semi-structured interviews with local policy actors	✓	✓	✓	✓	
Structured research team reflection	✓	✓	✓	✓	✓
Policy stakeholder workshops and focus groups	✓	✓			✓
Semi-structured interviews and focus group discussions in communities	✓	✓	✓	✓	
Literature review/use of internal process documentation				✓	✓

policy change. Each team began with three broad areas of focus: the national poverty reduction policy context, the utilization of findings and the impact of the Consultations at different levels of the policy process. These broad areas were developed according to our priorities, contexts and capacities. In Viet Nam, for example, the follow-up was able to draw on ongoing work to evaluate the PPA, and to convene a key stakeholders' workshop to contribute to both processes. In Somaliland the follow-up study was an integral part of the continued activities of the Sanaag and Togdheer regional CBOs, and provided space for reflection at the village level. Table 4.1 summarizes the methodological approaches taken by each team in addressing the three broad themes of the follow-up study.

The reflections and findings of the five study teams were synthesized and summarized at IDS, with the aim of illustrating the multiple ways in which an initiative of knowledge creation can influence the thoughts and activities of different individuals, groups and institutions in the process of poverty reduction policy. By examining the dynamics of change through examples of different kinds of impact, we identify a range of ways in which knowledge is constructed and used in the poverty reduction policy process, and thus begin to identify spaces and potential strategies for change.

CONTEXT: PARTICIPATORY RESEARCH AND POVERTY REDUCTION POLICY

At the turn of the century, the reduction of poverty has once again moved to the centre of the mainstream development agenda. In order to receive debt relief, for example, the governments of many poorer countries must demonstrate that they have a coherent national strategy for poverty reduction. Consultation processes, which bring together different stakeholders from government and civil society to discuss issues of poverty reduction, are becoming increasingly common in the process of elaborating such strategies. Research processes using participatory methodologies are often used as a vehicle to introduce 'the voices of the poor' into such processes and the policies they aim to inform.

The design and implementation of the Consultations fieldwork owe a great deal to almost a decade of experience with consultative and participatory processes for poverty reduction, particularly the evolution of PPAs (see Brock, this volume). Like PPAs, the Consultations fieldwork used consultative and participatory methods to engage local people in sharing their experiences, opinions and priorities about poverty.

Most of the 23 Consultations national studies are closest in resemblance to first-generation PPAs, principally aimed at the collection of information about poverty from the perspectives of the poor for delivery to policy-makers. In terms of the five countries discussed here, the studies in Bulgaria, Ethiopia and Brazil perhaps conform most closely to this model. In Viet Nam, however, the Consultations study was one output of a second-generation national PPA, a process that has had considerable impact, largely due to the dense networks of policy-makers it has convened. In Somaliland, by contrast, a partnership between ActionAid and two regional CBOs led to the Consultations study being carried out by community members engaged in wider processes of local action and reflection. As such, our five country studies illustrate very different experiences and models of partnership and implementation.

The Consultations initiative must be historically situated in the evolution of methodologies for knowledge production employed by powerful Northern development actors. The development of consultative and participatory approaches to poverty research is partly a response to the rapid spread of participatory approaches to development, particularly within the project context. PPAs, and similar initiatives like the Consultations, appear to offer 'invited spaces' for the participation of a range of actors, including the poor themselves, in the policy process for poverty reduction (Brock et al, 2001). To better understand the nature of these spaces, and how they were occupied by different actors in the Consultations process, it is to the policy context of each country that we now turn.

Viet Nam

Poverty reduction and equitable growth are centrally important goals of the government of Viet Nam. But the poverty that is often defined in planning and policy documents refers mostly to economic deprivation and limited access to social services. The phrase 'poverty reduction' is often equated with the government's hunger eradication and poverty reduction (HEPR) pro-gramme, which is a framework of targeted support to groups defined as vulnerable or poor by the Ministry of Labour, Invalids and Social Affairs. As such, poverty reduction is often seen more in terms of social safety nets than in terms of addressing constraints on change at the macro, structural and sectoral levels.

The timing of the Viet Nam PPA could hardly have been better from the point of view of influencing policy. During 2000, the government was drafting its new five-year plan, a new socio-economic plan for 2001–10 and its longer-term vision to 2020. These plans, discussed at the ninth party congress in early 2001, have a strong influence on the direction that Viet Nam takes over coming years. This was the right time to be undertaking poverty-related research work.

Multilateral and bilateral donors are key actors in the poverty reduction policy process in Viet Nam. The World Bank identified the need for a new poverty assessment in its Country Assistance Strategy (CAS) in early 1998. The first poverty assessment, published by the World Bank in 1995, was based on household survey data collected in 1992–93. There was very limited use of qualitative information and little ownership of the analysis by either government or the wider donor community. The CAS identified a need to do the second poverty assessment differently, focusing on partnerships between a range of stakeholders including central and local government, and collecting and incorporating qualitative information. The World Bank therefore initiated the process of designing a PPA, supported by other donors.

The process of designing and implementing a PPA with multiple stake-holders to influence policy needed to be responsive to the policy context in the country. In theory, the participation of poor households in the govern-ment's planning process can take place through the role that the Communist Party of Viet Nam and the people's councils play as their representatives. In some localities with active and consultative leadership, this can work well. In many places, people do not feel informed about the government's plans, less still consulted during the formulation stage. Civil society is underdeveloped and does not generally play an active role in policy formulation.

There is, however, substantial room for manoeuvre for local authorities to define the local policy environment; some provinces are known to be more progressive than others because of the way in which they have interpreted central policies to promote growth at a local level. Others are identified as being more conservative and slower to implement reforms initiated at the centre, often hampered by the limited resources at their disposal. All provinces are required to have their own HEPR plans, although the resource constraints often mean that these are restricted to implementing activities funded under the national HEPR. The local HEPRs are not generally based on strong analyses of the local causes and problems of poverty or the important local constraints on development. There is a strong emphasis on collecting quantitative data to inform planning exercises, but very little experience at the local level in conducting any kind of qualitative research that might broaden policies and programmes addressing the needs of the poor.

The international Consultations initiative coincided with the implementation of the Viet Nam PPA process, which itself emerged from the combined strategies of donors and a potentially conducive policy environment. The thematic and methodological structures of the two studies were compatible enough for the four regional synthesis reports of the PPA to provide a Viet Nam national report for the Consultations study. As such, the range of stakeholders directly involved in the Consultations process in Viet Nam is far broader than in the other four cases, and includes national and international NGOs, DFID, the World Bank and national and local government actors. The team was managed, and the follow-up study written up, by a member of the World Bank team.

Brazil

Poverty reduction policies in Brazil in the 1990s were dominated by a growth-based model that was focused on gaining fiscal equilibrium and monetary stability. The federal government does not have an explicit national poverty reduction strategy, although there is a federal agency that provides both emergency relief – such as the distribution of free food to very poor communities affected by adverse shocks – and oversees several targeted federal sectoral projects in areas such as education and capacity building. Many of the current federal government programmes consist of the scaling-up of successful municipal experiences, and it could be argued that Brazil's poverty reduction interventions are currently divided between a myriad of local initiatives carried out by municipalities.

The poverty issue is currently highly politicized at the federal level, and this has resulted in several legislative proposals for the establishment of an anti-poverty fund on the basis of earmarked sources of funding. Conservative and opposition politicians fought fiercely for the authorship of the proposals. While acknowledging the gravity of the poverty situation, the government opposed the idea of a fund because it would imply 'budget rigidity'.

A central issue in the poverty reduction agenda concerns the spatial concentration of poverty. Both intra- and inter-regional inequality in Brazil are very high. The Brazilian northeast, with some 30 per cent of the country's population, accounts for some 63 per cent of all those considered income-poor relative to a US$2-a-day poverty line. Poverty rates across the whole country are much higher in rural areas, in which over half of the population lives in poverty.

Understanding the role of government and the politics of poverty reduction in Brazil requires a consideration of the country's federal structure. The political dynamics underlying the formation of poverty alleviation policy operate at different levels. Sub-national governments are subject to different constellations of pressures than federal government. Municipalities and states in Brazil enjoy important fiscal autonomy and constitutional prerogatives. They have become not only the terrain of political struggle, but also places of innovation and experimentation in democratic governance.

Apart from national poverty reduction actions, other arrangements have been set up that impact on poverty by expanding poor people's capacity to influence public spending. Municipal participatory budgeting is one example of these arrangements. It has been recognized as one of the few approaches that makes explicit connections between the formal, top-down decision-making processes of city government and the bottom-up processes of claim-making and negotiation by communities. Recife and Santo André – in which four sites in the Consultations study were located – are examples of municip-alities in which participatory budgeting schemes have been set up. The other arrangement, which is also found in both cities, is the ZEIS[4] forum – a deliberative forum in which representatives take decisions regarding zoning and infrastructure issues in these areas.

Other important ways in which the poor can influence policy are the tripartite councils – involving civil society, the state and service providers – that were created by the Constitution of 1988. Through the decentralization of the 1990s, states were empowered to decide about the allocation of federal funds in the areas of housing and sanitation, which constitute a large proportion of social spending in Brazil. Considering that in the 1980s these resources were entirely centralized at the federal level, it could be argued that a revolution took place in the country in the area of intergovernmental relations. More importantly, this revolution was accompanied by the setting up of thousands of municipal sectoral tripartite councils mandated to authorize the allocation of resources.

In Brazil, the study was carried out by a research team from the Univers-idade Federal de Pernambuco, with the participation of an anthropologist from a local NGO. It took place in this context of heterogeneous initiatives for poverty reduction, which are not unified in the form of a single national strategy. The context and structure of decentralized government, however, meant that the study had the potential to make impacts through the local political spaces, which had already been opened up by the creation of structures like the tripartite councils.

Somaliland

Somaliland is unique among the five study countries in several ways. It is a territory that has no international recognition and therefore has no represent-ation at the UN or any other international legislative authority. Further, there is no World Bank presence in Somaliland. The study was conducted in the context of a country recovering from the destruction of prolonged armed conflict, where people were striving to rebuild not only the damaged relations among their communities, but also the basis of their livelihoods. They were also struggling to establish their own governance system.

The Republic of Somaliland was established in May 1991 in what had been the northern regions of Somalia. The creation of this new republic was a direct result of the civil war in Somalia, which began in 1982 when resistance to Siad Barre's regime was first mounted in the northern cities of Hargeisa and Burao by the Somali National Movement (SNM). Two decades of Barre's regime and the war that followed resulted in human rights violations on an unprecedented scale, which devastated the country. Cities in the north, which have traditionally been centres of trade, administration and education, were left shattered. In Hargeisa, for example, 80 per cent of the buildings were destroyed, supply infrastructures like electricity and water were smashed, the schools were left roofless and ruined, and the hospitals were devastated and lacked the most basic facilities. The cost was staggeringly high in any terms, with people dead, wounded, displaced and impoverished.

Since declaring its independence in 1991, Somaliland has made remarkable progress in achieving peace and stability, while the south of Somalia remains dominated by conflict. After the collapse of the Somali state, the people of Somaliland reverted to their traditional, clan-based forms of self-governance in order to resolve their conflicts, negotiate peace and establish a functioning government. Despite two inter-clan disputes, Somaliland moved on and clan militias were disarmed. An unusual parliament was created, mixing democracy with the traditional leadership of elders and clans. The Somaliland govern-ment, based in Hargeisa and headed by President Egal, has made progress in establishing administrative coverage and capacities since 1996.

The improvements in security and governance that have been achieved so far have been accomplished without much foreign help. Lacking international recognition, Somaliland has no access to multilateral or bilateral investment from the international community. The Somaliland government has outlined its lack of resources for the huge reconstruction needs and provision of social services at various meetings with international aid agencies. The two main international bodies that are attempting to provide aid to the country are the Nairobi-based Somalia Aid Coordination Body (SACB), which brings together international aid agencies working in Somalia, donors, and the UN agencies led by the UNDP. In order to improve coordination and efficiency among the aid agencies in the country, both the SACB and the UNDP have been encouraging the government to produce a national strategy for develop-ment.

The government has produced a plan of action, but this cannot be called a poverty reduction strategy. The document explains the country's need to prepare for repatriation and reintegration through a sectoral appraisal of the situation in 1999, and provides a snapshot of ideas and proposals that were available at the time of the report. The document is not an exhaustive list of government priorities and does not claim to provide prioritized or project-designed programmes. There is no indication that the document was based on any consultation with the people or communities, or the application of participatory methodologies in gathering data and information. All the indications are that the document was prepared by the personnel of the government line ministries, coordinated by the Ministry of National Planning with financial support from the SACB.

In Somaliland, the Consultations study was carried out by two regional CBOs acting in partnership with an international NGO, ActionAid. Local people with experience in the use of participatory methods for learning and action made up the study teams. The policy processes for poverty reduction that do exist are constrained in terms of the potential impact they can achieve, given that the government has few resources and limited structures for policy implementation. Given these two important background considerations, the impact of the study in Somaliland was particularly important at the local level.

Bulgaria

In common with the other countries of the former Soviet bloc, Bulgaria experienced a dramatic economic crisis during the 1980s. In 1989, the communist government of the People's Republic of Bulgaria collapsed, and the country entered a period of political and economic transition. The 1990s witnessed both economic depression and a change of government. Reforms during this period include a Local Self-Government Act, designed to shift the structures of government away from the rigidly centralized model of the communist era.

Transition has presented a huge challenge to processes of governance and policy-making. In the arena of poverty reduction policies, the legacy of centralized decision-making is felt partly in terms of the inherited attitudes that decisions are supposed to be made 'at the top' only, and that the opinions of the poor are not valid in the formulation and implementation of social policy. Essentially, the former centralized system was based on the presumption of social engineering, in which needs are defined from a position of expert knowledge about the well-functioning individual, and those who do not conform to this pattern are considered to be misfits, citizens who ought to be the recipients of patronage. Notably, this attitude still impedes the opening up of the decision-making system to poor and marginal groups, although now the poor are branded inferior by the new official liberal ideology precisely because they are a product of the former patronage system, a function of state care and, hence, seen to be incapable of individual achievement and initiative.

Even though many senior government officials remain in favour of the centralized model, the influence of international institutions has prompted some to suggest that other levels should also eventually be included in decision-making processes at the level of local government. This potential shift, however, would have to take place in the context of a legislative and legal system that continues to operate by government decree. In stark contrast to the Brazilian experience, there are no institutionalized mechanisms of consulting stakeholders in the decision-making process.

In the policy process in general, decision-making and policy-making are not evidence-based but assumption-based. The administration has a selective approach to research, tending to absorb findings that are in line with the current policies and neglect those that are critical. The intrinsic values of governance in Bulgaria do not attribute priority to transparency, account-ability and participation. Research might be used as a justification, but it is not perceived as an intrinsic part of the process of policy-making. The Consultations follow-up study, however, suggests that there is growing interest in poverty issues and poverty studies, and that the Ministry of Labour and Social Policy in particular is starting to use the findings of those studies increasingly. Recently, many government institutions have started to open up to more participatory methods of decision-making, mainly as a result of the requirements of influential international institutions like the World Bank, the European Union and the UNDP.

In Bulgaria the study was carried out by academics at the Department of Sociology in the University of Sofia, who had their first training in participatory methodologies as part of the Consultations initiative. The context in which the team worked was that of inherited attitudes and behaviours concerning policy and decision-making, combined with the contested nature of decentralization and local government, which presented multiple barriers to the impact of a participatory poverty study.

Ethiopia

Ethiopia is one of the poorest countries in the world, with a predominantly rural population that mostly makes a living from rain-fed subsistence agriculture and livestock production. As the Consultations national report notes, 'a majority of the respondents interviewed for this report have experiences of three radically different state systems, the last of which is the present federal government.' (Rahmato and Kidanu, 1999, p14.) The imperial regime of Haile Selassie was overthrown in 1974 in a coup that resulted in the establishment of a Marxist military government, the Derg. The Derg relied heavily on Soviet support, and implemented policies of collectivization and the nationalization of agricultural land. Towards the end of the 1980s, with

Soviet resources diminishing, some liberalization of government policies occurred under the rubric of the creation of a 'mixed economy'.

The Derg was overthrown in 1991 after the intensification of long-running civil conflicts in Eritrea and Tigray. Following a period of transitional government, elections were held and a new constitution provided a framework for a federal government system, which restructured the administration of the country in ethnically-based regions. The system was intended to provide an alternative to the long period of centralized government (Keeley and Scoones, 2000). Structures of policy-making and governance continue to evolve, and the degree of regional autonomy to develop and pursue policy agendas varies across sectors and regions (Carswell et al, 2000). The post-Derg government quickly committed itself to policies of economic liberalization, which were continued by the current government, elected in 1995.

Keeley and Scoones suggest that despite these changes in government, underlying continuities exist in the Ethiopian policy arena. Firstly, the severe food shortages that have affected the country in every decade since the 1960s have ensured that a concern with food production and food security has been a central policy focus of each successive government, although each has approached the issue very differently. Secondly, all three governments have tended towards authoritarian, hierarchical and centralized policy styles, which have translated into a bureaucratic structure that is predominantly top-down in its approach to policy formulation and implementation.

Under the military regime Ethiopia was out of favour with the international donor community, and most of the massive inflow of aid that followed the famines of the mid-1970s and mid-1980s was channelled through NGOs rather than through government. External assistance increased dramatically when the transitional government came to power.

Poverty studies were initiated by the government and donors in the early 1990s and their findings were presented for public discussion in the second half of the decade. Prior to that, while there was a good deal of concern regarding the poverty situation in the country, there was very little sustained debate on the subject and very limited documentation of it. Initially, the stimulus for debates on poverty was the economic reform programme of the transitional government, which was keenly promoted by the major donor agencies, in particular the IMF and the World Bank. The World Bank and other donor agencies provided both the initiative and the finance for poverty studies as part of their support to the economic reform programme. One outcome of this was the establishment of the welfare monitoring system in 1994, under which the Central Statistical Authority was charged with the collection of poverty information and monitoring changes in the poverty situation in the country. The debate therefore became anchored in the framework of structural adjustment and in the context of a social action programme to alleviate poverty. Another characteristic of this debate is that it has been dominated by the work of economists. The result has been an almost exclusive concern with the quantitative measurement and distribution of poverty.

The present government in Ethiopia has sectoral programmes for poverty reduction, which do not constitute an integrated poverty strategy. The information basis of these strategies is largely provided by the outcomes of 'standard' instruments that may fail to capture the totality of livelihood deprivation, powerlessness and socio-cultural marginalization. While the policy environment regarding poverty reduction has improved to some extent, the development of a comprehensive poverty reduction strategy is inextricably linked to the negotiation of a PRSP with the international financial institutions, which reflects the continued governmental belief that economic growth will serve as the chief engine to propel improvements in living standards among all sectors of the population, including the poor.

In Ethiopia, the study team was managed by academics who undertook the project as a consultancy. The policy context in which the study took place is dominated by top-down bureaucratic approaches and predominant attitudes that frame poverty as an essentially economic and quantifiable phenomenon, and these restricted the prospects for the potential impact the Consultations process might have.

USE OF RESEARCH TO INFLUENCE POLICY

The overview of poverty reduction policy contexts in the five countries illustrates the diversity of opportunities for the Consultations study to have an impact, and the range of obstacles that such a process may confront. The policy contexts are summarized in Table 4.2, and linked to the broad level of impact the study attained at different levels. The impacts are discussed country-by-country in the following section.

Viet Nam

The policy impact of the PPA was the subject of reflection at a stakeholders' workshop. Participants concluded that the impact of the PPAs on *policy-making* had been greater than the influence on *policy* to date. They argued that the impact on policy-making has come about through broadening the poverty policy debate, the elevation of qualitative research in national poverty assessment, the promotion of bottom-up approaches to planning and policy-making, and creating more places at the national policy-making table. Several months after the stakeholder workshop evaluated impact, the PPA findings have begun to have a greater influence on *policy*. Perhaps most notable in this

Table 4.2 *Actors, contexts and impact*

	Range of actors involved in implementing Voices study	Enabling factors in the policy context	Constraining factors in the policy context	Type of impact
Viet Nam	World Bank, donors, local and international NGOs and local and national government, acting as a multistakeholder partnership managed from the World Bank Country Office	Poverty reduction is the central goal of government. Strong donor coordination and advocacy for a partnership-based PPA. Potential room for manoeuvre by local government in decentralized structure	Dominant narrative of poverty reduction defines poverty as economic deprivation, to be tackled through economic growth and the provision of social safety nets. Relatively weak civil society, which does not generally play a role in policy formulation	At the national government level, impact through inputs to formal national policy processes. Limited impact at the level of local government. PPA process feeding in to ongoing and new programmes of implementing NGOs
Brazil	University academics with some involvement from NGOs and World Bank Country Office	Decentralized structures of local government with innovative participatory structures. Credibility of participatory poverty research	Dominance of growth-based approaches to poverty. Poverty highly politicized within national policy discourse	Majority of impact at local level, but only in certain institutional contexts. Impact of study at national level constrained by question of credibility
Somaliland	Community members, regional CBOs and international NGO. No World Bank Country Office	Partnerships between local communities and NGOs that address poverty reduction issues at the level of community governance	Post-conflict system of government, with few resources; lack of effective policy structure	Principally at local level, with particular impact on institutions of governance and local planning. Some impact at government level, principally in the form of information provision
Bulgaria	University academics with some involvement from NGOs. Little involvement with World Bank Country Office	Some donor-initiated movement towards participatory and consultative processes in government	Recent transition from command model of policy. 'Experts know best' approach to policy-making. History of systematic ideological exclusion of the poor from decision-making	Some impact from inclusion of team members in national policy formulation fora. Some impact at the local level, mostly facilitated through individuals or existing NGOs
Ethiopia	University academics acting as independent consultants. Little involvement with World Bank Country Office	Enduring policy concern with issues of basic food security	Strong tradition of top-down policy-making; strong quantitative bias in poverty assessment; limited credibility for participatory research	Minimal impact, with study encountering multiple obstacles to dissemination and influence

Higher impact ← → Lower impact

regard is the interim PRSP, which refers to the PPAs and picks up on many of the themes that were raised by their findings.

Achieving impact on policy and policy-making in the Viet Nam PPA has been a complex and iterative process. The follow-up study identified three aspects of this process as particularly important: the network of policy actors, which was catalysed by the PPA; the establishment of credibility; and the creation of spaces for debate and discussion of poverty issues.

Policy actor networks: Alliance and partnership

A key guiding principle of the implementation of the PPA was a focus on partnership within a network of policy actors, including central and local government, NGOs, donors and the World Bank. The broad objective of initiating the PPA was to work towards a commonly owned assessment of poverty that could serve the needs of all these groups, and thereby enhance the effectiveness of poverty reduction policy. In addition to this broad consensual objective, different actors in the partnership entered the process with different objectives for policy influence, which shaped the spaces in which the impact of the PPA would be felt.

For the World Bank in Viet Nam, the decision to carry out the PPA was taken after reflection on previous experiences of poverty assessment, which had relied largely on quantitative data. Through internal linkages at the World Bank, the Viet Nam PPA team was given the chance to take part in the Consultations project, and thus to feed their findings into an exercise in international policy influence. Although the PPA would have happened without the Consultations, the involvement did result in a national synthesis report being written, which might not have happened otherwise. Taking part in the global exercise helped to strengthen the legitimacy of the PPA findings at the national level.[5]

The UK DFID became an important source of funding and technical assistance for the PPA. DFID was seeking to strengthen its own understanding of poverty issues in Viet Nam and, following the spirit of recent UK government policy change on development assistance, was adamant that this should be done in partnership with others. The PPAs were therefore backed up by resources and funds that were unusually supportive and unconstrained. Of the five cases discussed in this chapter, the Viet Nam PPA was the most costly in terms of financial and human resources, and access to those resources was one of the factors that allowed it to achieve a high profile and wide impact.

The international NGOs that carried out the research were also motivated by the objective of seeing whether certain issues raised by poor households during the PPAs could be addressed at either a national level or during the development of the province's HEPR plans. The NGOs' interest in producing high quality research that accurately reflected local conditions lay in taking their own programme and advocacy work forward, rather than in simply satisfying the terms of a research contract.

NGOs were also interested in demonstrating to their local authority partners the benefits of opening up direct lines of communication with poor households during the formulation of local policy. As one NGO team member reflected, the collaboration on the PPA with a local authority partner 'allowed [the NGO] to participate in local policy dialogue at a more serious level'. The PPA fieldwork was therefore only one part of a much broader dialogue and process of policy influence, which was complemented by the use of a partnership model in the implementation of the PPA.

Like many national PPAs, the Viet Nam process maximized the involvement of government staff in the research stage, as partners in the participatory episode of the research (as advocated by McGee, this volume). The establishment of the Poverty Working Group involved government officials from central ministries and allowed them to feel a high degree of ownership of the overall process. The PPA research and dissemination of findings at the regional level involved a variety of different government actors. The PPA process was therefore able to create horizontal linkages across central government agencies working towards poverty reduction, and vertical linkages from the local authorities up to central government agencies. Both sets of linkages enabled policy influence.

According to reflections at a stakeholder workshop, it was the opportunity to strengthen and build linkages between actors within and beyond the stakeholder partnership which was widely perceived as a positive aspect of the PPA process. As this brief discussion of the different actors shows, the process of building such linkages was an important factor in shaping the opportunities that the PPA had to influence the policy process.

Establishing credibility and legitimacy
An important aspect of the PPA process was the attempt it made to challenge dominant attitudes towards poverty and understandings of it. On the one hand, this attempt took the form of the provision of information through the dissemination of research findings. Establishing the credibility of the research was a key factor in maximizing the impact on policy and policy-making. Although there has been a considerable amount of qualitative information on poverty produced over the past ten years, it has rarely seized the attention of policy-makers, who have tended to view such information as unscientific and lacking in credibility.

The challenge of establishing credibility for the PPA was tackled through various channels. It was critical that implementing agencies were able to build on longstanding partnerships with local authorities in the study sites, as familiarity with local areas meant that study teams were able to cross-check and triangulate information as it emerged. The processes that surrounded the implementation of the PPAs – the workshops, the presentations, the meetings with local government – were also important in establishing the credibility of the research methodology and findings in the eyes of policy-makers.

The link with the international Consultations exercise provided a further opportunity to establish credibility. The step of writing a national synthesis report, collating the findings of the four regional PPAs, was originally included so that the findings from Viet Nam could be included in the Consultations project. However, the national report turned out to be a valuable document in terms of providing an opportunity to reinforce findings that arose across the different sites in a variety of different social, economic and geophysical environments. Many of the problems of poverty were found to be just as crucial in Ho Chi Minh City as in remote, upland villages. This in turn helped to answer some of the criticisms that the PPAs were simply collecting anecdotes that were isolated or extreme cases. Where findings crop up repeatedly, although different research teams in different areas using different methodology are presenting them, it suggests that the analysis is cutting through the biases of any one particular research team.

The international development institutions involved in the PPA were instrumental in establishing the credibility of the PPA findings in the eyes of government actors. As well as providing leadership and a significant commitment of resources to dissemination activities, the uptake by donors and multilaterals of the key messages emerging from the study itself enhanced the legitimacy of the information. Due to the effective links that had been established with government throughout the process, the PPA findings fed directly into the World Bank's Viet Nam poverty assessment, in which they were integrated with national household survey data. This PA has provided the government of Viet Nam with a rich source of information, which has been used in the formulation of an interim PRSP. Establishing the credibility of the PPA messages among Vietnamese government policy actors has been part of the process of transferring the ownership of findings from external to government actors.

Space for debate and argument

A second important aspect of changing dominant attitudes towards poverty was the creation of spaces for debate and argument in the policy process, where different actors could come together to discuss the process and findings of the PPA and the implications of the findings. One example of a mechanism that created space for attitudinal change among policy-makers is the regional workshops, which were held at the end of the PPAs. These were often quite large, with up to 100 participants attending, including members of the national Poverty Working Group.[6] The attendance of a range of partners confirmed to local authorities that central policy-makers and donors were taking this kind of information seriously in policy formulation, lending implicit endorsement for local authorities to do the same. It benefited national policy-makers to see local leaders agreeing with the research findings, thereby assisting in the shift of attitudes necessary to establishing the credibility of the research in the national policy arena.

The workshops also gave the opportunity for vigorous debates on issues and concerns that had emerged from the research, but which had not been adequately addressed by existing policies, or which were previously considered politically inappropriate for public discussion. Examples of such topics included how to bring households closer to decision-making processes and how to deal with their lack of information, the need to investigate policies and procedures around revenue-raising at a local level, the need to re-think the status of migrants, and the need to look at equity issues within households and across ethnic groups. The workshops contributed to a broadening of the poverty agenda through the involvement of a combination of stakeholders at the regional level. These activities were consolidated by debate at key policy events and meetings at the national level. Now that these previously challenging topics are out in the open, in a published document that has the endorsement of government, there is a sense of greater legitimacy in pursuing them in policy formation and programme design.

The mainstream view of poverty among policy-makers has previously been related to hunger or income poverty. Through stimulating processes of debate and discussion, the PPAs have raised a number of topics that were not previously seen as part of the poverty agenda. At the launch of the Viet Nam poverty assessment, one official commented:

> *Poverty might mean social or cultural gaps between people. It might mean lack of information, transportation, knowledge and experience in dealing with hardships. It might mean severe vulnerability, so that health shocks or crop failure lead to a cycle of asset sales and indebtedness. It might mean not being able to influence the decisions that affect your livelihoods. Or it might mean being less advantaged within your own household.*

Such an understanding represents a real shift in the mainstream definition of poverty.

Brazil

In Brazil, our discussion of the impacts of the Consultations study focuses at the level of national policy influence, and at the level of two of the communities in which the process was carried out. At the national level, the complexity and politicization of the poverty reduction agenda is reflected by the perspectives of different implementing actors on the impacts of the process. At the community level, the spaces offered by the local political context give very different opportunities for impact.

Actor perspectives on impact

Perceptions of the impact of the Consultations in Brazil were mediated by institutional position. From the World Bank's perspective there were many positive impacts, but interviews with policy actors and reflections by team members suggest that for other actors, the impacts were contested and fragmented.[7]

The Brazil Consultations study was facilitated by the World Bank Country Office, which was in the process of designing an urban improvement strategy when the decision was made to engage with the Consultations process; they felt that the study was well designed to inform this ongoing work. The Bank's Country Office funded more than half of the study, and drafted a lead economist to assist in the sampling process, which was focused on urban areas in accordance with ongoing operations.[8] The field research process, analysis and writing up of the study were carried out by a team of academics, but the study was closely identified with the World Bank.

The World Bank Country Office emphasizes that the Consultations study had an influence on the content of the CAS,[9] particularly its advocacy of exploratory work on poverty and violence.[10] The findings have been used in the preparation of a Bank-supported urban project in Recife, and were presented at a retreat of all the Bank's Brazil team leaders, where their implications for the Bank's work programme were discussed. The external profile of the project was heightened by the presentation of findings at a global forum on government by the Consultations team leader from Washington in May 2000, as well as in other policy settings at the national level.[11]

The follow-up study was undertaken before some of these impacts had been felt. Nonetheless, interviews with other policy actors, which discussed the way in which the study was used in the process of the government negotiating a CAS with the Bank, suggest some alternative understandings of the impact of the study.

There was no significant government involvement in the Brazil Consultations process. This lack of involvement was a double-edged sword: it ensured that the research process was not seen at the local level to be controlled or co-opted by government, but reduced the probability that the process might influence current poverty reduction strategies. At the time that the Consultations study was carried out, the Bank and the government of Brazil were engaged in a dialogue to negotiate a CAS, which was finalized in March 2000. As noted above, the Consultations study was seen by Bank staff to have influenced the *content* of the CAS. It was also, however, used by other actors to influence the *process* of elaborating the CAS.

The CAS negotiations comprised a closed set of 'consultations' held under a confidentiality rule. The Brazilian Network on Multilateral Financial Institutions had been lobbying for an opening of this dialogue, and in March 2000 a senator undertook to obtain a copy of the CAS and make it public.

A national seminar of NGOs, CSOs and Congress members was convened at which the CAS was distributed. At the same seminar, the Consultations research report was also distributed by the lobbying group, which called for its findings to be incorporated into the CAS. The use of a Bank-sponsored report by the network, in an attempt to advocate a change in the formulation of a Bank-sponsored policy, demonstrates not only the complexity of the policy process in this case, but the difficulty of drawing clear conclusions about how – and through the agency of which actors – the study influenced policy.

A similar difference of perception arises around the urban focus of the Consultations study. Although the choice was made for clear reasons, consistent with the Bank's operational objectives, semi-structured interviews with policy actors also found that the urban focus had increased the difficulty of establishing the credibility of the study more widely, in a country in which poverty is largely concentrated in rural areas. It also limited the number and the type of institutional actors who became involved in the process of debating the findings. The public remark of a senior World Bank Country Office staff member, who stated that the decision to focus on urban sites was taken on no specific criteria or technical grounds,[12] showed little appreciation of the clear operational and technical motives of sampling, and contributed to the challenge of establishing wide credibility for the study.

According to the reflections of the study team, this example of different and perhaps contradictory approaches to policy influence is illustrative of a more general lack of coordination and communication between the different actors involved in the study process. The follow-up study found that poor communication between the study team and the operational branch of the Bank involved in the implementation of the urban project resulted in the impact at the project level being slow to develop. This may be related to the structure of the Bank itself, and a gap between operations and policy divisions, which cautions against drawing conclusions about the Bank as if it were a single, homogenous entity. In interviews for the follow-up study, Bank staff and their partners both expressed the view that research like the Consult-ations has a legitimization function rather than an operational one. One partner commented that 'the Bank is putting the icing on the cake. . . with no practical impact in terms of how priorities are decided and projects are managed.'[13]

The perspectives of the study team, World Bank staff and other policy actors who used the Consultations study to inform their poverty reduction activities draw our attention to difficulties with the partnership structure of the study. They also suggest that different actors pursue strategies for using and acting on the information which are not always complementary, and may even be in conflict. These inherently political dynamics point to the dangers of seeing the process of influencing policy processes with 'new knowledge' as linear, and suggest instead a policy process in which the existing interests, agency and priorities of policy actors are at least as important in catalysing change as the production of new information.

Decentralized local government: A space for action?
As discussed earlier in the chapter, decentralized local government has increasingly offered spaces for local people to participate in policy processes. The study team returned to two research sites, Vila União and Morro da Conceição – both *favelas*[14] in the city of Recife – to discuss the impact of the study at the local level. Understanding the impact of the study involved contextualizing the process in the configuration of local political institutions, particularly the activities of the neighbourhood associations of the two *favelas*.

The Vila União Neighbourhood Association is highly representative and active. The current leader was elected for two years following elections with a turnout of 230 people, and the association has become centralized around him. Although the community has not been subject to NGOs interventions – because it is small and relatively newly settled – the interface between the community and larger, city-wide social movements in Recife is guaranteed by the neighbourhood leader's participation in the directorship of the Federation of Neighbourhood Associations of Pernambuco. He was also the delegate from the area to the city-wide participatory budgeting scheme. The learning from this experience was translated into his ability to identify the channels and actors that were crucial for the advance of community demands following the Consultations research.

The Morro da Conceição Neighbourhood Association, in contrast to its centralized equivalent in Vila União, is organized along a collegiate structure. It is very pluralistic, and operates according to a strict division of labour. There are 13 'sectoral commissions', which specialize in issues such as youth problems, culture, football and gender relations. There are over 40 active coordinators distributed in these 13 commissions. This is a result of the complexity of the community in terms of its lengthy history of settlement, size and associative life. Several NGOs have been active in the area in addition to the Church, which is extremely influential.

In Vila União, the most impressive impact of the Consultations process had to do with the effective use of the site reports by the community to navigate a course through the dense institutional arrangements that exist in Recife. Apart from the instrumental use of the information gathered in the reports in the various fora in which the neighbourhood association has a seat, the reports were also cited on an impressive number of occasions in the process of formal contacts made by neighbourhood association leaders concerning the problems of the community.[15]

In discussing the impact of the Consultations, the neighbourhood leader cited several episodes in which his previously unsuccessful attempts to make appointments with key officials, such as government officers and the mayor, were transformed by using the Consultations report to negotiate opportunities for meetings. The site report was also used during an interview with the press about the lack of water supply to the *favela*, which prompted an unusually quick response from the water utility company. According to the neighbourhood leader, 'the most important outcome of the World Bank study is the site report that we can use to make our demands more credible. . . it was a great help'.

The research in Morro da Conceição had a very different impact. Here, members of the community had already been exposed to other participatory research in the past and the Consultations study was felt, in the words of one resident, to be 'another experience of that type'. Due to the size and complexity of the neighbourhood association, it was many months before the site report was read by more than a handful of councillors. At the time of the follow-up the process had not resulted in any direct impacts.

A range of factors affected the contrasting ways in which the study was used in this case. The differences in size and organizational capabilities are very significant. While Morro da Conceição is much older and complex, Vila União is a small, new settlement with pressing problems. People here were exposed to participatory research for the first time. Expectations were consequently higher and the exercise attracted more attention from residents. In addition, because the team had had previous experience in the area, the process built on the trust and confidence that was generated in the past. The situation in Morro da Conceição, in which a dense network of CBOs existed, could have produced a much less encouraging environment for the work, if not 'participation fatigue'. In addition, unlike Vila União, community people have other established mechanisms for gaining access to government, including close links to councillors.

The organizational structure of Morro da Conceição is decentralized, while in Vila União centralism prevails, with a strong focus on the charismatic and dynamic community leader. Easy access to this leader by residents and the lack of a bureaucratic structure, however, made the centralized model appropriate for the effective advocacy of community needs and priorities in this case. While the pluralistic structure in Morro da Conceição potentially could have produced much more effective and comprehensive outcomes, a number of factors blocked this happening. The research in Morro was carried out in a fragmented way, with a range of separate focus groups, and thus it was not possible for a single group or leader to grasp the whole process. The extreme time constraints under which the Consultations took place exacerbated this fragmentation.

One key enabling condition for effective impact at the community level in the Brazil case is suggested from this experience. This is the importance of the effective harnessing of the process by a key group of local people, which can take an overview and plan strategic activities accordingly. If the focus group discussions occur in different places and the process as a whole is not clearly captured by each of the groups, the probability of successful learning and strategic use of the knowledge generated is reduced. Other factors that facilitated the successful exploitation of the process include community trust and good community access to the research team.

The discussion of the Brazilian case shows that in both the community and the national policy arenas, the spaces for the impact of the study were not limited to the information it produced, but by the particular features of the spaces in which key actors were able to make use of this information. Perhaps the most successful example of direct influence, in the Vila União case, owed a great deal to existing experience of creating and occupying spaces for action in advocating community needs. Examples of restricted influence were related at both levels to the sometimes conflicting objectives of different actors and the difficulties of communication between them.

Somaliland

In Somaliland, the World Bank agreed to work through an international NGO and two CBOs to obtain the opinion of the residents of a country whose previous government had collapsed, and whose nascent government has yet to be internationally recognized. Given the government's hopes of attaining international development assistance, the symbolic recognition of the country by an international financial institution was a unique and singularly important channel for impact, and one that did not rely on the existence of dense networks of policy actors that characterized the Brazilian and Viet Namese cases. In other respects, the impact of the Somaliland study can be discussed in terms of the action-based partnership between the implementing actors, the absence of a national policy arena and government planning, and the development activities of the local communities that carried out the study.

Actors in partnership for local change
ActionAid, the international NGO that acted as a channel to facilitate the study, had an existing relationship with the CBOs in Sanaag and Togdheer. They had several stated objectives for taking part in the Consultations initiative: to increase their understanding of poverty in the Somaliland context, to further their own and Somalilanders' knowledge of participation, and to demonstrate that communities could feed directly into policy thinking and formation through assessments that they conducted themselves. Action-Aid staff, reflecting on the process with hindsight, also noted that several objectives emerged during the course of the study. Firstly, when it became clear that the Somaliland report was the only national study to reflect pastoral

livelihoods, it became important to the ActionAid team that pastoral issues should be reflected in the outputs of the Consultations process. A second objective, which was not clearly stated but was certainly in some people's minds, was the desire to put Somaliland on the map by consulting Somalilanders.

For the Somali implementing partners, Sanaag Community Based Organization (SCBO) and Toghdeer Community Based Organization (TCBO), the findings of the study immediately fed into the formation of long-term development strategies, such as the three-year plans that both organizations presented to their donors. They have also used the results for the allocation of projects and resources in their programme coverage areas. The board members of the CBOs have also reported that the study has increased the knowledge and capacity of their members as regards participatory methodologies, quite apart from the useful data and information obtained from their constituent communities.

The SCBO and TCBO study teams were entirely composed of residents of the Sanaag and Togdheer regions, including women, elders and intellectuals. The follow-up findings reveal that, at the community level, the study was an extremely valuable piece of work that has contributed to the ongoing process of reconstruction. It stimulated debate and generated inputs into the long-term development thinking of the local people, who are organizing their communities to tackle their immediate needs in the absence of effective government. The primary ownership of the information, debate and findings remains local.

The absence of a resourced and fully active state structure negated the possibility of impact on national policy, at least in the short term. However, all the development actors who were interviewed one year later noted that a major impact of the Consultation process was that it provided information that defined poverty from a Somali pastoralist perspective, in a country in which all national records were destroyed in the civil war, and where no national institutions exist to collect this kind of information. Despite the lack of a resourced dissemination strategy, the Consultations study was distributed as widely as possible. The director general of the Ministry of National Planning stated that he regularly shows a copy of the study to the international organizations doing business with his office. The director of International Cooperation for Development stated that his staff use the document regularly, and found it particularly useful during a feasibility study for starting a programme in Togdheer region. Although the agency of government policy actors in Somaliland is severely restricted by the lack of resources, an impact on future policy content could be achieved by the provision of credible information in a situation in which very little currently exists.

In such a policy context, the implementing partnership for the Somaliland Consultations study relied on existing networks of the long-term participatory work being carried out by community institutions and their advocates. As such, rooted in essentially action-oriented partnerships, the major impact of the study was felt at the local level.

Spaces for local action

In the context of the existing structure of community institutions, what space did the Consultations study create for local action in Somaliland? According to participants in focus group discussions, the study introduced questions and analysis that were not directly linked to any possible funding proposal, and this lack of a link to funding provided local people with a space for discussion that was perceived as having 'no strings attached'. The existence of this space stimulated debate on subjects otherwise not debated or regarded as taboo, particularly concerning gender issues.

Members of the participating communities[16] reported that the study process provided them with appropriate venues to discuss and analyse their own problems, which led to an increase in cooperation between various groups in the community. In an exercise that updated the priority problem ranking carried out in Ceel Bilicile as part of the Consultations study, the issue of local governance – a high priority problem in the original exercise – was not included in the updated priority problem ranking. Meanwhile, the village committee – which did not exist when the study was carried out – ranks highly in the updated institutional ranking and analysis. The headman and his committee were selected and put in place in late 2000, after the study. Members of one focus group stated that the formation of the village committee was actually one of the outcomes of the study, because the study provided the community with an opportunity to come together and discuss their common problems, since other community meetings usually concentrated on solving a specific problem or issue. They further explained that the institutional analysis exercise included in the study was instrumental in initiating community debate and discussions on the type of leadership that the community needed and the qualities such leadership should have. They added that the criteria for evaluating institutions that were generated by the discussion teams were taken to the wider community to initiate the formation of the village committee and its selection process.

In Qoyta village, improvements in community cohesion and cooperation were illustrated by a new community-owned shallow well. The construction of the well was the result of a general community mobilization led by the elders and the women's group. Almost all the members of the village contributed to the construction of the well, and a management committee has been established. Residents attributed the initiation of this community project to their membership of the Togdheer CBO, which they joined last year after the Consultations study. In the Somaliland case, in which the Consultations formed part of an ongoing process of learning and reconstruction at the local level, it is difficult to isolate the study process as the single cause of any of the developments described by local residents. In the case of the Qoyta well, for example, the Consultations process was one link in a causal chain of activities and events which, in combination, led to a change. Despite this difficulty in attributing causality, there is a broad consensus among participants that the study provided a space for discussion and negotiation at the community level which encouraged existing processes and catalysed new ones.

Beyond the boundaries of the community, there is a potential for spaces that might open up as the nascent structures of government evolve. Residents of Ceel Bilicile village noted another impact of the study: less suspicion of outsiders and development agencies. They stated that although they receive no support from outside development organizations or the government, they would now be willing to welcome them and work with them.

A similar shift in attitude is reported by the regional planning coordinator for Sanaag in Somaliland, who was interviewed by a CBO member for the follow-up study. When asked for his first impressions of the Consultations study, he replied

> *I raised my eyebrows in surprise, as experience tells me that a study of such magnitude can be conducted only by government or multilateral institutions like the World Bank, with a lot of preparation. Therefore I could not believe that a local organization like Sanaag CBO could handle such a huge task.*

Commenting as an observer of the process, he continued

> *I appreciate the simple and easy methodologies being employed to develop a very distinctive and clear definition for the word poverty in Somali context, because I had the impression that it could never be defined.*

In this case, a shift in attitude about the possibility of local people carrying out the impossible task of defining poverty has led to a concerted effort by one local government official to use the findings within his limited sphere of influence. The study produced a great deal of information that has been used in the planning and prioritization of regional needs, and the findings of the study have been used to develop a checklist for approving proposals presented by local NGOs. Other agencies visiting the region are advised to use the study as a basis for their own assessments.

At the community and regional levels, the impact of the study in Somaliland can perhaps be characterized in terms of governance. In the domain of internal community governance, the study was one episode in an ongoing process of development activities that provided space for a range of local actors to discuss common problems, in turn influencing institutional change. In terms of more formal relationships of governance, such as they are, influence

was felt in terms of changing attitudes among local government officials
towards the development knowledge capacities of communities.

Bulgaria

Participatory poverty research in the Bulgarian context can be characterized
as a challenge to the centralization of existing policy processes, because it
presupposes a real decentralization of decision-making processes, and
receptivity to the opinions of different stakeholders and the requirements of
the fast-changing social environment. In other words, a participatory process
demands that decision-making processes are turned into dynamic, collective
acts that are both bottom-up and top-down, and which presume a constant
exchange of information and transparency, and proactive and responsible civic
and administrative action. Consequently, if we want to assess the impact of
the Consultations study on poverty reduction policy in Bulgaria, in which
the traditional approach to policy is inimical to participatory policy-making,
we must first examine whether it has helped to bring about a change in the
principles of policy-making or the attitudes of policy-makers to the inclusion
of formerly excluded actors in the policy process. Secondly, we need to
examine the dynamics of local change experienced by study participants and
their allies in civil society.

Influencing national policy: Challenging the principles of policy-making?
The Bulgarian Consultations study took place in the context of a polarized
policy arena. Interviews with government officials, poverty researchers and
NGO activists for the follow-up study saw a broad agreement among
respondents that social policy is made at the top level of government, and has
no serious relationship to poverty studies. Most government officials remained
committed to the centralized model, although a few argued that decision-
making could be opened up to include local government; NGO activists and
poverty researchers were adamant that the centralized model should change.

In the context of such polarized domestic opinions concerning policy-
making, donors and international financial institutions are advocating a range
of mechanisms for poverty reduction policy which are associated with
evidence-based planning and policy processes, including an expanding
portfolio of programmes and research processes that use participatory
methodologies. The impacts of these initiatives are beginning to be felt at the
level of local NGOs and government.[17] It is important to situate the Consultations study in this wider process of change.

Although these donor-driven strategies can be characterized as an attempt
to include a broader range of previously excluded actors in the policy process,
their implementation raises issues about the dissemination and use of 'new

knowledge' generated by participatory research exercises like the Consultations. Studies have been largely tailored to donor needs, and research reports
are usually in English and get limited publicity. In the absence of a traditional
link between research and policy, there are considerable barriers to impact,
which can be reinforced rather than challenged by participatory processes that
do not challenge the mindsets of policy-makers concerning the use of
information.

The informants in the follow-up study identified a range of difficulties in
establishing links between research and policy. Research in the domestic
context is widely perceived as being commissioned and conducted to confirm
current official social policy. Research that is carried out using different
methodologies, and the apparently contradictory findings to which such
research gives rise, led policy-makers to argue that they did not know whom
to trust. Finally, dissemination is generally weak, and there is no link between
researchers, donors and policy-makers, who seldom speak the same language.

There is some evidence to suggest that the Consultations study formed
part of an attempt to address some of these issues. It was able to build on the
existing donor-driven popularization of social assessments to present findings
at a range of seminars and to contribute to the elaboration of strategies with
a range of policy actors. The seminars include an academic workshop on
understanding and building social capital in Bulgaria and participation in a
meeting of the Carat Coalition on gender at the World Bank. In addition, the
study findings were used as part of a World Bank Poverty Retreat with the
government, and have allowed a richer and more substantive analysis of the
situation of the Roma in the Europe and Central Asia PRSP.[18] In January
2000, senior Bulgarian policy-makers met World Bank officials to discuss ways
of mainstreaming social development and poverty reduction in government
activities. Although Consultations researchers were not invited to this
meeting, the study findings were presented and debated. The result of the
meeting was a decision to develop a national poverty reduction strategy.

This process suggests that efforts are being made to address the problems
of lack of communication and coordination between government and
donors, and to disseminate research findings. The government, after the World
Bank-sponsored poverty retreat, organized a round table dedicated to
elaborating a long-term strategy for monitoring poverty and the reintegration
of underprivileged and vulnerable groups. This combines the efforts of the
Ministry of Labour and Social Policy and NGOs. The round table has had
its profile raised by parliament, which initiated a debate on poverty in
Bulgaria.

In 2001, the government, together with the IMF and the World Bank,
worked on the definition of a poverty line and the formulation of a strategy
and plan of action for poverty reduction in the medium term. The poverty
reduction strategy covers three levels: on the one hand, it applies a classical

approach in defining an adequate poverty line, established through quantitative economic methods, which sets the general national framework of the strategy. The second level specifies different policies towards the most vulnerable groups, relying on social needs assessment methodologies. The third level covers the consolidation of the NGO community, the improvement of information policies, and the promotion of regional initiatives; the focus here is on changing policy-making principles so as to increase the participation of all groups. In addition, the UNDP financed a project with the Ministry of Labour and Social Policy, which has established an anti-poverty information centre that sets up networks for NGOs working on poverty alleviation, and serves as a mediator for civil society engagement.

The national poverty reduction strategy will be completed by teams of consultants, working within the framework of programmes organized and financed by the UNDP and the World Bank. So far, the policy-making system has been opening up towards the issues of poverty and its own change in terms of heeding more Consultations in decision-making under external pressure, not as a result of internal development and need. The Consultations study, identified with the World Bank, has been an important part of this process of attempting to open up the poverty reduction policy arena from the top down. As one of the study researchers reflected, one of the dangers concerning the implementation of participatory assessments is that they are conducted in name only, with the intention of complying with donor demands. The result can be that findings, supposedly established in a democratic and consensual way through the process of the research, represent the views of powerful minorities. This situation might arise in the context of a lack of adequate training in participatory methods and the attitude and behaviour changes that accompany them, and of the dominant culture of research and planning. Although the Consultations had considerable impact within the arena of donor poverty reduction activities, there is little evidence that they had direct influence on national government outside the domain of donor–government negotiations on policy. The 'voices of the poor' were therefore almost exclusively mediated through the lens of donor priorities for poverty reduction.

Catalysing changes: Dynamics of local government and civil society
Beyond the dynamics of the national poverty arena lie spaces for change that participatory research can occupy at the local level. In contrast to the opportunities presented by interactions with local government in the Viet Nam and Brazil cases, Bulgarian decentralized local government is a recent phenomenon, with little power. There was no involvement of local government personnel in the Consultations study; study participants flatly refused to take part in joint meetings with the local authorities, either because they assumed it was pointless, since all decisions are seen to be made at the top,

or because they saw local government as part of the 'mafia' on which they depended for the informal livelihood activities that had become increasingly crucial to their survival. Citizens' perceptions of government are a key determinant in deciding whether involving government staff in participatory poverty research will be useful in enhancing policy influence. In those cases in which trust between government and citizens is very low, governmental involvement might be detrimental to the process or credibility of the research, and thus to the likelihood of impact.

Beyond the domain of local government relations are civil society actors who are directly involved in poverty reduction issues at the community level. The follow-up study provides two examples that illustrate the dynamics of impact on civil society initiatives. The first example is a group of homeless youths who were sleeping rough at Sofia's central railway station, who made up one of the focus groups in the Bulgaria Consultations research. A member of the research team was also member of an NGO working with street children, and he dedicated himself after the study to working towards finding solutions to a number of the problems identified in the study, and to incorporating the findings of the study into the ongoing work of the NGO. As a result of this partnership, and particularly through use of the research report, a day centre has been founded with support from an international NGO partner. This impact is the product of a combination of the Consultations of the homeless, with the analysis of the researchers, the commitment of NGO activists in searching for donors, and the involvement of people with experience of turning proposals into concrete social policies. As in the Somali case, it is difficult to attribute direct causality to the Consultations study. Instead, this outcome should be characterized as one of a series of episodes and events – including the personal commitment of a poor people's advocate, the availability of donor resources and the agency of the homeless youths themselves – which catalysed action.

The second example from Bulgaria relates to the desire for self-organization among a group of Roma[19] people, which resulted from the open-ended discussions undertaken as part of the Consultations study. During the discussion, the members of the group arrived at the conclusion that there was no alternative to self-help, and decided to establish an NGO. Members of the research team provided advice about how they could go about forming an NGO, and put them in touch with already-established Roma organizations. These organizations were, however, far from supportive, and tried to dissuade the group from creating an organization of their own, arguing that they could count on the one that was already in place. Despite this lack of support, the group held a meeting to elect a governing body, which team members attended as guarantors of a fair election, and set about finding a lawyer. Then, somewhere along the way to court registration – someone had to pay the lawyer and the registration fee, and there was some caution about offending the established Roma organizations – the process was halted. The research team, occupied with new work, could not pursue the process and the Roma group themselves had lost confidence and momentum. A good beginning was not brought to a good conclusion.

The case of the Roma reinforces the lessons from the case of the homeless youths in Sofia. Advocates with adequate human and financial resources are critical in catalysing action which has arisen from the initiatives of a new network of actors, which has coalesced around an issue arising from participatory research. In both cases, personal commitment by members of a study team of academics, who lack the capacity, training, resources and time for strategic advocacy work, was a key factor in maintaining momentum for bottom–up initiatives.

The Bulgarian Consultations study can be seen as attempting to occupy two principal spaces for change in the policy process, one at the level of donor–government national poverty reduction policy, and the other at the level of civil society and community self-help initiatives. In both of these spaces, the impact that was achieved took place through the mobilization and creation of informal networks of actors, brought together at the micro level around substantive issues arising from the research, and at the macro level through a broader shift towards widening the poverty reduction agenda. In both spaces, impact was constrained by poor links with government, and the considerable inertia of centralized policy-making.

Ethiopia

In Ethiopia, the follow-up study found that impact was minimal. In contrast to the other countries discussed, the Consultations field research was very rapid and was carried out as a consultancy by a team of academics who were isolated not only from the World Bank but from broader policy and advocacy networks. In addition, the context of top-down policy-making was not conducive to influence at the national level.

Barriers to impact at three levels

The follow-up study returned to two of the communities in which the Consultations research was carried out. There, discussions with participants focused largely on difficulties with the Consultations methodology. The research team cited lack of time for engagement with communities as a serious constraint on impacts: the team spent only a day in each of several communities to collect the study findings.[20] They felt that many of the questions in the process guide for the study were drafted with the South Asian experience in mind, and that although the questions were adapted to the Ethiopian context, the fit was not comfortable. Participants commented that there were too many visual tools in the research. The lesson to be drawn from the lack of local impact in the Ethiopian case is fundamental: if the methodology used for an interaction between local people and researchers is not appropriate to the context – whether because of cultural considerations or lack of time – the chances of meaningful impact are reduced.

In the Consultations process, relationships with local government were carefully negotiated. Following established tradition, it was necessary to formally request the cooperation of the zonal administrative councils, and these requests were transmitted to wereda[21] administrative councils and kebele[22] chairs. The contact people throughout the study were the wereda representatives, who played a crucial role in facilitating the consultations. The kebele peasant association chairpeople were key actors in organizing the focus groups and providing information on community characteristics. None of these officials, however, took part in the actual collection of information. On the contrary, the team ensured that no officials were present during the consultations, fearing that they might influence the process and the discussions. This dilemma can be characterized as a trade-off between the need to maintain the open nature of discussions, and the need to include enough local actors to allow the research process to have a direct impact on poverty reduction at the local level. In this case, the potential for establishing networks for impact was reduced in the pursuit of credible research findings.

Considerable barriers to impact were also discovered at the national level. The team had no resources for dissemination, and did not receive from Washington the copies of the national site report on which it was expecting to base its own, informal efforts to disseminate findings.[23] The World Bank Country Office was reluctant to meet the research team during or after the Consultations study was carried out, although a member of World Bank staff presented a certificate of appreciation to the research facilitators.

Despite these barriers, the findings were presented at a university research seminar to which government officials were invited, and at a seminar of invited social scientists. A shortened version of the findings has been published, and is being sold at a subsidized price in order to reach as many people as possible. The team conclude that, despite a very weak overall dissemination strategy, those who are in a position to shape the country's poverty strategy and policy have access to the findings produced by the Consultations process, or have heard about them. The question posed by the Ethiopia team concerns whether or not these policy-makers are willing to listen to the poor. In particular, the research team cite two of the main messages in the draft PRSP, which run completely contrary to the findings of the Consultations study. The first is that poverty has declined in the 1990s; in contrast, the Consultations findings presented poor people's analysis of increased poverty in the 1990s. Second, the PRSP states that there is no landlessness in Ethiopia, while the Consultations findings suggest that landlessness is a major cause of poverty.

Such apparent discrepancies are explicable. In the first example, the divergence of opinion on the direction of poverty trends can be traced to methodological differences, and has stimulated debate in other countries in which qualitative and quantitative poverty monitoring exercises tell different stories. In the second example, the hugely politicized nature of the debate on land reform in Ethiopia has given rise to entrenched positions and narratives, which are largely unrelated to the interaction between poverty and landlessness. The implication of these apparent discrepancies lies less in their detail than in understanding why they have failed to stimulate debate or change.

The Ethiopian case raises a further general point about understanding impact. The team there notes that there is very little to say about the impact on policy content of the Consultations since it has only been just over a year since the study was carried out, and it takes longer than that for government offices – at least in Ethiopia – to respond to the outcome of research on any issue. In all five cases, it is important to note that policy influence takes time, and that a one-year time frame is too short to fully understand impact in this area. It does not, however, seem premature to suggest that the degree of difficulty the Consultations study in Ethiopia encountered in achieving impact implies considerable challenges for future activities of this kind in the absence of broader changes in the way policy is made, and the implementation of participatory research initiatives.

CONCLUSION

The very diverse range of political environments examined in this chapter suggests that some contexts are more conducive than others to the acceptance of the perspectives of poor people in the policy arena. For a participatory research process to effectively and strategically influence policy, an understanding of contextual factors and entry points needs to be reached and applied, both in planning and implementation.

The diverse routes to impact identified in the five follow-up studies – and the different levels of impact achieved by the Consultations process – are illustrative of the very wide range of entry points for impact that a study can have in any scenario. These entry points are firstly related to scale: whether the impact takes place at the level of the community itself; or at the interface of the community and the other institutions and authorities with which it interacts; or at the national level. Such entry points are not always mutually exclusive but have sometimes proved mutually reinforcing, as the Brazilian case illustrates.

Secondly, they are related to different kinds of space within the policy process. The Viet Nam case, for example, illustrates the opening of a policy space at the level of central government through the establishment of a carefully composed Poverty Working Group, which slowly developed a sense of ownership of the PPA process and advocated the use of its findings in national planning processes. In traditionally centralized policy environments like those in Bulgaria and Ethiopia, spaces for effective community action provided by the decentralized local government structures are absent. In Brazil, more space in this arena is on offer, but the opportunity to occupy it is mediated by local institutional configurations.

Within the spaces opened up in the structures of government or local institutions, the acceptable rules and norms of citizen action were also a determining factor in the impact of the Consultations studies, ranging from the activities of local communities in Somaliland to facilitate their own development in the absence of effective government, to the refusal of study participants to work with local authorities in Bulgaria. The importance of such norms is perhaps best illustrated in the Brazilian case by the contrast between Vila União and Morro de Conceição, where communities with different approaches to local governance and action had very different approaches to using the Consultations findings. Such norms for action are an important part of determining the kind of impact a participatory research episode might be able to have.

A principal mechanism for influence employed in the Consultations research was the attempt to occupy spaces opened up by existing programmes and projects. Attempting to link the Consultations study with ongoing processes compensated for the lack of built-in strategic resources for policy influence at the country level. The strength and nature of this link was an important determinant in the type of impact the process was able to make. The closest linkages were in the Viet Nam and Somaliland cases. Linking the Consultations study to the Viet Nam PPA maximized impact at the level of the national policy agenda, while the partnership with ActionAid and CBOs in the Somaliland case gave an opportunity for the work to contribute to local understandings and ongoing processes of change.

The experiences of the other countries with less integrated links are equally instructive. In the Brazilian case, the intended links to ongoing Bank projects developed slowly and were impeded by difficulties with communication and coordination. However, opportunistic links to ongoing processes of changing local governance, mediated through local activism, allowed a strong impact in Vila União. In the Bulgarian case, the inclusion of an NGO worker on the research team provided the homeless youth in Sofia with an advocate for change, rather than a systematic link between the research and an ongoing programme. For the Roma, the lack of such an advocate contributed to the failure of their initiative. In the absence of integrated links with ongoing processes, individual advocates become particularly important impact mechanisms, especially at the local level.

Regardless of the contextual backdrop of the policy process, the use of participatory research to influence policy is often described in terms of the production and dissemination of information. As such, policy-makers are provided with information about poverty as it is experienced and analysed by poor people, and this information helps them to make better policy to reduce poverty. The follow-up studies have shown that the production and dissemination of the study findings remained a basic factor in determining impact; where dissemination largely failed, as in Ethiopia, the prospects for impact were minimal. Examples from Viet Nam and Brazil, however, also highlight the idea that adequate dissemination alone is not enough: the credibility of the methodology and the findings being disseminated needs to be established. The broad lesson that the case studies suggest is the importance of viewing participatory research as a process, rather than as an episode of research whose findings need to be disseminated. This process needs to be based on an understanding of the local context, and designed accordingly.

Clearly, it is not just the existence of policy spaces and the production and generation of new knowledge within the policy process that mediate the impact of participatory research, but the actions and agency of different policy actors within those spaces. This chapter has discussed the motivation and strategies of a range of different actors: the World Bank, multilateral donors, national and local governments, civil society organizations and study participants in local communities. In those cases in which the Consultations study had the most impact, the work was situated in existing networks of policy actors or local activists who were able to use the process and findings of the study to advocate for change within and beyond their existing action spaces. In some cases it allowed actors to strengthen existing links with different kinds of actors, thus creating new partnerships around poverty reduction issues. In some cases, the absence of the involvement of a particular kind of actor – particularly government officials – presented a key challenge in facilitating impact.

The case studies suggest that the best potential for impact lies in the engagement of a range of actors in a process of constructing poverty knowledge. As noted in the introduction to this chapter, PPAs have had three main functions: to increase the quality and relevance of information on poverty, to support the rights of poor people to be involved in the definition and analysis of poverty, and to open spaces in which poor people's perspectives can influence policy-makers' perspectives. Whichever of these functions a participatory research process aims to fulfil, its impact will depend in large part on how well the process is understood as an integral part of the wider policy environment it is trying to influence.

NOTES

1 Our thanks to Robert Chambers, Robin LeMare, Rosemary McGee, Deepa Narayan and Patti Petesch for comments on earlier drafts of this chapter.

2 Consultations with the Poor is the 23-country study that was one element of the 'Voices of the Poor' project; its findings were published as Narayan et al, 2000a. The other element consisted of reviews of existing PPAs and other participatory research on poverty; findings were published as Narayan et al, 2000b and Brock, 1999. The whole initiative was originally called 'Consultations with the Poor' but adopted the title 'Voices of the Poor' in late 1999.

3 Thanks to funding from DFID, Sida and SDC.

4 *Zonas Especiais de Interes Social* – special zones of social interest.

5 Experience with other PPAs suggests that the production of a single aggregated national report might contribute favourably to policy influence (see Norton et al, 2001).

6 The World Bank staff who implemented the PPA were members of the Poverty Working Group.

7 A draft of this chapter was reviewed by the Consultations of the Poor team at the World Bank in Washington, who contested some of the claims and assertions of the Brazil case study. The chapter was revised to show as clearly as possible where World Bank views of the study impact differed from those of the research team, and how.

8 Petesch, personal communication, 2001.

9 Finalized in March 2000.

10 von Amsberg, personal communication, 2001.

11 Petesch, personal communication, 2001.

12 The World Bank's chief country assistance strategist in the seminar 'O Banco Mundial e o Combate à Pobreza no Brasil', World Bank Brazilian Office, Brasilia, May 30 2000.

13 Interview with Prometropole staff, who asked not to be identified.

14 Poor urban communities lacking infrastructure and/or secure land tenure.

15 19 out of 31 official contacts concerning the problems of the community made between the production of the report and the follow-up study made explicit reference to the Consultations site report.

16 Residents of Qoyta, Ceel Bilicile and Bihn villages, and Erigavo town.

17 The Ministry of Labour and Social Policy, for example, has commissioned an ongoing large-scale participatory assessment of Bulgaria's social assistance system, which includes open-ended discussions and interviews with the directors of welfare offices, social workers and beneficiaries.

18 Launched in March 2000.

19 Roma are 'gypsies', and have a long history of persecution, exclusion and marginalization from Bulgarian society.

20 The Consultations Methodology Guide recommends a minimum of five days in each community, and the Ethiopia example is not typical in terms of the length of Consultations fieldwork in other countries. The point here in terms of the wider study process may well be about the need for training and backstopping.

21 This is equivalent to a district.
22 The lowest unit of administration in the rural and urban areas under the federal system.
23 Although the Consultations of the Poor team in Washington have stated that the Ethiopian team declined to apply for dissemination funds, which were offered to all Consultations teams, the Ethiopian team states that they did not receive the 200 copies of the site report that were promised.

REFERENCES

Brock, K (1999) 'It's not only wealth that matters, it's peace of mind too: A review of participatory work on poverty and illbeing', unpublished paper for 'Voices of the Poor' workshop, Washington, DC, World Bank

Brock, K, Cornwall, A and Gaventa, J (2001) *Power, Knowledge and Political Spaces in the Framing of Poverty Policy*, IDS Working Paper 143, Brighton, IDS

Carswell et al (2000), *Sustainable Livelihoods in Southern Ethiopia*, IDS Research Report 44, Brighton, IDS

Keeley, J and Scoones, I (2000) 'Knowledge, power and politics: The environmental policy-making process in Ethiopia', *Journal of Modern African Studies*, Vol 38, No 1, pp89–120

Narayan, D with Patel, R, Schafft, K, Rademacher, A and Koch-Schulte, S (2000a) *Voices of the Poor: Can Anyone Hear Us?*, New York, Oxford University Press

Narayan, D, Chambers, R, Shah, M and Petesch, P (2000b) *Voices of the Poor: Crying Out for Change*, New York, Oxford University Press

Norton A, with Bird, B, Brock, K, Kakande, M and Turk, C (2001) *A Rough Guide to PPAs: Participatory Poverty Assessments – An Introduction to Theory and Practice*, London, Overseas Development Institute, Centre for Aid and Public Expenditure

Rahmato, D and Kidanu, A (1999) *Ethiopia, Consultations with the Poor: A Study to Inform the World Development Report 2000/2001 on Poverty and Development*, Addis Ababa, World Bank

World Bank (1999) *Methodology Guide: Consultations with the Poor*, Washington, DC, World Bank

CHAPTER **5**

POWER, KNOWLEDGE AND POLICY INFLUENCE: REFLECTIONS ON AN EXPERIENCE[1]

Robert Chambers

Poverty is the central issue of our time. . . Don't underestimate the importance of confirming within the World Bank that poverty is the central issue. . . [Voices of the Poor is] extraordinarily important to me and to the Bank. . . extra-ordinarily important to us in terms of direction. . . I need the voices you are unleashing. . . Hold me accountable for seeing this through the system. . . The first thing we have to do is move our institution. . . [I am] looking for an army to help me. If you will become part of that army I will be delighted. . . Be constructively critical. . . I am willing to make my time available to this group. You need to raise your voices. . . [This is] a straightforward offer. It is what I am here to do. I am not here to preside over the status quo. (From remarks by James Wolfensohn, President of the World Bank, to the Consultations with the Poor Workshop, World Bank, Washington, DC, 22 September 1999)

INTRODUCTION

THIS CHAPTER REFLECTS on personal experience of research, analysis and representation designed to influence policy and practice. The

23-country participatory Consultations with the Poor[2] project was managed from the World Bank and undertaken to influence the *World Development Report (WDR) 2000/2001*. This study illuminates methodological, epistemological and ethical challenges, dilemmas and trade-offs which are common to much policy-oriented research. In the Consultations these were sharpened by the aim to privilege and represent the voices and realities of poor people, consulted on a large scale and in a short time. Researchers had power to determine how open or closed the process was. Knowledge was formed iteratively through interactions of researchers' and participants' priorities, concepts, frames, realities and patterns of analysis and representation. Academic values and practices in part conflicted with the ethics of policy influence. The findings of the Consultations had power to outrage and inspire. Practical lessons can be drawn from the experience and impact of the study.

In this chapter I seek to draw practical lessons concerning power, knowledge and policy influence. It is based on personal reflection on a process and an experience, relating these to a wider body of ideas and evidence. This includes some of my own motivations and limitations, and trade-offs between conflicting values. Much of the material is what I recollect of my behaviour, and the method is critical reflection, embracing error more than celebrating success. I do not pretend to give a balanced overview. Those who criticize qualitative research will find grist to their mill. My challenge to them is also to recognize its strengths, and to be at least equally self-critical and transparent about their own methods and work. It is tempting to quote the Bible and say that whoever is without sin should cast the first stone. But that is not entirely appropriate. Let stones be cast, but after beating one's own breast with them first.

In fairness to the co-authors of *Voices of the Poor: Crying Out for Change* – Deepa Narayan, Meera K Shah and Patti Petesch – I wish to place on record that I know from personal communications how much more systematic they were than I was. This is an autocritique, not a critique of my colleagues. I shall conclude that a good way forward is a combination of critical reflection, action to offset distortions arising from power relations, and methodological pluralism. I hope these reflections will be of interest and help to others.

CONSULTATIONS WITH THE POOR

Consultations with the Poor was a 23-country study, part of a project known as Voices of the Poor (Narayan et al, 2000b). The intention was to contribute to the concepts and content of the *WDR 2000/2001* on poverty and development. Apart from the section on impact below, which considers Voices of the Poor as a whole, this chapter is concerned with the Consultations.

By any standards, the training, fieldwork and initial in-country analysis and synthesis of the Consultations were a considerable practical, logistical and methodological effort.[3] In a few months in late 1998 and very early 1999 two methodological workshops were held, methods pilot-tested in four countries, and a process guide devised. In the first half of 1999, country teams were found and trained; broadly comparable participatory methods of analysis, both verbal and visual, were facilitated with groups of women, men, youths and sometimes children in some 272[4] sites in 23 countries; site reports were written; national workshops were held; 21 national synthesis reports were completed; and an international synthesis workshop was held near Delhi. A global synthesis (Narayan et al, 1999) and 21 national synthesis reports were published and presented at the World Bank in September, and a final fuller analysis and synthesis came out as a book *Voices of the Poor: Crying Out for Change* (Narayan et al, 2000b) a year later.[5]

The process of the Consultations was managed and led within the World Bank. The Participation Group at the IDS at the University of Sussex was contracted separately by DFID to contribute technical assistance.[6] My own part was to engage on behalf of IDS in the early discussions and negotiations with the World Bank, to take some part in preliminary workshops, and then to be involved in analysis and writing as one of the authors of *Voices of the Poor*.

In the course of this experience I was a participant in the exercise of power in the construction and use of knowledge. This brought home dilemmas and choices involving costs and benefits, trade-offs and a search for win–win solutions in research, analysis and policy influence. It highlighted some ways in which power shapes knowledge. And it pointed to the importance and difficulty of reflexivity. I use reflexivity to mean self-critical epistemological awareness, entailing critical reflection on the part one plays, and one's relationships and interactions play, in the formation, framing and representation of knowledge.

TO ENGAGE OR NOT TO ENGAGE

A first choice was whether to engage or not to engage with the Consultations. I was not alone in having reservations about collaborating in research with the World Bank.[7] Previous experience had shown how power, impatience and preconceived ideas and priorities on the part of Bank staff could lead to systemic distortion and deception. I had already written about this as part of the theme that 'all power deceives' (Chambers, 1988, pp54–59; 1992; 1997, pp71–73 and 97–100). I knew of cases in which Bank staff had appropriated and taken credit for the work of others, and where Bank staff or editors had infuriated and frustrated researchers by heavily red-pencilling their drafts. I had myself had the title of a paper changed by a Bank editor.[8] There was, too, a sense of a legal bottom line limiting critical comment. I had also had the privilege of being invited to facilitate a workshop at the World Bank on values and incentives in that organization, and what I learned from that experience did not encourage optimism about early change in its culture and behaviours. At the same time, I had been asking myself deeper questions about the very existence of the Bank, and whether it was or could be on balance a force for good in the world. I might not have been the only person who toyed with the idea of an alternative world development report on poverty and development, to be launched at the same time as the official one.

However, the World Bank, like Everest, is there. It exists. For some, the right course may be to criticize and oppose it from outside. For others it is to engage with it but still from outside. Yet others, including able and committed people whom I know and respect, have joined it to work for change from within. For our part in the Participation Group at IDS, we consulted colleagues in the South and North. They thought we should engage. At the same time they stressed that the decision was in the end ours.

As incentives to engage, there were the challenges of trying, however modestly, to help develop a new approach to giving voice to poor people on a global scale, and of influencing the World Bank, the WDR and perhaps development thinking, policy and practice more widely. Against engagement was the danger of contributing to the legitimation of the World Bank, which might use the exercise for public relations. This might help to cover up its deficiencies and delay recognition of the need for radical change in its staffing, culture, funding and relationships.

In having such a degree of freedom of choice, we were unusually fortunate. For many researchers and consultants, whether in the North or South, choice is more constrained: work commissioned by the World Bank is relatively well paid, raises one's professional status and might lead to further contracts. Some want the work and income to augment already adequate lifestyles. For them to turn down a contract for ethical reasons ought not to be too problematic. For others – academics and consultants struggling to gain a livelihood, educate their children, care for relatives, pay a mortgage or build a house – it is harder, though some to their credit do so.[9]

The decision was evenly balanced. The counterfactual is unknowable. The Bank side accepted our amendments to the draft outline for the Consultations project. It also seemed that under the leadership of Ravi Kanbur the WDR 2000/2001 would be a major and good step forward in policy thinking. It deserved to be supported and if possible influenced. Within our Participation Group at IDS there was a range of views. However, our core funding from DFID, SDC and Sida, and DFID's willingness to fund us directly for work on the Consultations, seemed to promise a relationship with the Bank of partnership rather than that which I had observed in some other cases of funding patron and client. The assurance of independent funding was a factor in tipping the balance. So some of us did engage.

DILEMMAS IN PRACTICAL TRADE-OFFS

From the start it was clear that with the usual constraints of time and resources there would have to be painful trade-offs. Some of the more challenging and interesting concerned time, resources, scale, representativeness, methods and follow-up. In brief, these were as follows.

Time and resources versus scale and representativeness

There was a tension between paradigms: the dominant statistical canons of validity and those of qualitative research. The former argued for more and the latter for fewer countries, communities and groups of poor people. At an early stage the proposal being explored was for a focused comparable study of possibly 15–20 communities, rural and urban, in each of 30 countries. The latter favoured a smaller number of communities and countries bearing in mind issues of logistics, finance, quality, feasibility of analysis and follow-up with communities: a range of 5 to 12 countries was discussed. As one who favoured fewer countries and fewer sites, I underestimated the ability of those in the World Bank to make things happen quickly on a large scale. It was remarkable that in the event, 23 countries were involved, with some 272 communities. The opportunism of running with those countries in which there was interest, willingness and capacity was a practical trade-off between feasibility and other constraints. There were obvious gaps, but the final tally of countries gave a better spread of representation than might have been expected:

- In Latin America and the Caribbean: Argentina, Bolivia, Brazil, Ecuador and Jamaica.
- In Africa: Egypt, Ethiopia, Ghana, Malawi, Nigeria, Somaliland and Zambia.
- In Asia: Bangladesh, India, Indonesia, Sri Lanka, Thailand and Viet Nam.
- In Eastern Europe and the former USSR: Bosnia, Bulgaria, the Kyrgyz Republic, Russia and Uzbekistan.

Scale and financial resources, time, training, fieldwork and in-country analysis

The time taken in early negotiations, the amount and timing of funding, and the deadlines for completion constrained the training of field teams and their work. As an observer who did not take part in this phase, my main reflection is that the scale and quality of the work were beyond reasonable expectations, and this was largely because of the intense commitment and sacrifices of those involved. More time and money would have been better, but the urgency and pressure brought out the best in many people.

Scale, time, resources and orientation versus community-level follow-up

The combination of a large scale, a shortage of time and resources and the orientation of the study made local-level follow-up difficult in most cases. In the practice of PRA[10] and also in PPAs, a recurrent concern has been that there should be follow-up at the community level; if this is unfeasible, it should be made abundantly clear from the outset. With PRA, a common abuse has been raising and then disappointing local people's expectations (see Yates and Okello, this volume). The process guide was clear on this point:

> **Avoid generating expectations.** *Another issue to be kept in mind is that of generating any expectations. A consultative process, like the one being adopted by this study (and with the focus on understanding people's problems and priorities), can create expectation of some sort of benefits in people's minds. It is important to explain clearly at the very outset that this is only a study to understand poor people's perceptions. There are no direct benefits or follow-up to these discussions. However, it is possible that the results from the study could influence national policy, and in turn have a positive impact on the people's lives in an indirect manner. However, whether or when this will happen can not be predicted. This may have to be reiterated several times during the course of the fieldwork, as it is highly undesirable to generate any false expectations.* (World Bank 1999, p51)

In the event, there were a variety of practices and forms in which there were some local benefits. In Bolivia, unemployed workers were paid for their time. In Bangladesh where NGOs (ActionAid, Concern and Proshika) themselves funded the Consultations, there was immediate follow-up in at least one community, Khaliajuri, with a housing programme. In Brazil one community leader used multiple copies of the site report to apply pressure for better services (see Adan et al, this volume). Also on the positive side of the balance, it is quite common for participants in processes of this sort to say that they gain from meeting and talking to one another, from being listened to with empathy and interest, from their shared analysis, and from finding a sense of solidarity. All the same, the ethical issues of taking people's time and of raising their expectations were and remain a worrying concern, not just in this research but in poverty research generally, whether participatory or not.

Scale, number of aspects and open-endedness versus analysability

From the beginning, we all recognized that the larger the scale, the greater the number of aspects covered and the greater the open-endedness, the more difficult would be the analysis. This was addressed in part by reducing the number of sites in each country to a norm of some eight to ten; in part by restricting the core topics to four (see below); and in part by a degree of standardization of method. An early proposal that the process should include a questionnaire survey was abandoned. The open-ended and participatory process adopted instead was intended to allow poor people's concerns and categories to emerge from their own experience and analysis.[11] There were still dilemmas of language. Closed categories and narrow concepts would impose 'our' realities on 'theirs'. The process guide, moreover, had to be written in English (but was translated into Amharic, Bulgarian, Indonesian, Russian and Spanish, among others).

POWER TO OPEN AND CLOSE

Limited time and resources accentuated dilemmas over how much to open or close the participatory processes. As in all research, planning the methodology entailed the exercise of power to set boundaries on what would be found. In our planning workshops we were acutely aware of these issues, and took pains to choose and recommend participatory approaches, methods and behaviour which would offset biases and limit the extent to which research design determined categories and content. But limits had to be set. After much debate, convergence led to closure on four areas on which poor people were to be invited and facilitated to reflect, analyse and share their experience and ideas. These were:

- Wellbeing and illbeing, poor people's ideas of good and bad quality of life, degrees and categories of wellbeing and illbeing, and how relative numbers in these groups had changed.
- Problems and priorities, their relative importance, and how they had changed.
- Relationships with institutions of the state and of civil society, including institutions within communities, with rankings, and how these had changed.
- Gender relations, and how these had changed.

In all cases the approach was initially to be open-ended, with naming and listing by participants, rather than categories suggested by facilitators. There were, though, topics and aspects that were felt to be so important that they should be specified, both to ensure inclusion and to enhance comparability and ease of analysis. The text in the process guide concerning wellbeing and illbeing can illustrate this: first the process was to be more open-ended to enable people to express their own words and values, and then to be more specified in terms formulated for the researchers:

> *How do people define wellbeing or a good quality of life and illbeing or a bad quality of life?. . . Local definitions of wellbeing, deprivation, illbeing, vulnerability and poverty. Since these terms do not translate easily in local languages, it is better to start by asking the local people for their own terminology and definitions that explain quality of life. Local terminology and definitions must be included in the analysis. Different groups within the same community could be using different terms or phrases for the same subject.* (World Bank, 1999, pp15–16)

A later section in the guide was more specific:

> *Having discussed people's definition of wellbeing and poverty/illbeing, we need to introduce some discussion around four pre-determined categories of critical importance to the study. These include:*
>
> 1 *Risk, security and vulnerability.*
> 2 *Opportunities and social and economic mobility.*
> 3 *Social exclusion.*
> 4 *Social cohesion, crime, conflict and tension.* (World Bank, 1999, pp15–16)

These categories had the potential to focus and simplify analysis, as to some extent they did. At the same time, they presented the well-known problems of preset categories, and getting out what you put in, compounded by the difficulties of translating terms into local languages.

That said, the researchers' site reports from the communities are a remarkable read. The straitjackets of academic theory, jargon and categories are little in evidence. The reports come over as faithful in reporting the realities and values that poor people presented. They manifest an honesty and vivid realism that shines through and carries conviction.[12]

SYNTHESIS AND SOSOTEC

To synthesize so much material generated by participatory processes is not easy. For the national synthesis workshops, guidelines were prepared in Washington. For the international synthesis workshop held at Surajkund near

Delhi in June 1999, we invented, improvized and drew on experience from elsewhere.[13] We had to minimize obvious dangers like overloading a plenary with presentations of some 20 country reports, failing to capture key insights, and simply reproducing pre-existing categories. We needed also to exploit opportunities. These included enabling country team leaders to share what they felt to be most significant, collating materials in categories and forms that could be used by the writing team, and benefiting from synergies of discussion and sharing.

Combinations and sequences of the following were used:

- Verbal presentations by team leaders to small groups (based on the experience that we say things we do not write, and often express them more vividly).
- Each member of a small group having responsibility for collecting insights and points on a particular subject and writing these on cards (based on the principle of active listening and active questioning concerning the subjects).
- Members of different groups with the same subject meeting to share what they had harvested (as a means of collating and comparing experiences).
- Card sorting on the ground to encourage the rapid and flexible emergence of categories.
- Subject groups setting up stalls or collecting points with their cards and other materials, to which others then added.

Part of this was a day-and-a-half of SOSOTEC (self-organizing systems on the edge of chaos). SOSOTEC describes a family of processes based on minimal rules and a skeleton timetable within which individuals act as they see fit.[14] It presupposes participants with something to share and strong motivation. In the form we used, there were collecting points in different rooms for the four main themes of the Consultations. Each theme had one or more coordinator or hunter-gatherer. Scissors, paste, paper and boards were available. Every participant then contributed what and where she could and wanted. Once set up, the system ran itself. Variants of SOSOTEC can be very effective. In the right conditions, under white-heat pressure, participants contribute freely and frankly to a harvest of experience and ideas for a synthesis or report. In the Surajkund workshop we went to great lengths not to limit contributions simply to the topics of the collecting points. This was done by creating a separate place for reflections and contributions that did not fit the other categories.

Immediately after the Surajkund workshop, the four of us who were to be authors of the book met again and spent a day recording on cards the points of greatest significance that had struck us, organizing these into topics, and then allocating responsibilities between ourselves. This iteration proved useful in giving sharper focus, and bridging between the (considerable) SOSOTEC outputs, which we shared and used, and the next stages of analysis and writing.

DILEMMAS AND DECISIONS IN ANALYSIS

The analysis and synthesis of the enormous volume of material – the outputs from the Delhi workshop, many of the 272 site reports which progressively became available, and 21 national synthesis reports – posed huge problems. A book was meant to be in draft by mid-September, giving a mere three months. After the Surajkund workshop, and through most of the summer of 1999, further analysis and synthesis took place both in Washington and at IDS. At IDS, six of us were engaged in parallel, mostly on a part-time basis.[15] In the division of labour with Washington, we were concerned mainly with part of wellbeing/illbeing and with institutions.

Our method was continuous interaction between the material and categories and subjects that seemed important. We assembled extracts of reports by subject on pinboards. The categories multiplied to accommodate the material, some of it not anticipated. I also started sheets of paper on which we listed evidence and sources for particular issues, like 'documents and the poor', where these came up or where I felt there might be significant insights. In doing all this we were exercising power in selection and categorization – 'Shall we have a heading for "shelter"?' was a typical question. We tried continuously to select for 'significance' but of course it was unavoidably 'we' who were deciding what was significant. There was, too, a sense of discovery and excitement when something new emerged or was powerfully illustrated.

In Washington, Meera Shah's approach was more systematic. She read all the site reports for their sections on gender and analysed them, not once, but eventually four times. In this way she evolved and cross-checked categories and insights. This was especially important because of her initially controversial finding, confirmed in a fifth check by research assistants, of a reported overall decline in domestic violence against women (Narayan et al, 2000b, pp124–131). In Washington also, a team of full-time research assistants trawled through the material for particular topics, and in some cases wrote synthesizing notes.

In my own work I can identify circularities, self-validations and biases. These were most evident during the deadline pressure of the summer of 1999. These were less than they would have been with the preset categories of a questionnaire, and we did try to be aware of them and offset them. Nevertheless they were inescapably there at different stages in the whole process. There are lessons from three in particular: looking for evidence, hidden circularity and mental templates.

Looking for evidence

Ideally, I would have read all the site reports. But this was out of the question. My part-time colleagues trawled through them as they were sent on to us and selected extracts. But even these were too voluminous for synthesis. Moreover it became clear that in order to assess extracts, one needed a fuller context. Forced to compromise, there was an element of 'he that seeketh findeth'. We tried to be open to surprises and new topics and insights. The aim, after all, was to represent the realities of poor people, not to box these into our preset categories. There was some success in this. To illustrate, at different stages both those in Washington and those at IDS picked up the following points:

- poor people's negative experiences of the police;
- how small improvements can mean a lot to those who have little;
- the importance of kinship networks, friends and neighbours of the poor;
- the widespread identification of those we described as the 'bottom poor';
- the emergence of the 'new poor' in Eastern Europe and Central Asia; and
- cases in which poor people said they were better off than they had been.[16]

These emerged strikingly from the evidence.

At the same time there simply was not time to allow everything just to emerge. I felt forced to collect for certain topics. In searching my memory, the clearest example of looking for evidence concerns the importance of the body. On the basis of past experience I believed that the significance of the body as the main asset of many poor people was neglected. This was then a category or concern that I brought to the analysis. I was alert for 'good' quotations or examples, which might make or illustrate the theme. They were enough to seem to justify the focus. But I wanted a good summary quotation to make the general point. Somehow I gained the impression that someone in Egypt had said 'Our bodies are our capital'. This was so apposite that we searched for it again and again. We never found it, and yet I believed it was there. Whether I had imagined what I wanted to hear, or whether perhaps it had been said in a workshop by the team leader from Egypt, I simply do not know. Whatever the case, I wanted to find an apt quotation on those lines.

Written like this, a search for evidence to illustrate a theme or a quotation to make a point looks reprehensibly unprofessional. But we can ask whether, unacknowledged, and even without critical awareness, this is not quite common practice. We can ask how frequent such behaviour is, how much it matters and how it should be treated. Reflective readers will have hints from their own behaviour about how common such search and selection might be. To what extent do we search for and notice what will fit our preconceptions? To what extent do we pick out, remember and repeat words, phrases and quotations that stand out because they either fit our frames of reference, or make points we want to make, or give us material with which to disagree?

That it matters should be beyond dispute. The danger is that it packages realities in conventional forms, excludes discordant evidence and prevents new understandings. It can be responsible for academic and scientific conservatism and for serendipity overlooked.

The practical conclusion is to be alert to what one is doing, and especially alert for evidence that does not fit preconceptions. If all one's ideas are confirmed, something is likely to be wrong. A good test is how many surprises there are, how many times one exclaims 'aha!', how many reorganizations of categories, how many changes of ideas. Those we did have in quite good measure.[17]

Hidden circularity

At one stage in writing we were excited at the emergence of 'places of the poor' as a category. It began as part of the chapter on powerlessness. At the same time, infrastructure – water, roads, housing and other services – came out as a priority of participants which did not fit in the structure of the book. It was an 'aha!' experience, so obvious with hindsight, when we saw that these two could combine to become a chapter. I allowed myself smug satisfaction that here at least was a category and a set of insights which had been generated freely by poor people's expression of their realities.

Later, I reread the process guide on site selection and sampling. Site meant community or neighbourhood, village or urban settlement. I found 'The sites should be chosen to reflect two to three of the most dominant poverty groups in a country'. Then I had a second 'aha!' moment, jumping to the conclusion that the category was in part an artefact of the methodology, the result of a hidden circularity: if you look for places in which poor people are conspicuously concentrated, such as remote villages and urban slums, then of course places of the poor will tend to come out as an organizing idea. But there are other poor people who live in places of the rich and less poor, and who would be left out. This, I thought, would make a good example to parade as an insight from self-critical reflection: a category generated by the methodology itself.

A third, more muted and slightly disappointed 'aha!' moment revealed that it was not so simple. An earlier paragraph in the process guide runs 'The selection of sites will be influenced by the ongoing processes in a country. . . In case the study is being linked with an ongoing project, the choice of sites will narrow down to the project area. Similarly, if this study is being linked with another ongoing study in the country, the sites will be chosen from those already selected.' In fact, and sensibly, the basis for selection varied.

My best judgement now is that despite its origins, 'places of the poor' is a good organizing concept, justified both analytically and practically: analytically it integrates spatially many interlinked aspects of deprivation; and practically it is a focused source of recommendations for policy.

Mental templates

The process of analysis made me aware of mental templates. These are mentally embedded diagrams into which realities are fitted. Some like Buzan (1974), Waddington (1977) and de Bono (1981) are versatile and use many patterns. Others, like myself, repeatedly use one or a few patterns only. My IDS colleagues were not slow to identify me as a pentaphiliac, a lover of five circles connected with double-headed arrows. I like drawing this pattern. It has a pleasing symmetry. So if there are four or six emergent categories, I try to expand or conflate them to become five. An early symptom of this now-chronic personal condition was a deprivation trap (Chambers, 1983, p112), linking physical weakness, poverty, isolation, vulnerability and powerlessness. It just so happened that the last two of these resonated with security and empowerment, which – together with opportunity – were the three main themes of the draft WDR made public in January 1999. This only served to reinforce the pattern. So later, in August of that year, during an intense week in Washington in which our writing team had to organize our tasks, the diagram surfaced again. We kept the structure but changed the content to fit emergent categories and analysis. So the circle of isolation became bad social relations, poverty became material lack and want, and vulnerability became security, while physical weakness and powerlessness remained as they were.

The four of us authors fitted our division of the work into these categories, each taking one, with powerlessness shared. In the global synthesis summary (Narayan et al, 1999) presented in Washington in September, the diagram represented development as good change, from five circles of illbeing to five of wellbeing. The central pentagon formed by the doubled-headed connecting lines was characterized as the experience of living and being, of bad and good quality of life.

As analysis proceeded, pentaphilia came under pressure from complexity. In writing about powerlessness, the five broke right open and became (temporarily) 12,[18] as a web of multiple dimensions of disadvantage. Many interactions within the writing team led to the version that appeared in the book *Voices of the Poor* (Narayan et al, 2000b, p249).

A practical conclusion is for analysts to be aware of their mental templates, to reflect critically on how they may distort the framing of realities, and to expand personal repertoires of analytical diagrams for wider choice and a better fit with complexities.

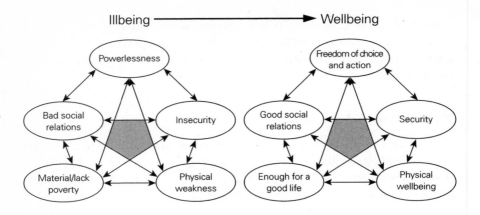

Psychological – the experience of living and being, bad and good quality of lie

Source: Narayan et al, 1999, p5

Figure 5.1 *Development as good change: From illbeing to wellbeing*

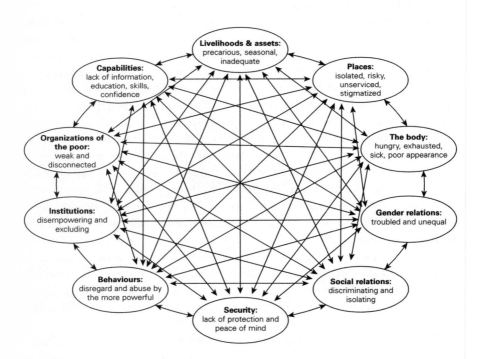

Source: Narayan et al, 2000b, p249

Figure 5.2 *Dimensions of powerlessness and wellbeing*

Professionalism, presentation and policy influence

Among the most thought-provoking trade-offs are those in which canons of normal and narrow professional correctness conflict with effectiveness in influencing policy and practice. The values are incommensurable. There is almost endless scope here for casuistry and controversy. Some issues concern numbers, syntax, selecting, editing, summarizing and simplifying.

Numbers: qualitative versus quantitative analysis

We experienced a classic ambivalence over numbers. On the one hand, in policy influence numbers count, and especially in the culture of the World Bank where macro-economists are still king. Statistics carry with them an authority and conviction that qualitative information has been considered to lack. There was therefore an incentive to generate numbers from the data. On the other hand, the nature of much of the data and the large number of sites meant that numbers would require many judgements of classification (which might be questionable or challenged) and would take a lot of time and effort.

There were times when opinion favoured limiting ourselves to qualitative findings only. But there were numbers generated by the processes, and many potentials for counting. I was engaged with the Bangladesh and India field teams briefly when they were struggling in new territory methodologically to identify and put numbers on trends. This they showed to be possible but time-consuming. Subsequently, all the site reports were analysed centrally by Karen Brock for changes in the top and bottom wellbeing categories, and for causes and effects of poverty and illbeing. Her numbers were not, however, included in *Voices of the Poor*. Other kinds of numerical analysis were undertaken by teams in Washington, notably on two areas of critical debate, again going back to the original site reports. These were trends in domestic violence and institutional rankings by community groups (for the results see Narayan et al, 2000b, p125 and pp201–202 respectively). The numerical analysis of data generated through participatory and visual methods remains a frontier with huge potential for providing alternatives to questionnaires, and where the work on the *Voices* process deserves further analysis to contribute to existing experience and techniques.[19] The Consultations confirmed yet again that much work that is participatory and qualitative can generate numbers to inform policy.

Syntax, summary and simplification

Words and syntax pose dilemmas. Care is needed to avoid over-generalizing. The first chapter of *Voices of the Poor* (Narayan et al, 2000b, p18) concludes with a cautionary discussion of what we felt could and could not be said. We had to avoid expressions like 'everywhere' and 'all over the world'.[20] The evidence from the 272 sites was varied, demanding interpretations that were qualified and nuanced. Through using the terms 'the poor' and 'poor people' we were always in danger of implying misleading homogeneity. Much of what we were discussing could not be reduced accurately to single-sentence or single-phrase generalizations. We resorted to 'often' and its synonyms to convey an appropriately indeterminate degree of significant prevalence.

Pulling in the opposite direction are ethical imperatives for impact. To be remembered, repeated and have an effect, a message is best kept simple and memorable. Through ease of absorption and repetition it might then lead to changed perceptions, priorities, policies and actions.

Much caution is, though, needed here in what is passed on to policy-makers and their speechwriters. It is notable how quickly and deeply easily remembered erroneous statistics become embedded in international discourse, and then how difficult they are to dislodge once they have been frequently repeated.[21] Precisely because of the voluminous material and the need to be concise, we were vulnerable to over-generalizing. Analysing the many site reports for a theme was a formidable task. Nevertheless, for two key issues – trends in domestic violence and institutional rankings by community groups – the individual site reports were analysed in Washington to derive accurate generalizations. The resulting diagrams (Narayan et al, 2000b, pp125 and 201–202) do indeed carry clear but qualified messages, and vindicate the huge effort that went into them.

Shortening and editing were problematic. I found it painful and extraordinarily time-consuming to shorten three chapters by 25 per cent each, as required. Such major shortening presents many agonizing choices of selection and elimination, unavoidably changing the balance and content of what is presented. More problematic still is passing responsibility for further editing to someone who has not been a colleague in the process and who is not familiar with the material. One editor returned a chapter I had drafted and redrafted many times, and then unhappily shortened, after he in turn had further reduced it, with the message that he had cut out the 'emotional' parts.

Soundbite ethics and 'disembodied voices'

Some of the conflicts and dilemmas can be illustrated with a story against myself.

In a draft for this chapter I wrote as follows about James Wolfensohn's speech to the Board of Governors of the World Bank in September 1999:

> *Of the poor he said, Let me share with you their world in their own words. An old woman in Africa: 'A better life for me is to be healthy, peaceful and to live in love without hunger.'* (Wolfensohn, 1999)

Mr Wolfensohn cannot be expected to have known that the Ethiopian woman who said this was reportedly only 26 years old. Nor is he likely to have known that she went on to say:

'*Love is more than anything. Money has no value in the absence of love.*'

These may, indeed, have been sentiments to which he would have subscribed. But for whatever reason they had been edited out. Nor is such editing so unusual. I have done it myself. When faced with a long quotation, only part of which is relevant to a context, I have shortened it, leaving dotted lines to indicate where cuts have been made. For Mr Wolfensohn to have used the whole quotation would have distracted attention from the punchy sequence of voices of the poor he was quoting, and detracted from the impact of his speech. Which arguably was far more important than pedantic faithfulness to the words and meanings of the Ethiopian woman. I wonder what she would think. She might be annoyed, indifferent, flattered, approving or some mix of these. I wonder, too, what you, dear reader, think?'

At that stage I knew that in *Voices of the Poor* (Narayan et al, 2000b, p22) the 'full' quotation above appeared at the head of a section 'Wellbeing is multidimensional'. Since I was the main drafter of this section, I accept responsibility for this, and for the form in which it appeared. It was such a favourite quotation that we had debated among us authors where to place it for best effect.

To be on the safe side, however, I sought out the original in the Ethiopia National Synthesis Report (Rahmatu and Kidanu, 1999, p60). This indicated that the woman was a divorcee who had been educated to secondary level and then stopped learning because of marriage. I was then dismayed to find the following in a question–and–answer sequence:

What about the future? In the future I have the idea of improving my level of education, go to a town and lead a better life. A better life for me is to be healthy, peaceful and live in love without hunger. Love is more than anything. Money has no value in the absence of love. (Rahmatu and Kidanu, 1999)

My first reaction was annoyance: to include the first sentence of her response would weaken the force and impact of my critique. But this was overtaken by a wry smile. For I had caught myself doing precisely what I was criticizing, using an abbreviated quotation, moreover without dotted lines, when the fuller one would not have made my point as effectively. At issue also is the use of quotations without their full context. On the one hand there were those who considered that 'disembodied voices' could mislead when presented without an understanding of the processes and conditions which led to what was reported to have been said, and even sometimes of what sort of person had been speaking. They could be dismissed as decontextualized anecdotal snippets. On the other hand, there was the thought that a 'good' quotation might make an important point forcefully and contribute to good change. The anecdotal snippet could be an apt illustration.[22]

The issues of syntax, quotation, abbreviation and decontextualizing, and so of disembodying the voices, involves trade-offs between professional and social values, which are in part incommensurable. On the one hand there are the professional and academic values of the social scientist who wants to know the context and fuller meaning; on the other there are the values of those who want to make the world a better place for poor people. Professional correctness in adherence to technical and fully qualified accuracy can diminish practical pro-poor effects. The full quotation above would have detracted from the impact of Wolfensohn's speech. The shorter extract was punchy and powerful.

The dilemma lies in the ethics of the intermediary and the soundbite. In development practice, many of us find ourselves being intermediaries between people and data on the one hand, and those with power on the other. There are two big traps. For clarity and contrast these can be caricatured. The first is pedantic and long-winded inclusiveness, heavily and cautiously qualified, sometimes combined with over-consultation. These are more likely to have negative than positive effects: a provincial commissioner in Kenya, presented with a big tome of survey findings, exclaimed 'You expect me to read *this*! And it is only a *draft*!' The trap here is failure to communicate. The second trap is self-regarding selection, shortening, manipulation and even misinterpretation of data to produce simple messages that those in power want to hear, and will reward.

The challenge is to find and walk the narrow path between these two. It involves balancing and trade-offs. It demands keen concentration, honest observation and, at times, courage. The two key questions are: What do the data show? And what can make a change for the better? The answers come in a myriad of decisions, most of them small in appearance and almost invisible. Together they come to make up the representation. The tensions and temptations might be most acute at the interface between those who write speeches and need soundbites and those who supply them with qualified and nuanced information. No easy judgements can be made.

In weighing and balancing these incommensurables, there will be different personal positions. Being trained as a historian, I am inclined to side with the social anthropologists who want more information, more context, more qualifications, more nuanced interpretations, and strictly keeping faith with reported facts. I can also understand, though I might not agree with, the actions of some of those concerned, working under pressure, to achieve pithy relevance to policy. They might justify selecting, shortening and simplifying in order to make a difference for the better. They might argue that all knowledge is socially constructed anyway. In reconstructing knowledge for a good political purpose, they might say, they are expressing a higher value than pedantic faithfulness to earlier constructions of that knowledge.

There is a need here for codes of behaviour. It would help to identify and agree non-tradeables – that is, non-negotiable principles or behaviours. These would provide an ethical bedrock to which practitioners could anchor, giving security in the sea of relativism. I shall not try to sketch out such a code: it would best come from a pluralist and participatory process rather than from any one person. There is, though, a meta-level. I would argue that there is an imperative to strive for honest and self-critical epistemological awareness. This means repeatedly examining how information and knowledge are generated. It means critical straining for honest reflection on how one's own ego, mindset, institutional context, and social and political interests combine to select and shape both personal knowledge and the form it is given when passed on to others.

The power to outrage and inspire

Codes of behaviour demand commitment. For some academics, commitment can be clinically intellectual. For many of those engaged in development, commitment is inspired more by outrage. Even though, to my shame and chagrin, I was unable to take part in the fieldwork, I was shocked and moved by material and evidence from the Consultations. There are moments when one exclaims 'Hell!'. For me and for others, there were many such moments with the Consultations. Their impact on how we see and feel things should not be underestimated.

In any critically reflective review of research, the convention is to conceal what we feel. The vocabulary of disparagement includes 'subjective', 'anecdotal' and, worst of all, 'emotional'. Saying what shocked and shook me has invited ridicule, and a response on the lines of 'But of course. . . we have always known that. . .I am surprised that you are surprised'. Obvious and well known though they may be to others, here are four findings that touched and moved me. Perhaps at some level I knew them in part already. But living and working with the evidence brought them home with a stark sharpness.

1   The weak, hungry and desperate are paid less (Narayan et al, 2000b, p96). A group of men in a fishing community in Malawi were reported to have said:

> . . .we get some K5,[23] buy some maize for one day's consumption; when it is finished we go again. . .The problem is that these boat owners know that we are starving. As such we would accept any little wages they would offer to us because they know we are very desperate. . .we want to save our children from dying.' (Khaila et al, 1999, p66)

Of the 'helpless poor' the Bangladesh national synthesis report observed: 'They accept low wages in lean periods. They cannot bargain with the employers given the fact that they will starve without daily wage.' (unNabi et al, 1999, p25)

2 Reluctant crime for livelihood (Narayan et al, 2000b, pp60–61). The Consultations presented examples of risky livelihoods contrived on or beyond the fringes of legality such as sex work, growing marijuana, drug peddling, selling women and children, and theft. Theft of food appeared extraordinarily widespread, especially in Eastern Europe, the former USSR and rural sub-Saharan Africa. It was described as a risky strategy, undertaken with reluctant desperation. In the reported words of a discussion group participant in Sarajevo:

> Criminality is a result of poverty. When you're hungry, you have to find a way. Hunger doesn't ask. (Lytle, 1999)

3 Police who oppress the poor. I had not realized just how widely and badly the police hurt and hinder poor people, and keep them poor. There were exceptions, outstanding among them the Deputy Superintendent in charge of the Cassava Piece Police Station in Kingston, Jamaica, Rosalie McDonald-Baker, who was warmly praised by a group of poor women. But again and again, the police were experienced as oppressors who persecute the poor and add to the insecurity of their lives and livelihoods. In India they were characterized as 'a licensed evil?' (PRAXIS, 1999, p35). A group of youngsters in Sacadura Cabral, Brazil, said of the police: 'They hit [first], then they question you. . . they get near you and tell you to raise your arms and open your legs. Then they hit your legs. Then they call you shit and demand your documents.' (Melo, 1999, pp37–38)

4 The bottom poor. Some of the very poorest and worst-off did take part in the Consultations, but often participants identified a group separate from and below themselves as the poorest, variously pitied, feared and looked down upon. The group was diverse, including widows, divorcees, orphans, the chronically sick, very old people, the disabled, the homeless, those without relatives, the mad and mentally disordered, drug addicts, the destitute and simply those who were very, very poor. A women's group in Malawi identified the 'stunted poor', whose bodies are short and thin and do not shine even after bathing, whose hairs are thin, who have frequent illnesses and who severely lack food (Khaila et al, 1999, p38).

There are many other illustrations in the site reports, in the national synthesis reports, and in *Crying Out for Change*. As with these four, it was not just the finding or reaffirmation that made a personal impact; it was also the immediacy of the evidence. The vividness of what poor people were reported to have said vindicated the participatory methodology as a means of influencing as well as of learning. Reading about starvation wages, or stealing to feed children, or police brutality, or the bottom poor, is not the same as meeting poor people and hearing about these things directly during fieldwork. Nor are meeting and hearing about them the same as experiencing them personally as one of the victims. But whether through reading, meeting or experiencing, feelings of anger and outrage can be provoked, and feelings like these are drivers for personal commitment to change. They inspire action. The personal impact of disturbing detail can be superficial. It can also be deep. When powerful people and policy-makers are moved, the links between poor people and policy change are shortened and strengthened (see also McGee, this volume).

IMPACTS: MAKING A DIFFERENCE?

The ultimate justification for the *Voices of the Poor*, of which the Consultations were a part, has to be net good effects. A balance sheet would be premature. Questions about whether, how and how much there has been or will be a difference for the better or the worse can never be fully answered. Many impacts are invisible, and many are no doubt continuing and still working themselves out. What follow are simply some points that seem worthy of remark.

There were many impacts at personal, community and policy levels. Personally, those poor people who took part were surely affected, as were those who conducted the fieldwork, analysis and synthesis (Adan et al, this volume, and Narayan et al, 2000b, pp8–16). In some cases there was follow-up at the community level, and regional and national policies were influenced (Adan et al, this volume).

The original primary purpose of the Consultations was, however, none of these but to influence the *WDR 2000/2001*. The process guide expressed it thus:

> The purpose of the Consultations with the Poor study is to enable a wide range of poor people in diverse countries and conditions to share their views in such a way that they can inform and contribute to the concepts and content of the WDR 2000/2001. (World Bank, 1999, Introduction)

Influence on the concepts of the WDR is difficult to assess. Its opening sentence, 'Poverty is pronounced deprivation of wellbeing', and the paragraphs that follow which add security and empowerment to the definition of wellbeing, resonate with what came out of the Consultations, as does the stress on the multidimensionality of poverty. The conversion to this broader definition is reflected in the use in the first pages of the WDR of the term 'income poverty' to describe the narrower concept.[24] However, the words security and empowerment were at the core of the WDR draft before the Consultations took place. Possibly, though, the Consultations served to reinforce them in the WDR. The Consultations may also have served to limit any rewriting there might have been in the later stages of preparing the WDR after Ravi Kanbur, the director of the WDR team, had resigned.

Influence on the contents of the WDR is clearer to see. Six of the 91 boxes are derived from the *Voices of the Poor* as a whole, including the first box, which stands out prominently in the overview. The six are:

- 1 The voices of the poor
- 1.1 Poverty in the voices of poor people
- 1.4 Measuring voice and power using participatory methods
- 2.1 On interacting with state institutions: The voices of the poor
- 5.4 Locked out by health and education fees
- 6.1 Poor people are often harassed by public officials

These present some of the most acute and deeply felt concerns expressed by poor participants. There is also a visual impact from 30 quotations in green italics, many of these at the head of sections, and contrasting with the black roman text. In a sense these are, 'rather than data. . . treated as illustrations and flourishes' (McGee and Brock, 2001, p34). But even decorations have their effects. Anyone skimming the WDR will have their eyes caught by these remarks. They might remind them that poverty and the bad life are not just words, but the experience of real people. The prominent quotations point towards policies, but their impact might be more through affecting policy-makers personally as people.

Not all the voices got through. One big concern of many poor people was the police. Here the message in *Voices of the Poor* (pp162–166) is strong, stressing police brutality, harassment, extortion, corruption and unrespons-iveness. Yet the WDR, strong though it is on legal systems and reforms, has little to say on the police.[25]

Perhaps the most conspicuous early effects of the *Voices of the Poor* have been on policy-makers. Among international leaders who have quoted them, James Wolfensohn stands out, as with the words at the head of this chapter. He has repeatedly referred to the *Voices of the Poor* and himself repeatedly amplified some of them. In a sense, he has enabled poor people to ventriloquize through him. Moreover, his many repetitions must have internalized them for himself[26] and impressed and influenced others. Big changes in development orientations and practice can be levered and catalysed by simple ideas. This one was that poor people's voices matter and those in power should listen to them. Coming from the President of the World Bank it carries weight and supports the big shift in development towards enabling poor people to express their realities and influence policy and practice.

That said, in the longer term and in a wider perspective, a troubling question remains. It is whether or to what extent the *Voices of the Poor* has served as camouflage or cosmetic. Some might argue that it has been a disservice to poor people to allow the World Bank to present itself as a caring and listening bank. They might ask: has the wolf been helped to pose as a sheep? *Voices of the Poor,* they might say, can be seen as a diversionary tactic, a distraction from the main and major issue of whether the international financial institutions should continue to exist in their present form. A tough litmus test here is whether the *Voices of the Poor* affects the middle management of those institutions.

To conclude on a positive note, there has been much useful learning about methodology (see, eg, Narayan et al, 2000b, Chapter 1 and Appendix 3). The methodology guide is available as a source of ideas for others. There was a healthy debate as to whether the Consultations have led at times to over-simple generalizations. Renewed discussion of the complementarities and tensions between qualitative and quantitative poverty assessment has resulted.[27] The critical reflections of this chapter and elsewhere in this book have been provoked. Participatory methodology was spread to new countries and to researchers to whom it was new. The ethical issues of taking poor people's time and raising their expectations have once again surfaced.

Participatory appraisals and policy influence are increasingly localized – at national or sub-national level – or concentrated on categories of marginalized and deprived people such as pastoralists, slum dwellers, street children, widows, sex workers and landless labourers. For these, there is much to be learned from the Consultations concerning methodology, analysis, represent-ation and influence.

PRACTICAL LESSONS FOR OPTIMIZING: TRADE-OFFS, BALANCES AND WIN–WINS

Of the practical lessons from the Consultations, some are old, some somewhat new:

- **Assess whether to engage.** When decisions are taken to engage in research there is usually some assessment of costs, benefits and risks, but less often of opportunity costs. Yet engaging in one research project can mean foregoing other opportunities to learn, influence and make a difference.

- **Self-critically reflect**. Perhaps the most important lesson is to be aware of one's power in the selection, organization and naming of knowledge. It helps throughout any research project to keep a self-critical and reflective diary and to revisit this. Much otherwise is forgotten. Much might also be distorted later through unconscious manipulation of memory, especially if there have been differences of opinion. The very act of writing a diary also helps reflection, optimizing trade-offs and identifying and adhering to principles which should be non-negotiable.
- **Optimize trade-offs**. Recognize and make conscious decisions about trade-offs both in the use of scarce resources, and in optimizing between incommensurable values. Some of the more obvious are:
  1 Scale and representativeness versus quality – the larger the scale the greater the level of representativeness, but the greater the difficulty in assuring quality.
  2 Scale versus timeliness for training, fieldwork and analysis – the larger the scale, the more time and resources are needed for training, fieldwork supervision and analysis.
  3 Scale versus resources for follow-up – for a given level of resources, a larger scale diminishes the scope for follow-up with communities, and for policy-related workshops.
  4 Standardization and analysability versus open-endedness and difficulty of analysis.
  5 Care and comprehensiveness of analysis versus timeliness in influencing policy.
  6 The qualifications and nuances of academic standards versus simplified messages for policy influence.
- **Adopt, invent and use win–win methods in analysis**. Seek to minimize or avoid trade-offs by looking for win–win solutions in which there are gains all round:
  1 Develop and use a wide repertoire of diagrams, choosing those that fit the nature of the material rather than fitting the material to the diagram. Consult de Bono (1981), Buzan (1974) and Waddington (1977) to extend the range and inspire inventiveness.
  2 Make verbal presentations. Do not limit communication and learning to the written word. Talk about experiences. In talking we say things that we do not write, and often express them more vividly.
  3 Write on cards. Note striking points while others talk. On other cards write impressions and understandings, what stands out, what seems to matter.
  4 Sort cards into emergent categories on the ground. Express, cluster and analyse disparate information in self-organizing ways, which also allow and encourage committed participants to contribute from their experience and critical reflection.

5 Revisit primary sources. Maintain self-critical doubt about conclusions, and return repeatedly to the originals to check, correct and reinspire.

CONCLUSION: REFLEXIVITY, POWER AND PLURALISM

The biggest lessons I draw from reflection on these processes concern power and knowledge. This is not the common truism that knowledge is power. It is that power forms and frames knowledge and that interpersonal power distorts what is learned and expressed. There is no complete escape from this. Each one of us has to take responsibility for our part in the methodological, epistemological and ethical struggle to achieve representations of realities which optimize a multitude of trade-offs. There is no simple answer. But this chapter underpins three affirmations that help in finding good ways forward.

The first is honest reflexivity. Self-knowledge is so difficult that 'honest reflexivity' is almost an oxymoron. But difficulty is no reason for not trying. Degrees of understanding can be gained through introspection, and through observing, remembering and interrogating the interactions that fashion knowledge.

Unfortunately, the public expression of reflexivity, and hence our collective learning, is inhibited in three ways. The first constraint is personal, the fear of exposing oneself. Here social anthropologists have often set a fine example,[28] describing their own experiences, emotions and limitations, and reflecting on how they learn and mislearn. Those in other disciplines might feel more constrained by anxiety that self-criticism will ricochet.

The second constraint is collective loyalty to colleagues and friends. This can apply in any collaborative venture. In a research project in South Asia in the early 1970s I never sought to publish a paper entitled 'Up the Garden Path'. It would have shown that in interpreting part of the results of a questionnaire survey, the investigators themselves appeared to be the most powerful independent variable. As a finding it was important but disturbing. It would have upset colleagues and might have cast doubt on other analysis which we were publishing together. Rightly or wrongly, faced with this conflict of incommensurable values, I opted for personal relationships over professional responsibility. One can ask how many shortcomings of collaborative research are under-reported and under-recognized for similar reasons.

The third constraint is space and time. In their late stages, books and articles often lack space. They are considered too long. Editors and publishers demand shortening. Where are the cuts to be made? Methodological issues were the last part of the book or article to be written. They are also the easiest to cut.[29] Writing has taken longer than expected. The author or authors have run out of time and energy to argue. Further critical reflection is out of the question:

the team has dispersed; new research projects are in hand, or new jobs started, and neither time nor funds are available for further writing. So methodology and critical reflection are abbreviated, relegated to appendices or footnotes, or excised altogether.

The practical conclusion is to give space, time and rewards for critical reflection, and for collaborators to accept methodological criticism in a spirit of trying to help all of us to do better.

The second affirmation concerns how power distorts. Much power resides in patronage and the ability to bestow prestige. Anyone with these forms of power is disabled by how they attract and reward others. In this context, the World Bank is especially disadvantaged.[30] Perhaps the most painful but for me most important reflection concerns ego. Others will know whether they are also vulnerable and vain. It is flattering to be invited to Washington. It is great to be able to return to one's institution and write a trip report, as I did, saying that our workshop had been addressed by James Wolfensohn at a time when he was exceptionally busy, including in it the quotation at the head of this chapter, glowing with pleasure that he had said that our work was immensely important to him, and that he needed us to help him. 'Where have you been?' 'Oh, I see you were at the Bank.' And then casually dropping names. The very way in which we talk of 'the Bank,' as I have in this chapter, reflects its extreme status and power: there is only one 'the Bank' and everyone knows which it is.[31]

A recurrent theme in this chapter, and in this book as a whole, is another form of power: the power to frame the realities of others. As described, one of my activities was searching for material and quotations concerning themes or aspects I had identified as important. The example I have given of The Body as a neglected aspect of deprivation illustrates the point. I was alert for and sought relevant evidence. The evidence was there to be found. But the process and its dangers, in my hands or in those of others, must be recognized. Nor are these dangers at all limited to qualitative data. Indeed, the authority commanded by statistics can make quantitative data even more vulnerable at times.

When these two manifestations of power combine, hazards are compounded. The incentives and temptations to please power are strong. The selection and manipulation of data are later invisible. Consultants and researchers show what is wanted and are not shown up. They then get further contracts. Prestige and promotion follow, in whatever organization. So it is that a synergy of patronage and the power to produce knowledge fabricates fantasies. As a postmodern Lord Acton might have said 'Power tends to deceive and absolute power deceives absolutely.'

The third affirmation is pluralism. When there is consensus among those with power, warning lights should flash. Disharmonies are of the essence in much great music: progressions of discord resolve in transient harmonies, not once but again and again. So disagreement and debate are of the essence in learning to do better in development. In this context, those with power have learning disabilities to recognize and overcome. The experience of the Consultations with the Poor has proved a source of practical lessons. Not least, it has shown what participatory approaches can achieve and how important it is to reflect on power, process and representation. In the methodology, epistemology and ethics of participation and policy influence there are no simple solutions. Rather, there is a struggle without end to optimize trade-offs between conflicting values and to find good ways forward. For development to be better, many voices will always need to be raised, both of the poor and of self-critical development professionals.

NOTES

1 For stimulating comments presenting a range of views, suggestions and corrections based on drafts of this chapter I am grateful to Karen Brock, John Gaventa, Rosemary McGee, Deepa Narayan, Andrew Norton, Raj Patel, Patti Petesch, Jules Pretty and Meera K Shah. The experience with Consultations with the Poor, and the time to write this chapter, were supported variously by DFID, SDC and Sida. Responsibility for opinions, errors and omissions is mine alone, and should not be attributed to any organization or other person.

2 Consultations with the Poor describes the 23-country study that was one element of the Voices of the Poor project; its findings were published as Narayan et al, 2000a. The other element consisted of reviews of existing PPAs and other participatory research on poverty; findings were published as Narayan et al, 2000b and Brock, 1999. The whole initiative was originally called Consultations with the Poor but adopted the title Voices of the Poor in late 1999.

3 As team leader, the study was led and managed by Deepa Narayan, at the time lead social development specialist in the World Bank's Poverty Group. As consultants, Patti Petesch played a major part in coordination and logistics and Meera Shah in methodological guidance and training. All three were involved in analysis and synthesis. The process guide can be accessed at http://www.worldbank.org/ poverty/voices/reports.htm. For a description of the study process, experiences in the field and critical reflection, see Narayan et al, 2000b, Chapter 1. Chapters 2–11 of that book present findings. Chapter 12 is 'A Call to Action: The Challenge to Change'. Appendix 1 acknowledges many others who contributed to the study, Appendix 2 lists countries, sites and criteria for selection and Appendix 3 provides an overview of study themes and methods.

4 272 is the total number of sites listed in Appendix 2 of *Voices of the Poor: Crying Out for Change* (Narayan et al, 2001b) and the figure used for consistency in this chapter. However, the actual number of site reports available was somewhat fewer: for example, the 40 sites in Viet Nam were summarized in four regional reports. If these regional reports are taken as site reports, the total is only 236. There were no national synthesis reports for Egypt or Sri Lanka. The Sri Lanka work followed a slightly different methodology but was broadly comparable.

5 In a three-volume series entitled 'Voices of the Poor', the first was a parallel book based on comparative analysis of participatory poverty assessments (Narayan et al, 2000a). *Voices of the Poor: Crying Out for Change* is the second. The third (in preparation) will be *From Many Lands*, with contributions from countries that took part in the Consultations.

6 While contributions were made by other members of the Participation Group at IDS, those most concerned were John Gaventa, who provided overall management, Karen Brock and myself.

7 The World Bank is staffed by people who combine to an extraordinary degree intelligence, ability, drive and a range of views regarding 'development'. 'The World Bank', as I use the term, refers to characteristics that are repeatedly manifest, and which damp down or over-ride individual idiosyncratic deviance.

8 The word 'shortcut' was introduced by an editor into an earlier version before it reached Michael Cernea, in whose book it then appeared as 'Shortcut Methods of Gathering Information for Rural Development Projects' (Cernea, 1985).

9 For example, a trainer who refused a contract because it required PRA training to be conducted in three days. She insisted that a longer period with fieldwork was essential. She was told that if she would not do it, someone else would be found who would. Someone else was found, and she lost the contract.

10 PRA, originally participatory rural appraisal, now sometimes participation, reflection and action, is an approach, methods and behaviours for enabling local people to undertake their own appraisal, analysis and action. For a fuller descriptions see Chambers, 1997, Chapter 6 and http://www.ids.ac.uk/particip

11 The process guide was prepared by Meera Kaul Shah under the overall supervision of Deepa Narayan, team leader, and is available on http//:www.worldbank.org/poverty/voices/reports.htm

12 Sceptical readers are invited to read and judge for themselves. The national reports are on the same website.

13 Sources included card sorting for emergent categories in PPAs in South Africa (Attwood and May, 1998, p125), in Shinyanga, Tanzania (Gaventa and Attwood, 1998), and in the Empowerment Zones Programme in the US (Gaventa et al, 1998).

14 For another example of SOSOTEC see Kumar, 1996. This is a report compiled on the basis of 25 people's experiences shared over 36 hours. For a more detailed description of SOSOTEC visit http://www.ids.ac.uk/particip for the 21s (see 21 of the Best) or for hard copy, contact Jane Stevens, IDS, University of Sussex, Brighton BN1 9RE, UK. Much remains to be learned about the strengths and weaknesses of SOSOTEC approaches. For example, Meera Shah (personal communication, 23 Jan 2001) found the 'Ahas' or surprising and significant insights from the presentations of the team leaders more useful as starting points than the outputs of the SOSOTEC process.

15 Kath Pasteur, Anna Robinson-Pant, Damien Thuriaux, Kimberly Vilar and myself, with support from Karen Brock.

16 This is part of a listing by Meera Shah (personal communication, 23 January 2001) which had overlaps with what those at IDS also found striking. From her analysis of gender relations she added: the reported trend of decreasing violence against women; the perception of many women that they felt an improvement in their status; and male frustration and anxiety.

17 Sequences vary. Andrew Norton has described (personal communication) a process that starts with the material. '1. Writer picks up an issue from the material. 2. Writer creatively formulates the issue in a way that makes it come alive personally in the light of own experience, concepts, values. 3. Use of the new concept enables writer to uncover other elements of the material which she would not otherwise have seen.'

18 It is bemusing to note that a regular dodecahedron has regular pentagons as its faces.

19 Other numerical analysis was conducted in parallel by a team at the University of Maryland. Details are not known of their objectives, methodology or findings. Examples of conventional tables with large numbers generated through participatory methods include a survey of utilization of services in some 130 villages in Nepal (ActionAid Nepal, 1992) and research into how poor people coped with the drought of 1992 in 20 districts in Malawi, Zambia and Zimbabwe (Eldridge, 1998). Both these generated tables similar to those from questionnaire surveys. See also Mukherjee, 1995; Chambers, 1997, pp122–125 and Rademacher and Patel, this volume.

20 In spite of this, the usage crept into the *World Development Report 2000/2001*. On p146 it says 'In every part of the world participants in the *Voices of the Poor* study mentioned child labour as an undesirable coping strategy.' This is misleading as the study was not in every part of the world and child labour was not mentioned in every report.

21 An extraordinary example was the widespread belief that post-harvest losses at the village level were of the order of 30 per cent. This had a life of its own in the 1970s and 1980s, persisting long after scrupulous field research had shown it to be a wild exaggeration.

22 I am grateful to Caroline Moser (2001) for the term and concept 'apt illustration', which comes from the work of the social anthropologists Max Gluckman and Clyde Mitchell some 50 years ago.

23 5 kwacha is approximately equivalent to US$0.07.

24 The old usage of income poverty described simply as 'poverty' slips back, however, in later sections of the WDR, eg in Box 1.8 'Tracking poverty in India during the 1990s'.

25 In the 17 paragraphs of the WDR on poor people and the rule of law, only two sentences mention the police (on p103).

26 Catechists and teachers know how repetition embeds words and ideas, and any politicians who are critically reflective will recognize how this forms and distorts their beliefs.

27 Personal communication, Ravi Kanbur, who said that without the Voices of the Poor and its impact on the World Bank the March 2001 Cornell conference on Qualitative and Quantitative Poverty Appraisal: Complementarities, Tensions and the Way Forward would probably not have taken place.

28 I am grateful to Paul Spencer for many anecdotes about his own work. See also Evans-Pritchard's classic account in *The Nuer* pp 9–15, Barbara Harrell-Bond's description of her own behaviour in *Imposing Aid* eg pp116–117; and McGee (this volume). Another remarkable illustration is Elenore Smith Bowen's *Return to Laughter*, based on the experience of her fieldwork but written as a novel where

'the truth I have tried to tell concerns the sea change in one's self that comes from immersion in another and alien world'.

29   For example, when the edited chapters (Farmer, 1977) from a research project on agrarian change in rice-growing areas in India and Sri Lanka had to be shortened, it was the one on methodology that was cut in length.

30   See, eg, Chambers, 1997, pp97–100.

31   Apologies to the African Development Bank, the Asian Development Bank, the InterAmerican Development Bank, and other banks. The statement here concerns fact of usage, not institutional reality.

REFERENCES

ActionAid Nepal (1992) *Participatory Rural Appraisal Utilization Survey Report Part 1: Rural Development Area Sindhupalchowk*, July, Kathmandu, Monitoring and Evaluation Unit, ActionAid Nepal

Attwood, H and May, J (1998) 'Kicking down doors and lighting fires: The South African PPA' in Holland, J with Blackburn, J (eds) (1998) *Whose Voice? Participatory Research and Policy Change*, London, Intermediate Technology, pp119–130

Bowen, Elenore Smith (1956) *Return to Laughter*, London, Victor Gollanz

Brock, K (1999) 'It's not only wealth that matters, it's peace of mind too: A review of participatory work on poverty and illbeing', unpublished paper for 'Voices of the Poor' workshop, Washington, DC, World Bank

Brock, K, Cornwall, A and Gaventa, J (2001) *Power, Knowledge and Political Spaces in the Framing of Poverty Reduction Policy*, IDS Working Paper 143, Brighton, IDS

Buzan, T (1974) *Use Your Head* (1989 edition), London, BBC Books

Cernea, M (ed) (1985) *Putting People First: Sociological Variables in Rural Development*, Oxford, Oxford University Press for the World Bank

Chambers, R (1983) *Rural Development: Putting the Last First,* Harlow, Longman

Chambers, R (1988) *Managing Canal Irrigation: Practical Analysis from South Asia*, Oxford and IBH, New Delhi, and Cambridge University Press

Chambers, R (1992) 'The Self-deceiving state' in Murray, R (ed) 'New forms of public administration', *IDS Bulletin*, Vol 23, No 4, pp31–42

Chambers, R (1997) *Whose Reality Counts? Putting the First Last*, London, Intermediate Technology

de Bono, E (1981) *Atlas of Management Thinking*, Harmondsworth, Maurice Temple Smith (Penguin Books edition, 1980)

Eldridge, C (1998) 'Summary of the main findings of a PRA study on the 1992 drought in Zimbabwe', unpublished report, London, Save the Children UK

Evans-Pritchard, E E (1940) *The Nuer: A Description of the Modes of Livelihood and Political Institutions of a Nilotic People*, New York and Oxford, Oxford University Press

Farmer, B H (ed) (1977) *Green Revolution? Technology and Change in Rice-growing Areas of Tamil Nadu and Sri Lanka*, London, Macmillan

Gaventa, J, Creed, V and Morrissey, J (1998) 'Scaling up: Participatory monitoring and evaluation of a federal empowerment program' in Whitmore, E (ed) *Understanding and Practicing Participatory Evaluation,* San Francisco, Jossey-Bass Publishers

Gaventa, J and Attwood, H (1998) 'Synthesising PRA and case study materials: A participatory process for developing outlines, concepts and synthesis reports' in Participation Group, *Participatory Poverty Assessments Topic Pack*, Brighton, IDS

Harrell-Bond, B E (1986) *Imposing Aid: Emergency Assistance to Refugees*, Oxford/New York/Nairobi, Oxford University Press

Holland, J with Blackburn, J (1998) *Whose Voice? Participatory Research and Policy Change*, London, Intermediate Technology

Khaila, S W, Mvula, P M and Kadzandira, J M (1999) *Consultations with the Poor, Country Synthesis Report, Malawi*, Malawi, Centre for Social Research, University of Malawi (submitted to Poverty Group, PREM, World Bank, July)

Kumar, S (ed) (1996) 'ABC of PRA: Attitude behaviour change', report of a South–South workshop organized by ACTIONAID India and SPEECH, ActionAid India, Bangalore

Lytle, P (1999) *Consultations with the Poor, Site Report, Bosnia-Sarajevo*, Washington, DC, World Bank

McGee, R and Brock, K (2001) *From Poverty Assessment to Policy Change: Processes, Actors and Data*, IDS Working Paper 133, Brighton, IDS

Melo, M (1999) *Consultations with the Poor: Brazil – National Synthesis Report*, Washington, DC, World Bank (participatory poverty assessment prepared for PREM, May)

Moser, C (2001) "Apt illustration' or 'anecdotal information'? Can qualitative data be representative or robust?', notes for the Qual-Quant Workshop, Cornell University, March 15–16

Mukherjee, N (1995) *Participatory Rural Appraisal and Questionnaire Survey: Comparative Field Experience and Methodological Innovations*, New Delhi, Concept Publishing

Narayan, D, Chambers, R, Shah, M K and Petesch, P (1999) *Global Synthesis: Consultations with the Poor*, Washington, DC, World Bank

Narayan, D with Patel, R, Schafft, K, Rademacher, A and Koch-Schulte, S (2000a) *Voices of the Poor: Can Anyone Hear Us?*, New York, Oxford University Press

Narayan, D, Chambers, R, Shah, M K and Petesch, P (2000b) *Voices of the Poor: Crying Out for Change*, New York, Oxford University Press

PRAXIS (1999) *Consultations with the Poor: India 1999: Country Synthesis Report* Washington, DC, World Bank (study undertaken by Institute of Participatory Practices, 12 Patliputra Colony, Patna 800 013, Poverty Group, PREM)

Rahmatu, D and Kidanu, A (1999) *Ethiopia, Consultations with the Poor: A Study to Inform the World Development Report 2000/01 on Poverty and Development*, Washington, DC, World Bank

unNabi, R, Dipankara, D, Chakrabarty, S, Begum, M and Chaudhury, N J (1999) 'Consultation with the poor: Participatory poverty assessment in Bangladesh', prepared for Global Synthesis Workshop, 22–23 September, World Bank

Waddington, C H (1977) *Tools for Thought*, St Albans, Paladin

Wolfensohn, J (1999) 'Coalitions for change', address to the Board of Governors of the World Bank, 28 September

World Bank (1999). *Methodology Guide: Consultations with the Poor*, Washington, DC, World Bank Poverty Group (http://www.worldbank.org)

World Bank (2000) *Poverty and Development: The World Development Report 2000/2001: Attacking Poverty*, New York, Oxford University Press for the World Bank

RETELLING WORLDS OF POVERTY: REFLECTIONS ON TRANSFORMING PARTICIPATORY RESEARCH FOR A GLOBAL NARRATIVE

Anne Rademacher and Raj Patel[1]

When 'people' are involved in developmental discourse about civil society – whether the World Bank singing the praises of the ordinary African worker or the geographer lauding peasant science – who the people are, and how they are constructed, are precisely political questions. (Peet and Watts, 1996, p27)

We need to worry less about the unintended consequences of our study of local organizations and movements, and to worry more about the intended consequences of our relative lack of study of central institutions of power. (Dove, 1999, p225)

INTRODUCTION: TRADING CONTEXT FOR CONTINUITY

THIS CHAPTER ADDRESSES conceptual, political and practical concerns surrounding the use of participatory poverty reports to produce a story about 'global' poverty. Through reflections on methodological practice, it examines moments of abstraction from 'the local' to 'the global', a conceptual transition often overlooked in the effort to understand broadly defined social conditions like 'poverty'. Embedded in the local to global analytical transition lies a classic ethnographic and ethical question: when and how are social experiences removed from their historical, political and cultural contexts in order to view them as broader features of a more generalized human experience? Regarding the local–global transition itself as a trade-off, in which important specificities may be lost but broader analytical relevance gained, emphasizes certain choices facing researchers over what to include, and what to exclude, as being representative of a social condition at a generalized scale. Openly acknowledging this trade-off places the researcher and her choices at the centre of the knowledge creation process. It also points to the importance of a researcher's institutional context and turns our attention to the broader institutional agendas that 'global' narratives serve. The chapter concludes that researchers, particularly those claiming to be critical of existing power structures, need not necessarily reject global generalizations. However, we must recognize that in certain important respects, the broader our gaze, the *less* we may actually be able to know about specific experiences of poverty: knowledge generated by and for 'global' centres of power may in fact tell us very little about poverty as it is actually lived in everyday experience. We argue further for a critical imperative in research practice that takes our responsibilities as reflexive, knowledge-producing individuals seriously, and exercises informed caution when asserting social facts at a global scale. Finally, the chapter calls for institutional changes that will ensure that participants in participatory poverty studies are active not only in the generation of local studies, but also in the larger, 'global' knowledge-creation and policy-making processes that result from them.

THE UNIVERSAL/SPECIFIC TRADE-OFF

At the intersection of the humanities and the social sciences lies a common question in the investigation of social phenomena: how are observers to know whether what they see is idiosyncratic or part of a more general pattern? Disciplinary approaches to addressing this problem range from the application of probability theory and statistical treatments to a denial of the utility of generalization altogether. In nearly all social science practice, however, generalizations are employed at certain levels; it is almost impossible to talk about society and social processes without using broad categories to illustrate important features of collective behaviour and interaction. In certain respects it is generalization itself that affords a distinction between the social and the individual by emphasizing social practice and action as phenomena that can be observed, experienced and described in terms beyond those that are exclusive to individuals.

Yet analytical generalization involves homogenization; it is impossible to create and use distinctions in society without silencing, at least to some extent, the particular details of each person who comes to constitute a given analytical category. Social researchers are faced with the persistent challenge of how to demarcate clusters of social experience and how to generalize across individuals and groups, while at the same time preserving important realities of heterogeneity and difference. Particularly at a global discursive scale, analytical generalizations run the risk of burying or supplanting critical historical, political, geographical and cultural differences. For this reason, methodological choices and the institutional contexts within which general-izations take place are critical matters in understanding the processes by which 'global' knowledge is produced. Points where contextual data are scaled up can harbour important revelations about the exercise of power in research itself.

Distortionary abstraction is not monopolized by any particular ideology. In the case we explore in this paper, the World Bank, its critics, and we as authors, all use the term 'the poor' as shorthand for a heterogeneous, diverse and incommensurable set of conditions, circumstances and people. The very idea of a single global category within which we discuss poverty is rarely problematized, either by major development institutions or their critics. This chapter suggests that by focusing on how such categories are generated, defined and used we can understand more fully their utility as well as their limitations.

POWER AND THE PRODUCTION OF KNOWLEDGE

The calculus of advantage and disadvantage that accompanies generalization depends on *who* is carrying out the generalization, and *for whom* certain analytical insights are useful. In an exploration of institutional power in issues of representation, anthropologist Michael Dove (1999, p228) reminds us of Edward Said's provocative questions: 'Who writes? For whom is this writing being done? In what circumstances?' Dove suggests further that we must also ask, 'Who reads, for whom, and in what circumstances?' These questions emphasize both the representative powers of the researcher herself and the importance of the audiences for whom she is producing knowledge in the first place.[2] A researcher's own social and institutional context is as important as that of her informants and topics of study.

Trade-offs between specificity and generality are the product of negotiated encounters between ideology, the politics of the institutional context of knowledge production, and the agency of the researcher. Knowledge is not only produced, but it is itself a product with its own political economy of extraction, processing and distribution. Asking questions such as, Who gets to choose which details to amplify? and, Which institutional priorities does an individual researcher engage and honour? demonstrates how power relations shape knowledge as a product and how, in turn, this affects what we know – and believe we can know – about social conditions and experiences at a 'global' scale.

This chapter focuses on a methodological process of generalizing the experiences of poor people in dramatically different social contexts to derive broad conclusions about the global experience of poverty. We draw on our work as research assistants to the study published as *Voices of the Poor: Can Anyone Hear Us?* (Narayan et al, 2000)[3] to explore how locally collected contextual narratives assumed the form of a single, more generalized policy-oriented narrative. By focusing on the research process, we aim to draw attention away from the question of whether we 'hear' those living in poverty and towards the question of how we, as researchers and institutions, are 'listening' to our informants.

The purpose of this exploration is threefold: the first is to identify particular moments at which highly contextual data in this study were re-contextualized and transformed through generalization. In examining these moments of transition from 'local' to 'global', we aim to emphasize the power relations that inevitably co-exist with, and in many cases guide the creation of, institutional knowledge (cf Dove, 1999). The second purpose is to identify moments of mediation that rendered the research team agents of knowledge creation. In amplifying certain stories and silencing others, we exercised precisely the sort of power that makes knowledge production, and recent promotions of the World Bank as a 'knowledge bank',[4] central concerns of development practitioners and theorists alike. Reflecting on our own involvement in the research process (Long and Long, 1992; Emerson et al, 1995), while recognizing the multiple institutional actors and understandings that informed the global synthesis (Gardner, 1997), offers important insights into the complexity of the universalizing abstractions behind 'global' institutional knowledge.

Finally, by engaging these topics, we hope to articulate more fully the ethnographic and ethical challenges facing researchers and policy-makers who seek to synthesize qualitative social research. Abstracting local studies and placing them into policy contexts inevitably involves institutional constraints that condition the range of acceptable methodologies researchers can employ and the conclusions they can reach. The insights afforded by qualitative methods are of critical importance to answering questions such as the one posed by the *Can Anyone Hear Us?* study: How do the poor, themselves, define and experience poverty? A full answer to this question requires both candid reflection and an honest commitment to improving the research practices intended to create spaces for marginalized people to speak. By the same token, the institutional spaces that exist to 'hear' about poverty demand our attention and require reform.

By affirming that the translation of studies situated in specific historical, social and institutional contexts to a 'global' narrative is indeed a *transformation*, we are better equipped to explore the linkages between the social production of facts in one site and their reception in another (Pigg, forthcoming). The political terrain a narrative has travelled is as important as the 'knowledge' it conveys.

DEFINING 'LOCAL' AND 'GLOBAL'

Before proceeding, it is important to recognize the complexities subsumed by simplistic assignments of the terms 'global' and 'local'. Although these are actually fluid terms defined only in specific research practice, they are often applied in a naturalized way in development discourse: the 'local' tends to refer to smaller scales of social organization, like communities or regions, while the 'global' tends to imply both commonalities in human experience and social conditions shared over large scales. The problem with accepting these terms as given arises when 'the local' comes to imply a bounded place or social experience while the 'global' defies any single locality. Often, social features we take as 'local' in fact have extra-local origins; limiting an inquiry to a bounded locality can sometimes obscure the important non-local origins of problems like poverty. For global institutions or processes that might otherwise be implicated, bounding localities can serve as a convenient way to avoid inclusion in a social problematic. Similarly, our sense of the 'global' is often derived from the knowledge created by very specific institutions, and the universalizing narratives, ideologies and critiques that circulate through and from them.

It is precisely because there is nothing self-evidently meaningful about the terms 'global' and 'local' that an understanding of institutional knowledge-creation is important; it is often through institutional processes that definitions of 'local' and 'global' are stabilized and naturalized (Peters, 1996; Forbes, 1999). In our case, the World Bank functioned as a 'global centre', able to see things at a world level, while PPAs, the contextual data from which we were working, became, necessarily, knowledge of 'local' origin. In this chapter, we use the terms 'local' and 'global' as provocations to reflect critically on their origin and content.

In the case of aggregating PPAs, turning the 'local' into the 'global' entailed important contextual losses, but potential gains in promoting institutional reform. These trade-offs are only acceptable insofar as they are accompanied by a full and open acknowledgement of the content of the losses and the potential institutional goals that necessitate them. We must ask, in reflecting on transitions from local-to-global discourse: when does the global scale get invoked, and why? If we are suspicious of the global gaze as inclined towards reinforcing existing hierarchies, we are equipped to take stock not only of what a global narrative says, but of what it *does not* say and cannot accommodate. Recognizing that global knowledge is fashioned for global institutional consumption places appropriate limits on what we can say and understand about poverty at the global scale. Our own global synthesis (our contributions to the *Can Anyone Hear Us?* project), and the practice of creating it, reveals as much as an institutional knowledge product as it does as a partial look at the revelatory potentials of participatory methodologies.

CAN ANYONE HEAR US?

From March to July 1999, we worked as research assistants on a team based at Cornell University commissioned by the World Bank to conduct data analysis related to its *World Development Report 2000/2001* on poverty and development. The project[5] involved the analysis of hundreds of World Bank poverty assessments, conducted between 1990 and 1998, from nearly every country to which the Bank is a lender. After a brief initial review, 73 PPAs were selected for inclusion in the study, based on their use of participatory methodological approaches to addressing the question, 'How do the poor, themselves, understand and define poverty?' The final data set used in the analysis represented reports from 46 countries.[6]

Following the development of a coding protocol, the team coded and analysed the content of the 73 documents using a data analysis software package that facilitated a systematic content analysis on thousands of pages of text.[7] Researchers collated, cross-indexed and compared data from different PPAs, and drafted portions of what would ultimately become *Can Anyone Hear Us?* The final report produced in our phase of the project sought to describe poor people's own accounts of the condition of poverty; each chapter addressed a topic identified by the research team as important for determining social and economic mobility among PPA respondents.

In addition to serving as a synthesis of the findings of participatory research initiatives over the past decade, the report was intended to demonstrate the potential value of participatory research methodologies within the World

Bank. A recent World Bank publication advocated PPAs by arguing that they could

> *allow better technical diagnosis of the problem, as well as better design and implementation of the solution. [PPAs] have the potential to increase dialogue and negotiation at a policy level, and strengthen links between communities and policy-makers (that). . . could challenge existing power relations in the long term.*
> (Robb, 1999)

It is precisely because of the potential of PPAs to help researchers appreciate local details and complexity in the experience of poverty that it is imperative that we explore the transformations of those local details in a global rendering of PPA data.

The data set for *Can Anyone Hear Us?* presented a bewildering variety of possible approaches to, and content for, an overall synthesis. Precisely how and where the team drew the epistemological boundaries for the final report, and what guided our notions of where the boundaries should go, is a central question in mapping and analysing any knowledge production process. The methodological introduction to *Can Anyone Hear Us?* (Narayan et al, 2000, pp16–26) highlights many of the challenges encountered in the project. The present discussion is meant to elaborate these points and place them in a context of institutional knowledge production and authorization.

Two particular methodological features can serve as focal points for understanding the process of generalization in this case: the creation and regulation of a coding protocol, and the parameters within which a 'helpful', or acceptable, global report could be located.

CREATING CODE

A central objective of the *Can Anyone Hear Us?* exercise was to generate a report that emphasized the diversity of experience and definitions of poverty across countries, regions and respondents. Since it was impossible to capture the temporal, spatial and experiential diversity contained in 73 documents from 46 different countries in a global synthesis, the first challenge was to devise a coding scheme that would allow collation, comparison and the identification of informational patterns in the data. Although the stated intent was to 'let the data speak' insofar as was possible, certain features of the methodology limited our capacity for doing this.

An inductive approach to devising a coding scheme would have afforded the research team a chance to read through all of the data before identifying the main themes that would comprise a coding scheme (Emerson et al, 1995). Time constraints prohibited such a reading. Instead, the key features of our master coding scheme, around which most of our analysis later centred, were determined in brainstorm-style sessions very early in the project, at a time when data coders had read no more than a few reports. Inevitably in this set of circumstances, we 'spoke' to the data as much as it 'spoke' to us.

Still, we sought to mitigate the imposition of our own assumptions on the coding scheme by compiling a secondary set of codes that could evolve as the project progressed. The collection of these codes, which we called 'free nodes', allowed us to accommodate some previously unforeseen themes that arose as researchers simultaneously read and coded the data. Each researcher accumulated an individual list of secondary codes, and in subsequent meetings the team discussed them. In cases in which several researchers identified the same topic of interest, a new free node code was added to the team's shared coding scheme. While this method might have allowed more room for the data to 'speak' for itself, by only gradually instituting new codes at the group level it was impossible to ensure that all the documents in the data set had been read and marked for secondary codes.[8]

The practice of coding can easily obscure information not captured in a coding scheme, or de-emphasize those issues not shared across countries or regions. A topic that arises as absolutely central to respondents' descriptions of poverty in a particular report, but which is not repeated in other reports and thus not frequently coded, can be instantly erased or obscured by the act of assigning and aggregating data codes. In the critical moments of creating a coding scheme and assigning it to portions of text, then, a profound transformation takes place: coded data becomes dislocated from their context while uncoded data are lost. The consequences of this transformation can be particularly dangerous for those topics that are neither secured an a priori place in an analytical framework nor mentioned frequently enough across reports to warrant closer examination in subsequent analysis.

In coding qualitative data, researchers inevitably encounter problems of commensurability: text is collapsed into codes and codes are grouped and counted, giving those handling the data the power to determine what counts as 'similar' and what counts as 'different'. Of course, differences among coded data persist, but only insofar as they are able to withstand the process of collapsing data onto dimensions that have been decided, ultimately, by the researcher. An iterative process of coding and reintegrating categories can minimize this, but only within limits.

THE CATEGORY OF THE 'HELPFUL'

The process of coding and analysing the data set was shaped by practical and institutional constraints. Although we regularly held meetings to share our comments, opinions and ideas about the project and its methodology, these discussions assumed clear parameters implicitly drawn by regarding certain ideas as either 'helpful' or 'unhelpful'. Several concerns simply could not be accommodated by the project or the formal discussions meant to inform it. For example, questions about how to integrate the considerable body of scholarship that explores the limitations, problems and lessons learned about participatory research in practice (Mosse, 1994; Ribot, 1996; Pottier, 1997; Woost, 1997; Goebel, 1998; Michener, 1998; Hanmer et al, 1999) into our treatment of the data set were ultimately 'unhelpful' – and unresolvable – within project confines.

Critically reading each report would have introduced the complicated task of scrutinizing the very methodological tool our project was intended to advocate; far simpler, and more efficient, was the naturalized acceptance of each report and an uncritical reading and compiling of its contents. For instance, the following quotation, which appears in the conclusion to *Can Anyone Hear Us?*, was read and incorporated into the study at its face value:

> *After we had lunch with them, they sang for us. It is really amazing how they used songs to express themselves and their thoughts, expectations, fears, anxieties. The words of the final song were: 'Here they are, yes, we agree, here they are, our visitors who were sent by the World Bank, yes, there they are, they are here to help us and develop us, and we hope they won't forget us.'* (Narayan et al, 2000, p283)

This quotation can be read in many ways, ranging from a spontaneous outpouring of gratitude towards the World Bank to an example of the institution's power to coerce rehearsed responses in the places in which it operates. The implicit and explicit boundaries of the 'helpful' guided us to treat all of our data in the spirit of the former interpretation.

Unhelpful questions were thus suspended as researchers worked to read and interpret the data for a synthetic narrative that would bind 'localized' parts of PPA narratives into a 'global' whole. A searching analysis of each individual report and its conditions of production was impossible within the constraints of the project. Such an analysis would, moreover, have required a capacity for institutional reflection that remains underdeveloped within the World Bank.[9]

Hearing, listening, knowing

Creating a global narrative that would retain some of the 'voices' of people consulted in individual PPA studies often involved searching for exemplary quotations, moments in the global synthesis intended to amplify, in a living, breathing person's own words, some aspect of the struggle and suffering of living in poverty. Read uncritically, these quotations can punctuate research findings with moments that feel alive and 'real' – moments in which a voice considered powerless and remote is suddenly brought forwards and amplified in an institutional centre that has power to 'do something'. The entire *Voices of the Poor* initiative, on one level, provides an answer to long-held criticisms of development institutions' inability to 'hear' – learn about and respond to – the actual needs of those whom their projects are intended to help.

But the hearing of respondents is incomplete without attention to how they have been listened to. Understanding this 'how' entails articulating gains and losses, both at the local level itself and in the transition from local to global narratives. In assembling the global synthesis, we pulled decontextualized quotes from the data set – quotes that can hardly be thought of as voices in the usual sense of the word. In most cases these 'voices' were simply quotations – raw data material largely stripped of its original social and political context. Most of the quotations in the global synthesis are attributed only to a country name and year, and at times a gender identification or other general marker. As a consequence, it is impossible to discern the construction of self and deployment of agency in the global narrative; the placement of the speaker is largely lost, along with many local-level insights about what each speaker might have actually *meant*. This is to say nothing of the complexity of the local encounter, and local production of the PPA itself. As mentioned above, a great deal of scholarship has demonstrated that in practice, PPAs involve political, and sometimes highly problematic, processes.

What, then, is the utility in calling these the 'voices of the poor?' Certainly, at one level, the enrichment of a report with the actual words on which conclusions or observations are based provides the reader with an invitation to attribute the quote, and the experience, to a human being – a simultaneous agent, survivor and victim. The Voices of the Poor, as a concept, is radical in its assertion that connecting our understanding to real, lived experiences is critical to rethinking how development institutions understand and respond to poverty. At the scale of a global narrative of poverty, however, references to the quotations as 'voices' can be easily distorted, and should be read more as an aspiration to amplify a human experience than as an actual assertion that we have now reproduced, at the global level, the unadulterated, unmediated local voices of people living in poverty.

It is important to be clear about the losses incurred if we allow ourselves, or our institutions, to read the words and ideas behind these voices uncritically. The loss at this level involves not only the context that allows us to think about what is said versus what is meant, but also the reality that by the time the 'voice' reaches the global synthesis it has been processed through multiple layers of abstraction and mediation through the eyes, powers and agendas of first the field researchers themselves, then the editors of individual reports, then the combined layers of our research team, our coding and analysis, and the further analysis, writing and editing conducted at World Bank head-quarters. Without explicit attention to the definition and use of the 'localized' voice, the real contribution of participation as a theory and methodology is too easily obscured, redefined, and co-opted.

Rather than argue that this loss is somehow avoidable in any process of retelling what others have said, we mean to underline the importance of employing quotations as 'voices' only in a clearly contextualized and qualified sense. This qualification, one that informs the methodological discussion of *Voices of the Poor: Can Anyone Hear Us?*, is often downplayed at the centres of institutional power because the *imagination* of the voice intact, and of participation itself, allows the centre to congratulate itself, sometimes prematurely, for innovative reforms. Recognizing this institutional reality prevents us from making the dangerous assumption that we are suddenly able to amplify, unproblematically and fully, the true and unmediated voices of those living in poverty.

In the case of *Can Anyone Hear Us?*, without a critical and informed understanding of the use of 'voices' we leave open the possibility that the global synthesis will be used solely as an answer to critics who claim that the World Bank is incapable of either hearing those whom its policies affect or of transparent, rigorously participatory initiatives. Until the Bank is open to hearing the criticisms of development *and its institutions* in what it invites from the voices of the poor, and until it is equipped to receive more contextualized, actual 'voices', it is hard to refute the charge that narratives such as *Can Anyone Hear Us?* are simply using the appearance of listening to remake a World Bank image while avoiding the real work of re-making the institution (Lohmann, 1998). Is *Can Anyone Hear Us?* the institution's agenda made into local expression, or is it the other way around? A truly 'global' perspective on poverty would include the institution itself in its problematic of global and local poverty.

The institutional role played by a 'global' narrative, then, conditions its form and content. One way to understand this conditioning is through critical reflection. Provided that we recognize that this is the case and do not mistake or misrepresent a global synthesis for a globalized PPA,[10] we can use the global synthetic project to promote important institutional reforms.[11]

SPEAKING TO THE INSTITUTION: REQUIREMENTS FOR BEING 'HEARD'

Institutional expectations, requirements and norms exert control over any narrative created for an institution's own consumption and reproduction.

Even those projects that advocate reform and demonstrate the value of new methods, ideas and approaches – a project such as ours – must, at times, concede to these requirements in return for a chance to be taken seriously by those in positions of power. This is true not only in speaking to the World Bank, but also to its external critics who find themselves working within or through it. Reflecting on moments in the *Can Anyone Hear Us?* project during which these requirements were made explicit helps us to understand how abstraction and translation were guided, sometimes completely unintentionally, by institutional priorities. These conditions included the importance of numbers and the centrality of crisis narratives.

In preparing our initial findings for *Can Anyone Hear Us?*, we were acutely aware of the need to communicate with social scientists more familiar with positivist quantitative methodology. In anticipation of this audience, the research team produced numerical demonstrations of its findings, including matrices and frequency counts. Important limitations in the way our data was delimited and 'counted', however, made the numbers useful, at best, only as heuristics.[12] Nevertheless, the expectation was that numerical expressions of the data would make our report clearer and more legitimate to a wider institutional audience while cultivating a bridge from orthodox approaches to poverty to more pluralist treatments.

Yet, over time, a felt need to package the data for an institutional audience – some of whom, we expected, would not automatically accept our conclusions without numerical proof (nor, we assumed, would they automatically embrace the descriptive potential of participatory methods) – actually *drove* much of our treatment of the data for certain sections of the synthesis. Despite repeated recognition that our numerical data were inconsistent, at times we were guided by them. Matrices assumed a prevalent place among bundles of computer output on which later analyses were based. Often, we found ourselves confirming our conclusions with matrices containing possibly erroneous numbers. In our attempt to comply with the politics of knowledge at the centre, then, a key tenet of ethnographic, qualitative research – that human experience is not necessarily reducible to neutral, numerical metrics – had to be violated.

In addition to the need for numbers, institutional norms dictated a strong preference for crisis narratives. Such narratives are a regular feature of development discourse, and have been challenged by a number of critics (Wisner, 1993; Ferguson, 1994; Guthman, 1997, inter alia). In our case, the crisis took the form of a unifying theme: that of widespread and massive institutional breakdown.[13]

While the idea of institutional breakdown was not wholly inappropriate to describe the lives of those whose experiences we read and sought to write about, there are two important points to be made about the use of this crisis to construct our global narrative. First, defining crisis at the global scale involves selection: many of the very poor respondents whose stories are told in individual PPAs describe multiple forms of struggle related to their socio-economic circumstances. For the purposes of our worldwide synthesis, *particular* crises were identified, developed through the extraction of examples, and emphasized. Identifying which crises to deem 'global' has, inevitably, a connection to the knowledge-creating institution itself. In this case, ongoing policy-level debates about the appropriate relationship between states, lending institutions and markets were, perhaps, unstated factors in the choice of the particular narrative about state and institutional breakdown that was emphasized and developed (Caufield, 1996; World Bank, 1997; Hildyard, 1997). Paradoxically, while we were charged with exploring the breakdown of institutions in our work, the World Bank itself as an 'institution' was analytically off limits.

A second point about crisis narratives underlines the importance of the reflexivity of the global institution itself: assigning 'crisis' status to certain problems can divert attention from *systemic* problems leading to poverty, and instead create an impression that these problems are unnatural, out of the ordinary, or detached from issues of politics or history (or, in this case, the role the World Bank itself might have played in certain modern cases of state failure to provide social safety nets to its vulnerable populations). In a crisis mentality, extra-local forces contributing to a local problem tend to be ignored, and the focus becomes immediate acts of 'helping' rather than comprehensive consideration of the sum of acts of 'hurting' that brought about the crisis to begin with (Wisner, 1993). If read individually, PPAs might be able to refocus poverty analysis towards precisely these more systemic everyday experiences, complete with extra-local details and particular temporal and spatial locations.

CONTRIBUTIONS AND LIMITATIONS OF THE 'GLOBAL GAZE'

Can Anyone Hear Us? is a monumental and comprehensive aggregation of data from an enormous volume and range of materials. It attempts to bring together the 'voices' that emerged from over a decade of qualitative, ethnographic and participatory studies of poverty. In doing so, it seeks to illustrate the value of qualitative approaches to understanding poverty and how PPA data might be used to understand how it is differently, and specifically, experienced. 'The policy challenge that results', Narayan et al write,

> . . .is to formulate and implement poverty alleviation measures that succeed because they fit the detailed requirements of each case. Therefore, while we may

ask, 'What are the trends that unify experiences of the poor across regions?' we must never lose sight of the question these data are truly suited to help answer [namely] what is it about how poverty and social inequality are expressed in a given time, place and circumstance that must be reflected in policy measures?
(2000, p27)

Through this critical point – that policy must be flexible and sensitive to context in order to be effective – *Can Anyone Hear Us?* makes an essential contribution to the promotion of participatory studies as well as institutional reform. As a tool for demonstrating that poverty is indeed multidimensional, and far more complex than traditional economic indicators and exclusively quantitative approaches to poverty can convey, the book makes an invaluable contribution within the World Bank.

Yet even as it makes valuable policy points, the actual findings of the global synthesis remain perhaps surprisingly unremarkable as revelations about global poverty. Assertions that poverty is multidimensional, that it creates particular stresses on households, has gender dimensions, and can be related to failures of certain institutional structures, are not new. This may be a consequence of the fact that the dimensions of poverty PPAs are best equipped to address – contextuality and interconnection – had to be downplayed or eliminated to allow for generalization across reports covering such a wide range of social and temporal contexts. That the final conclusions we reached were unremarkable points to the losses sustained in the synthetic project. We must ask, then: if a global-scale analysis fails to yield new insights, how is the synthesis 'useful'?

The 'global gaze' is taken in institutional circles as the natural and desirable extension of localized studies: since poverty is a reality experienced worldwide, we should be able to discern what 'patterns' exist, and what realities are shared, in its experience. While we do not contend that there *aren't* shared aspects of poverty, we do suggest that by naturalizing the abstraction of knowledge from particular to universal, we might also assume, erroneously, that the most significant aspects of poverty would logically be the universals, the patterns that poor people 'everywhere' share.[14] If, on the other hand, we assume that the 'global' story is but a partial one – and one that might *not* contain the most important pieces of a fuller understanding of poverty – we are better positioned to identify the institutional and political momentum behind the very urge to gaze globally. In asking what is lost in the jump from individual reports to a single narrative, the question of *what counts as knowledge* at the centre becomes a proper one to ask. Through this, the character of the global scale – a scale without location, without history, politics or engagement with its subject – becomes clearer and requires explanation.

Both the limitations of a non-reflexive institution and the institutional requirement for an abstracted study exaggerate the losses incurred in any transfer of knowledge from one scale of reference to another. The urge to capture and tell the 'global' story can be as much a process of silencing, selecting and retelling as one of trying to convey 'local' realities to centres of power. Ideally, our project should not be a re-presentation and transformation of voices, but rather a struggle to construct institutional and political spaces in which the poor and marginalized can speak for themselves on their own terms (Spivak, 1988). The PPA might be a tool for creating that space, but when employed uncritically it runs the risk of becoming a device for managing, rather than 'hearing', the voices of the poor. The spaces in which researchers and institutions hear are as important as the spaces in which those who live in poverty can speak.

Similarly, until extra-local agents of development are free to include themselves in the construction of the problem of global poverty, there is room to question and suspect the current rhetoric of participation and PPAs. Until the boundaries of the 'global' imposed by the World Bank itself can be interrogated, the institutionalization of participation and PPAs is rightly susceptible to the criticism that through appropriation, PPAs have lost their theoretical force (Woost, 1997).

We are ill-equipped to grasp the institutional life of *Can Anyone Hear Us?* from our position as non-World Bank employees. But it is clear that as an advocacy piece for participatory methods the study plays an important role in promoting and further institutionalizing PPAs.[15] Could it be the case that in order to make PPAs more potent tools for social and institutional change, we must expect to disempower them and empty or transform their content for acceptance at the centre? In doing this, do we advance gradual reform? If so, it is even more important that the gains and losses incurred as knowledge is processed between and among these scales of reference be made explicit *in their entirety* among those who advocate PPA methodologies and their adoption. The global synthesis effort has great utility as an advocate of institutional reform and as a glimpse, albeit partial and limited, of the enormity of what has been missed in decades of defining poverty in narrowly economistic terms. This utility can only grow as we reflect on the imperatives for institutional change that it also represents.

CONCLUSIONS

Brosius et al (1998) usefully ask: 'When a unified discourse emerges from a range of regional contexts and under various guises. . . how might this make generic the ways local institutions are defined by external (ahistoricized) agents?' We are left to consider how the universalized narrative does just that: renders generic certain aspects of poverty even while it advocates a potentially powerful set of tools for understanding what is *ungeneric* about local experiences of poverty. On some levels, the very act of transferring PPA findings from a local to global scale lends an external ordering that contains the political, decontextualizes voices and experience, and in doing so, removes the institution itself from the problematic as constructed. Recall that individual PPAs might have the potential to describe very specific contours of poverty in particular contexts with distinct histories that the global analysis occludes. The differences between local reports and the global synthesis reveal as much about the institution, and the confines within which it can digest knowledge, as they do about human suffering and its causes.

Participation, and the institutionalized methodologies that purport to employ it, are 'moving targets' and cannot be taken out of history.[16] PPAs are tools that social scientists, planners and activists have been calling for in a quest for more democratic development strategies. Without a clear understanding of when and how they are applied, written about and later abstracted to central policy-level documents, however, the partial perspective of the global gaze is easily mistaken for complete knowledge. This 'knowledge' can then be used to pacify those who advocate genuine change and democratic processes. Perhaps our most important and responsible task is to keep careful track of the movements of this 'target'. We can do this by asking not only how PPAs are conducted at local levels, but how they change as they are aggregated and processed.

Scholarly attention to local–global transitions in development discourse has explored the divergences in global representations of local problems (Dove, 1998) and the impact of totalizing global narratives on local and regional experience, understanding and definitions of development issues (Pigg, forthcoming; Pigg, 1992; Buttel, 1992; Rangan, 1992). An unavoidable dimension of the question of just what constitutes the 'local' and the 'global' is an ongoing debate about the politics of representation[17] and the power of ethnography employed in the service of colonial (Asad, 1973) and post-colonial (Escobar, 1991) centres of power. If participation ideally represents a dissolution of the ethnographic subject and object – that is to say, if it is a truly collaborative exercise – *then the problem of power in representation centres precisely on the translations of that collaborative exercise for communication to more central, and more powerful, audiences.*

An emerging ethnographic focus on the experience of working within specific institutional orders (Pierce, 1999; Dove, 1999), including the development profession (Kaufmann, 1997), provides a guide for examining the researcher as an agent in this process of translation. These works query what is taken as 'natural' in institutional contexts and in so doing expose power relations and norms not openly acknowledged or understood. In studying the production of development discourse, this vantage point allows us a potentially constructive engagement with the idea of 'development' as a social process composed of agents – not the monolithic force producing hegemonic and totalising discourses that poststructural analyses of development have portrayed (Escobar, 1992, 1995; Ferguson, 1994), but a complex and multi-layered process of making and re-making 'knowledge'. Ferguson's (1994, p18) observation that 'the thoughts of development bureaucrats are powerfully shaped by the world of acceptable statements and utterances within which they live' is complicated in that this world exists at multiple scales; it is neither constant, singular nor bounded, nor indeed is it inhabited by single-minded professionals (Kaufmann, 1997). Multiple discourses exist and encounter one another in the complex flow of 'knowledge' and practice.

Thus an analysis of the creation of synthetic knowledge from a collection of local studies is not sufficient if it is to conclude that our end product, and the process that created it, simply confirms the existence of a singular dominated 'poor' and a monolithic, dominating World Bank. Rather, the problem involves a complex circulation of knowledge and intervention mediated by agents at every level and scale of analysis. Analysing the practice of creating a global narrative out of local reports is thus as much a reflection on the agency of individual researchers in an institutional context as it is a story of the built-in challenges of abstracting locally gleaned knowledge to a document focused on global patterns. Each individual's practice in this project (from the local-level interaction to the global synthetic initiative) was structured by a set of power relations and expectations that influenced, but did not always determine, which decisions were and were not taken. It is imperative to consider these conditioning realities seriously as they dramatically affect the nature of the 'knowledge' we glean from them (Pottier, 1997). Just as the collective – the institution – benefits from a reflexive imperative, so too do individuals in development practice. Perhaps our most critical – and most fully participatory – question should be: to what extent do our research endeavours serve existing power relationships and to what extent do they work to expose and seek to balance them?

The chances to challenge existing power relationships are substantially increased when there is opportunity for self-critical reflection. Much in the exercise of reflection turns on the ability to render previously taken-for-granted concepts problematic – that is, to recognize and interrogate the natural. Reflection is a tool for improving our understanding of the complex journey from local, lived realities to the products of knowledge that are produced, circulated and used by development policy-makers. Reflection is *not* an act of denying or distancing oneself from previous ideas or work; rather, reflexive engagement with past projects is an imperative feature of adaptive learning. As the social anthropologist Bruce Knauft (1996, p144) suggests: '. . .reflexive moments that look inward to our own forms of knowledge can stimulate, rather than preclude, reciprocal moments that appreciate the substance of ethnographic diversity. Moments of perspectival critique, and those of bracketed objectivity, can be mutually empowering rather than mutually deconstructing.'

Our own reflection, offered here, is thus in no way an attempt to disassociate from the work we undertook for the *Voices of the Poor* project. On the contrary, it is an exercise in engaging the project more fully and assuming accountability as researchers charged with the task of retelling worlds of poverty. In our view, reflection on the research process is an extension of our commitment to democratic forms of knowledge production.[18]

In conclusion, the production of a universal narrative in this case involved, more or less wittingly, a process of generalization that often seemed to owe more to the political circumstances in 'the centre' than to an accountability to the people whose words we wielded. Our argument has not been against abstraction per se, but rather for an active recognition that *every* abstraction involves an opportunity cost – some features are accentuated while others are diminished. The pattern of how opportunity costs fall is an urgent matter, and needs to involve the views of all those involved in the knowledge production process, not just those at the centre. Only in attending to this do we preserve the potential of participation to become engagement – and for that engagement to translate, fully and meaningfully, into institutional transformation. Without sensitivity towards, and dialogue with, those our global narrative claims to represent, the realities of those individuals and groups in participatory knowledge production can come to 'count' only in particularly biased and distorted ways. There is a need, to paraphrase Ribot (1996), for responsible, democratic abstraction, or 'no generalization without representation'. This is the crux of the ethnographic challenge posed by participatory methodologies and the very idea of aggregating them.

Notes

1 We are grateful to Jo Beall, Michelle Beesten, Christopher Brooke, Andrea Cornwall, Steve Curtis, Michael Dove, Shelley Feldman, Ravi Kanbur, Sarah Koch-Schulte, Phil McMichael, Deepa Narayan, Patti Petesch, Gretchen E. Schafft, Robert Torres, Annyce Turco and, in particular, Kai Schafft for wisdom, insight and support in writing this chapter. The views expressed, and any errors, are our own.

2 We refer to knowledge 'production' since knowledge is itself a practice insofar as it emerges within a particular set of social relations and institutional dynamics. Knowledge is not simply the revelation of facts; it is itself productive and reproductive of specific social and power relationships. In this case we intentionally refer to the global document as 'knowledge' rather than 'information'. The latter reserves some agency for the consumer while the former implies that the final product, the knowledge, has already been formulated and is delivered as definitive.

3 *Can Anyone Hear Us?* is the first volume of the three-volume Voices of the Poor series published by Oxford University Press and the World Bank. The second volume, *Crying Out for Change,* is a synthesis of data from methodologically standardized field studies conducted in 23 countries. Volume three, *From Many*

Lands, provides a series of country case studies and presents a discussion of region-specific patterns of poverty and vulnerability. We worked as research assistants to this project during its data coding and analysis phases (March to July 1999), performing tasks ranging from document coding and coding protocol development to data content analysis and writing. The draft report produced from this work was submitted to the World Bank in July 1999, where the volume was edited and reworked before its publication in 2000.

4   It is important to engage and understand the implications of the World Bank's growing interest in cultivating its identity as a 'knowledge bank'. Providing 'knowledge' is increasingly identified as a primary function of the Bank: the introductory pages of its website, for example, prominently feature a quotation from Bank President James Wolfensohn that reads: 'What we as a development community can do is help countries – by providing financing, yes; but even more important, by providing knowledge and lessons learned about the challenges and how to address them' (see also Hildyard, 1997, pii). The World Bank's emphasis on its role as a supplier of knowledge, rather than as a source of information, however, can easily obscure the bureaucratic and political filters through which Bank-produced 'knowledge' passes.

5   The Voices of the Poor process, also discussed by Adan et al and Chambers (this volume), was originally called Consultations with the Poor but adopted the title Voices of the Poor in late 1999. This chapter discusses the process of reviewing World Bank PPAs, published as Narayan et al, 2000.

6   The final published version of this report, *Voices of the Poor: Can Anyone Hear Us?* claims analyses of 81 PPAs conducted in a total of 50 countries, as an additional eight reports were added to the study after we concluded our research on the draft global synthesis for the World Bank.

7   For a period of about a week, consultants on the research team sorted through the boxes of documents sent to us from the World Bank's Washington headquarters. In general, we quickly skimmed the text, selecting reports that gave coverage to particular issues such as vulnerability, social exclusion and the gendered dimensions of poverty, as well as reports that contained relatively abundant direct quotes from respondents or otherwise incorporated ethnographic and/or qualitative data in their analyses. Reports were given a preliminary A, B, or C rating based on these criteria. All documents with an 'A' rating were included in the set, as well as some 'B' documents, while all others were disqualified.

8   It is important to note this and other weaknesses in our method. Although the coding tree evolved through the progressive reading of reports, we were not able to revisit the documents that had been coded with a first-iteration coding tree at the beginning of the exercise, in order to recode with a more sophisticated coding schema. Furthermore, there were inconsistencies in how the qualitative data analysis software program we were using delineated individual text units. These units could range from a single line in some documents to entire paragraphs in others, and the software rendered the task of tallying the number of text units coded for an individual topic of interest (for instance, 'social exclusion' or 'effective formal institution') a methodologically uncertain exercise. In many cases it was impossible to confirm that a frequency statistic for the occurrence of references to a given topic could be interpreted as a quantitatively meaningful number.

9 As a matter of course, the World Bank has tended to limit its reflections to internal discussion (the recent online public discussion of the Bank's *World Development Report 2000* is exceptional in this regard). Despite calls for greater transparency, the norm for reflexive critique within the Bank was made deeply explicit when the *Washington Post* printed an internal memo circulated by James Wolfensohn on his first day as President, which read: 'Dear Colleague: I expect from you loyalty to the institution and to each other. . . Criticisms must be internal and constructive. . . I will regard externally-voiced criticism of the Bank as a desire to find alternative employment' (quoted in Caufield, 1996, p312). In our case, not surprisingly, criticism considered constructive existed within particular confines, confines we in turn largely internalized.

10 The press release accompanying the launch of *Can Anyone Hear Us?* claimed that 60,000 poor people had been consulted. In a different press release, the number was a more modest 40,000.

11 For instance, a new World Bank initiative called 'Global Coalitions for Voices of the Poor' might provide more direct engagement between and among movements on behalf of people living in poverty. While this project is currently in its preliminary phase, it might be indicative of the wider institutional impact of a study like *Can Anyone Hear Us?*

12 As noted in Note 6, inconsistencies in how the qualitative data analysis software program we were using delineated individual text units – which could range from a single line in some documents to entire paragraphs in others – rendered the task of tallying the number of text units coded for an individual topic of interest (for instance, 'social exclusion' or 'effective formal institution') methodologically questionable. This point is noted in the methodological discussion at the beginning of *Can Anyone Hear Us?*

13 Once the data set had been coded, researchers produced data output of PPA text excerpts coded for particular topics of interest. In an all-team meeting that took place about two months into the project, it was decided that the central theme that would unify our treatment of the data would be the notion of 'institutions in crisis'; this theme became the guiding assumption for writing the report entitled *Crumbling Foundations, Conflicting Relations: Gender and Poverty in the 1990s*, the draft report submitted to the World Bank by the research team, which eventually became *Can Anyone Hear Us?*

14 While *Can Anyone Hear Us?* explicitly addresses the limitations of making statements about 'poor people everywhere' based on the study, publicity and official representations of the book went far to suggest that the book could do just that. The important point here is not just the accuracy of the claims, but that there is perhaps something suspicious about the need to accompany World Bank knowledge products with press releases at all. The exaggerated representation of these products lends credence to their role, in part, as tools to improve the public perception of the World Bank.

15 In correspondence following the launch of the book, one of the researchers, raising questions about the press materials, was told by a development professional to accept the content of publicity materials – correct or not – as 'inevitable'.

16 This phrase was used in an analysis of institutional adoption of cost–benefit analysis by Michael Dove at the Conference on Cost–Benefit Analysis, Yale University, 1999.

17 Dove (1999) offers a synopsis of the ongoing debate about ethnographic represent-ation: 'This debate commenced in the mid-1980s with claims by interpretive scholars, based often on analyses of the implicit premises of colonial-era anthro-pology, that representation is domination and therefore must be avoided (Clifford and Marcus, 1986; Marcus and Fischer, 1986; Roth, 1989). This critique of representation was countered with claims that the critics employ the same conceptual tools that they attempt to deny to others and that their work further inhibits the possibilities within ethnography for praxis (Parpart, 1993; Roseberry, 1996; Sangren, 1988; Spiro, 1992).'

18 It is important to clarify why we continued to work on this project even as we recognized its seemingly intractable challenges. The brief answer lies in a combin-ation of factors, all of which were the subject of continuous discussion and contemplation. They include: loyalty to our supervisor and to the belief that our continued contribution would be able to mitigate the more egregious distortions involved in the project; a genuine commitment to the decentering of knowledge production; and the high visibility of the project, first as a *World Development Report* background paper and, as we learned quite late in the project, a book. As graduate students, the financial inducements of the project were also an important factor. We are currently engaged in a more nuanced ethnographic exploration of the question of our own complicity in the process and problems described in this chapter; this will be discussed more thoroughly in a future paper.

REFERENCES

Asad, T (1973) *Anthropology and the Colonial Encounter*, London, Ithaca Press

Brosius, J P, Lownhaupt Tsing, A and Zerner, C (1998) 'Representing communities: histories and politics of community-based natural resource management', *Society and Natural Resources*, Vol 11

Buttel, F (1992) 'Environmentalization: Origins, processes, and implications for rural social change', *Rural Sociology*, Vol 57, pp1–27

Caufield, C (1996) *Masters of Illusion: The World Bank and the Poverty of Nations*, New York, Henry Holt and Company

Chambers, R (1992) *Rural Appraisal: Rapid, Relaxed, Participatory*, Brighton, IDS

Chambers, R (1994) 'The origins and practice of participatory rural appraisal', *World Development*, Vol 22, pp953–969

Chambers, R (1997) *Whose Reality Counts?* Bath, Intermediate Technology

Clifford, J and Marcus, G (1986) *Writing Culture: The Poetics and Politics of Ethnography*, Berkeley, University of California Press

Dove, M (1998) 'Local dimensions of "global" environmental debates', in Persoon, G and Kalland, A (eds) *Environmental Movements in Asia*, Surrey, Curzon Press

Dove, M (1999) 'Writing for, versus about, the ethnographic other: Issues of engagement and reflexivity in working with a tribal NGO in Indonesia', *Identities*, Vol 6, pp225–253

Emerson, R, Fretz, R and Shaw, L (1995) *Writing Ethnographic Field Notes*, Chicago, University of Chicago Press

Escobar, A (1991) 'Anthropology and the development encounter', *American Ethnologist* Vol 18, pp658–682

Escobar, A (1992) 'Imagining a post-development era? Critical thought, development, and social movements', *Social Text*, 31/32, pp20–56

Escobar, A (1995) *Encountering Development*, Princeton, Princeton University Press

Forbes, A Armbrecht (1999) 'The importance of being local: Villagers, NGOs, and the World Bank in the Arun Valley, Nepal', *Identities*, Vol 6, Nos 2–3, pp319–344

Ferguson, J (1994) *The Anti-politics Machine: Development, Depoliticization, and Bureaucratic Power in Lesotho*, Minneapolis, University of Minnesota Press

Gardner, K (1997) 'Mixed messages: Contested "development" and the "plantation rehabilitation project"', in Grillo, R D and Stirrat, R L (eds) *Discourses of Development: Anthropological Perspectives*, Oxford, Oxford University Press

Goebel, A (1998) 'Process, perception and power: Notes from "participatory" research in a Zimbabwean resettlement', *Development and Change*, Vol 29, pp277–305

Gow, D (1991) 'Collaboration in development consulting: Stooges, hired guns, or musketeers?', *Human Organization*, Vol 50

Green, E (ed) (1986) 'A short-term consultancy in Bangladesh', in *Practising Development Anthropology*, London, Westview Press

Grillo, R D and Stirrat, R L (1997) *Discourses of Development: Anthropological Perspectives*, New York, Oxford

Guthman, J (1997) 'Representing crisis: The theory of Himalayan environmental degradation and the project of development in post-Rana Nepal', *Development and Change*, Vol 28, pp45–69

Hanmer, L, Pyatt, G and White, H (1999) 'What do the World Bank's poverty assessments teach us about poverty in sub-Saharan Africa?' *Development and Change*, Vol 30

Hildyard, N (1997) 'The World Bank and the state: A recipe for change?', Washington, DC, Bretton Woods Project

Kaufmann, G (1997) 'Watching the developers: A partial ethnography', in Grillo, R D and Stirrat, R L (eds) *Discourses of Development: Anthropological Perspectives*, Oxford, Oxford University Press

Knauft, B (1996) *Geneologies of the Present in Cultural Anthropology*, New York, Routledge

Lohmann, L (1998) *Missing the Point of Development Talk: Reflections for Activists*, London, The Corner House

Long, N and Long, A (1992) *Battlefields of Knowledge: The Interlocking of Theory and Practice in Social Research and Development*, London, Routledge

Marcus, G and Fischer, M (1986) *Anthropology as Cultural Critique: An Experimental Moment in the Human Sciences*, Chicago, University of Chicago Press

Michener, V (1998) 'The participatory approach: Contradiction and cooptation in Burkina Faso', *World Development*, pp2105–2118

Mosse, D (1994) 'Authority, gender, and knowledge: Theoretical reflections on the practice of participatory rural appraisal', *Development and Change*, Vol 25, pp497–525

Narayan, D with Patel, Raj, Schafft, K, Rademacher, A and Koch-Schulte, S, (2000) *Voices of the Poor: Can Anyone Hear Us?*, New York, Oxford University Press

Nelson, N and Wright, S (1995) *Power and Participatory Development: Theory and Practice*, London, Intermediate Technology

Parpart, J (1993) 'Who is the "other"?: A postmodern feminist critique of women and development theory', *Development and Change*, Vol 24, pp439–464

Peet, M and Watts, R (1996) *Liberation Ecologies: Environment, Development, Social Movements*, New York, Routledge

Peters, P (1996) 'Introduction: Who's local here? The politics of participation in development', *Cultural Survival Quarterly*

Pierce, J (1999) 'Reflections on fieldwork in a complex organization: Lawyers, ethnographers, authority, and lethal weapons', in Imber, R and Imber, J (eds) *Studying Elites Using Qualitative Methods*, London, Sage Publications

Pigg, S (1992) 'Inventing social categories through place: Social representations and development in Nepal', *Comparative Studies in Society and History*, Vol 34, pp491–513

Pigg, S (forthcoming) 'Notes on the social production of commensurability: Science, facts, and language in the communication of HIV/AIDS information in Nepal', paper presented at the Agrarian Studies Conference, Yale University

Pottier, J (1997) 'Towards an ethnography of participatory appraisal and research', in Grillo, R D and Stirrat, R L (eds) *Discourses of Development: Anthropological Perspectives*, New York, Oxford University Press, pp203–227

Rangan, H (1992) 'Romancing the environment: Popular environmental action in the Garhwal Himalayas', in Friedmann, J and Rangan, H (eds) *Defense of Livelihoods: Comparative Studies in Environmental Action*, West Hartford, Kumarian Press

Ribot, J (1996) 'Participation without representation: Chiefs, councils, and forestry law in the West African Sahel' *Cultural Survival Quarterly*, pp40–44

Robb, C (1999) *Can the Poor Influence Policy? Participatory Poverty Assessments in the Developing World*, Washington, DC, World Bank

Roseberry, W (1996) 'The unbearable lightness of anthropology', *Radical History Review*, Vol 65, pp5–25

Roth, P (1989) 'Ethnography without tears', *Current Anthropology*, Vol 30, pp555–569

Roe, E (1991) 'Development narratives, or making the best of blueprint development', *World Development*, Vol 19, pp287–300

Said, E (1983) 'Opponents, audiences, constituencies, and community', in Mitchell, W J T (ed) *The Politics of Interpretation*, Chicago, University of Chicago Press

Sangren, P (1988) 'Rhetoric and the authority of ethnography', *Current Anthropology*, Vol 29, pp405–430

Spiro, M (1992) 'Cultural relativism and the future of anthropology', in Marcus, G (ed) *Reading Cultural Anthropology*, Durham/London, Duke University Press

Spivak, G (1988) 'Can the subaltern speak?', in Nelson, C and Grossberg, L (eds) *Marxism and the Interpretation of Culture*, Chicago, University of Illinois Press, pp271–313

Wisner, B (1993) 'Disaster vulnerability: Scale, power, and daily life', *GeoJournal*, Vol 30, pp127–140

Woost, M (1997) 'Alternative vocabularies of development? "Community" and "participation" in development discourse in Sri Lanka' in Grillo, R D and Stirrat, R L (eds) *Discourses of Development: Anthropological Perspectives*, Oxford, Oxford University Press

World Bank (1990) *World Development Report 1990: Poverty*, New York, Oxford University Press

World Bank (1997) *World Development Report 1997: The State in a Changing World*, New York, Oxford University Press

Wright, S (1994) 'Introduction: clients and empowerment', in Wright, S (ed) *Anthropology of Organizations*, London, Routledge

CONCLUSION: PARTICIPATORY POVERTY RESEARCH: OPENING SPACES FOR CHANGE

Rosemary McGee

BY BRINGING TOGETHER the perspectives of diversely situated practitioners and scholars involved in various ways with participatory poverty research, this book has sought to demonstrate one of the central principles behind participatory research: that multiple perspectives are enriching. This conclusion takes a step back from our main subject, participatory poverty research itself, to the domain that much of it seeks to influence, the poverty reduction policy process. It analyses this through the lenses provided by these six reflective contributions. Doing so gives rise to knowledge *about* policy which, when applied in participatory poverty research initiatives, becomes knowledge *for* policy – knowledge that can help those engaged in participatory research to change policy by various means in favour of the poor and excluded.

POLICY SPACES

Analysing policy processes, Grindle and Thomas (1991) draw attention to what they call 'policy spaces': those instances[1] in which 'interventions or events throw up new opportunities, reconfiguring relationships between actors within these spaces, or bringing in new actors, and opening the possibility of a shift in direction' (cited in Brock, Cornwall and Gaventa, 2001, p26). These can be described as either 'invited spaces' created by powerful actors from above – governments, for example – or autonomously created spaces in which less powerful actors set agendas and initiate engagement with the more powerful (Brock, Cornwall and Gaventa, 2001, p2). Spaces can be occupied by actors of just one type, or by a mixture of actors relating to each other in diverse ways. It is in these spaces that the opportunities arise to change the course of policy, through influencing its formulation, its imple-mentation or its monitoring or evaluation. The spaces can be used in various strategic ways: new policy actors can be allowed into existing spaces to replace or mix with those who previously occupied them; spaces can be used to develop counter-narratives with which to challenge dominant discourses; or institutional shifts towards more deliberative, participatory and inclusive policy processes can be promoted (Keeley and Scoones, 1999). Power relations, competing knowledge claims and the influence of dominant discourses in the broader environment all have a bearing on the room for manoeuvre that policy spaces afford those within them; some spaces exclude some actors or allow them little meaningful participation.[2]

Participatory poverty research seeks to open up policy spaces, or exploit existing ones, in ways that make policy more favourable to poor people. Poverty policy spaces differ from one another by origin, main function, the actors who occupy them, and the kinds of knowledge that dominate them. Since each of our chapter authors (or author groups) has a different vantage point on the participatory poverty research they describe and on the policy process it seeks to influence, each chapter identifies or emphasizes different policy spaces.

On the basis of the experiences discussed in this volume, then, certain characteristics and dimensions of spaces for pro–poor policy change can be discerned. Figure C.1 attempts to summarize them. By 'origin' I refer to the manner in which the space was created, and I would suggest that there is a spectrum of possible origins between the extremes of 'invited' and 'auto-nomously created', as well as many possibilities for complementarity between the two. 'Dynamics within spaces' are not mutually exclusive, nor necessarily fixed over time; they can be multiple and will relate to whether the origins of the space lie in invitation or autonomous initiative, with invited spaces tending to be somewhat less flexible and evolutionary. Categories of 'occupants' are not mutually exclusive either; the value of a space often lies in the co-existence of diverse actors within it, and the relationships and cooperation to which this gives rise. 'Dominant knowledge' refers to the kind of know-ledge or information that is considered legitimate and valid in a given space, and represents a continuum from quantitative poverty data and generalizable 'facts' to popular perceptions, priorities and forms of expression.

	Range of possibilities	Examples from this volume
ORIGINAL	Invited ↕ Autonomously created	Consultations with poor communities in 23 countries conducted by World Bank for Voices of the Poor project (Chambers; Adan et al)
		Advocacy-skills training programme set up by the UPPAP for civil society organizations (CSOs) – a space created within a government programme for non-governmental actors to develop autonomous advocacy initiatives (Yates and Okello)
		Community advocacy with local government in Brazil (Adan et al) – a space that was autonomously created at the local level within the invited, supranational space of the Voices exercise
DYNAMICS WITHIN SPACE	Policy deliberation	Civil Society Task Force, formed to contribute to the revision of Uganda's PEAP (Yates and Okello)
	Knowledge construction	Viet Nam PPA fieldwork (Adan et al); Myanmar case in which choices were made between methods, and PPA was adapted to meet conventional validity criteria (Shaffer)
	Inter-relational	Immersion experiences of members of WDR 2000–01 writing team, which can also open up spaces for *action* by influential individuals (McGee)
	Advocacy	Local institutional analysis in Somaliland in Voices research, leading to the formation of a village committee (Adan et al)
	Action for change	Founding of daycare centre for homeless youths in Sofia railway station, arising from Bulgarian Voices work (Adan et al)
OCCUPANTS	International donor actors	World Bank's role in Voices of the Poor initiative (Chambers, Adan et al, Rademacher and Patel); World Bank staff members undergoing immersion experiences (McGee); UNDP creating poverty knowledge in Myanmar (Shaffer); World Bank country strategy influenced by Voices reports in Brazil (Adan et al)
	Central government actors	Ministry of Finance officials championing the UPPAP project within government (Yates and Okello)
	Local government actors	District officials' involvement in the UPPAP fieldwork (Yates and Okello)
	Academics and analysts	Researchers involved in developing policy messages from PPA data for Voices initiative (Rademacher and Patel); researchers carrying out Voices research in Ethiopia (Adan et al)
	Participatory researchers or researchers using participatory techniques	All six chapters offer examples; Chambers and Rademacher and Patel focus on such researchers. In some cases, researchers worked as individuals without institutional affiliation; in other cases, researchers represented institutions
	NGO actors	International NGOs carrying out fieldwork for Viet Nam PPA (Adan et al)
	CBO actors	Vila União Neighbourhood Association leader in research site for Voices in Brazil (Adan et al); Somali CBOs (Adan et al)
	Poor women, men and children	Roma people taking part in focus groups for Voices in Bulgaria (Adan et al)
DOMINANT KNOWLEDGE	Generalizable quantitative poverty data	Myanmar PPA (Shaffer)
	Popular perceptions, priorities and forms of expression	UPPAP video and national report (Yates and Okello)

Figure C.1 *Poverty policy spaces: A preliminary typology*

By way of further illustrations of complementarity between different kinds of space, Yates and Okello reveal the potential synergy between what happens in *invited* spaces of *policy deliberation* and *knowledge construction*, and in *autonomously created* spaces of *knowledge construction*, *advocacy* and *action* taken up by non-governmental actors; and how the former can spark efforts to develop or claim the latter. Adan et al likewise depict situations in which *invited* spaces opened from above lead to actors at the grassroots creating their own spaces of *action, policy deliberation, advocacy* and *inter-relation*, and show how much the emergence and impact of these can depend on the commitment of single individuals. To illustrate how different actors' motivations or agency within one space can be contradictory, Chambers and Rademacher and Patel highlight the *knowledge construction* spaces that participatory methods of poverty assessment can offer at supranational as well as local levels, but illustrate cogently how in given institutional settings these are shaped by institutional imperatives and biases that crowd out dynamics of participation, empowerment and structural change in favour of the poor.

THE DYNAMICS OF PRO-POOR CHANGE

What are the dynamics of pro-poor change that take place in the policy spaces arising from the initiatives described in this volume? The spaces McGee focuses on lie within decision-makers themselves and in the relations between them and other actors. In these spaces, the inter-relation of actors unfamiliar with one another and with each others' contexts can generate a reversal in power relations. When this dynamic is accompanied by a structured reflection process, it becomes harder for 'normal'[3] power relations to resume subsequently. Perceptions alter; sets of previously opposed actors come to regard each other as potential allies for change. The kinds of knowledge that stimulate these processes are, on the one hand, new, non-technical and often intimate knowledge of the 'other' by each set of actors; and on the other hand, changes in outlook and insight engendered by a new self-knowledge on the part of the 'experts'. One dimension of the fluidity and dynamism of policy spaces is, precisely, this scope for experiential learning and the incorporation of lessons into later experiences of interaction.

Shaffer, arguing for PPA approaches to complement conventional econometric analysis, bases his case on the 'information loss' inherent in the latter, especially with regard to processes of poverty and diverse experiences of it among different social groups. Inherent characteristics of policy and policy processes predispose the major users of poverty knowledge to particular, dominant knowledges, but Shaffer shows how less conventional approaches such as participatory assessment can, in fact, meet qualifying criteria for gaining entry into methodological spaces of poverty knowledge creation, and secure credibility therein. Yet the dominant poverty policy discourse, favouring conventional assessment methods, remains unreflexive in its treatment of its own principles and practice, and reductionist in its treatment of participatory approaches, failing to recognize this or to acknowledge that participatory processes also provide other valuable spaces besides knowledge-creation ones. Technocrats exercise power and agency in selecting methods; choices are political and ideological as well as technical, though this fact is frequently obscured by an overwhelming preoccupation with technicalities. The dynamics of methodological choice, as Shaffer shows, are not inevitable and uniform, and researchers convinced of the usefulness of participatory poverty research can proffer technical solutions to win over detractors and build these approaches, with all their foreseeable and unforeseeable potentials for change, into the poverty assessment efforts of mainstream institutions.

UPPAP is a rare example of an initiative explicitly designed, by a partnership instigated from above, to create and open up policy spaces of various kinds. Knowledge construction was the primary rationale for UPPAP, but its designers, drawing on lessons from past PPAs, built in spaces for interaction between officials and poor communities, advocacy actors and academic 'poverty experts'; and spaces for community self-development actions, in partnership with government and non-governmental actors. In addition to the invited, planned spaces UPPAP offered, others arose, some of which were advocacy spaces championed by the non-governmental actors in the partnership, and others that were more informal but nonetheless influential spaces of interaction. The knowledge generated was not always new to either the researchers or the community members who co-created it, but the confidence and means to act on it frequently were. Knowledge was also shared 'downwards', as researchers used the same interaction and knowledge construction spaces to disseminate information on government policies and entitlements.

The UPPAP process thus held potential for a range of shifts in power relations. While one aim was to enhance the power of local government as a locus of pro-poor policy change, in the event aspects of the Ugandan policy environment and the politics of decentralization militated against this redistribution of power from the centre to the districts. Trade-offs between influencing central or local government were dealt with by means of pragmatic, realistic assessments of where the main opportunities for influencing policy lay. The flexible, evolutionary nature of UPPAP reflects in large measure the fluidity and dynamism of contemporary poverty policy processes in Uganda. As Yates and Okello's analysis suggests, there is no doubt that UPPAP has helped to institutionalize spaces for participation by non-government actors in policy processes and the consultation – if not participation – of poor communities, although it is less clear that the opening of such spaces represents any real lasting shift in power between donors, government and civil society.

Adan et al, Chambers and Rademacher and Patel offer different insights into the various dynamics that are set up when a powerful international institution initiates participatory poverty research at the micro-level. Power legitimizes or de-legitimizes knowledge, so whatever the pre-existing attitudes towards different poverty knowledges in a given country setting, the power of the convening institution confers a degree of acceptability on the knowledge-construction approaches to which it subscribes.

Nonetheless, the main understanding of the dynamics of pro-poor change which Adan et al offer concerns how heavily these dynamics depend on context – cultural, institutional, political, ideological and temporal. Entry points for participatory poverty research to influence policy present themselves at a range of levels, from the micro-level to that of international donor and creditor institutions. Some countries' political histories and regime types afford more opportunities than others, but spaces of sorts are opening up in at least four of the five examples discussed by Adan et al,[4] in some cases taking longer than the time frame of the Voices initiative. The scope for engendering pro-poor change in them depends partly on context-specific expectations about who is meant to take action against poverty – a paternalist state? Constituents in a decentralized participatory governance model? There are moments in a country's political evolution at which a participatory process or its findings can attain maximum impact: Viet Nam is a positive example, while Ethiopia illustrates how resistant to new poverty policy dynamics a government can be. In-depth understanding of the policy environment is thus critical to designing each participatory research initiative for maximum effect, a lesson confirmed by the UPPAP case. Unfortunately, the policy spaces arising in some countries, typically where these were created from above and under donor pressure, allowed changes in policy principles without concomitant changes in policy practice. Fortunately, although not systematically supported in the Voices exercise, micro-level actions and changes did result, and for many participants these incidental benefits will be the main or only impact they experience.

Chambers and Rademacher and Patel focus on the connections between knowledge creation and political momentum for policy change on the global scale to which the *World Development Report*, as the 'flagship document' of the World Bank (Wade, 2001, p1435), aspires. In the Voices, several forces were at work. Notwithstanding the framing of the Voices as an apolitical research initiative, the political forces – the might of the key institutional actor, the emotive power of the 'voices' and the accompanying public relations crusade within the Bank and outside it – were arguably more significant than methodological dynamics in triggering policy change. While these forces might combine to produce pro-poor policy change, there is clearly a risk of this happening at the cost of root principles of participatory research and practice, in particular ethical norms and epistemological integrity.

The dynamic of knowledge creation in the Voices, while spanning multiple levels, was claimed by the Bank to be a one-way process in which voices spoke and were listened to. This kind of dynamic is at variance with the co-creation to which most participatory researchers aspire. However, while the rhetoric surrounding the Voices presents it as the pure, unadulterated amplification of the poor's voices from the bottom upwards, these chapters disclose how deeply the commissioning agency and its contractors were implicated in the framing and creation of this knowledge. The agency of field researchers in the 23 country studies and, more significantly, of those analysing, synthesizing and writing outputs from the analysis of past World Bank PPAs, are absent from the final picture, giving a semblance of pure listening, so that the resulting policy messages appear to have arisen from 272 sites and 73 PPA documents with only minimal intervention from inter-mediaries. Such invisibilization is only possible, but is all the more detrimental, in the apparent absence of reflexive praxis or the sort of self-knowing process that McGee and Chambers advocate. Although the 'exposure' or 'immersion' of policy-makers in situations of poverty is becoming ever-more common in PPA practice, it would have been completely unrealistic for the Voices to attempt to forge these spaces for interaction. Had this been possible, it might have rendered visible the large power differentials between convenors and participants in the process, which would have raised questions about the degrees of influence of 'listeners' and 'speakers' over what was 'heard'. It would also have provided a route to the kind of institutional change that Chambers suggests could be 'the main and major issue', from which the voices may be but a diversion (this volume, p20).

THE SHAPING AND BOUNDING OF POLICY SPACES

This discussion of the Voices brings us to the question of what shapes and bounds policy spaces, affecting the potential they offer for pro-poor policy change. The Voices exercise was portrayed as a policy space being created for poor people to put their priorities on the global policy table. This portrayal draws on the principle behind efforts to scale up participatory research, that the creation of micro-level spaces to capture poor people's priorities can change the orientation and nature of the macro-level processes and structures into which they are fed (Gaventa, 1998; Gaventa and Cornwall, 2001). This assumed sequence of events, insufficiently theorized to date and all too often disappointingly elusive in practice, remains an article of faith among those who agonize over the dilemma 'to engage or not to engage' and eventually

decide to do so (Chambers, this volume). The Voices experience has inad-
vertently done the agonizers a favour, by revealing the extent to which the
macro- and supranational-level spaces, and by extension the micro-level
spaces opened up purportedly to influence them, are in fact crowded with
institutional imperatives that condition the possible outcomes of the process,
thereby calling into question the methodological value and the ethics of
conducting the exercise. This does not constitute a reason to refuse to engage,
nor a denial that the Voices had any positive effects; but the reflections of
Chambers and Rademacher and Patel now offer ex ante a detailed map of
the battlefield that is engagement. On this battlefield the objective of pro-
poor policy change through participatory research has to fight it out with the
other priorities of the dominant institution. If it wins, this is not without cost,
both to people who are powerless to hold the institution to account, and to
the reputation of a methodological approach that places a premium on
accountability and transparency.

Looking more broadly across the six cases discussed in this volume, we can
identify several sets of factors at the national level which shape and bound
the policy spaces in which poverty knowledge is made or applied. At the
broadest level there is the political and institutional context. The nature of
the political environment, prevailing and past political ideologies and the
model of governance in place, will first determine whether any invited or
autonomously created policy spaces actually exist; and, if they do, will 'push
in on' these spaces, imposing on them norms of behaviour and interaction,
openness, flexibility or rigidity.[5] The nature of relations between government
and civil society will affect whether spaces are opened or seized at all, and
whether government engages with actions occurring in autonomously
created spaces. The existence and nature of decentralized levels of government, their latitude and capacity, will determine the availability of spaces and
the effectiveness of attempts to influence resource allocation and planning.
Timing is critical: policy environments are more malleable and amenable to
the proliferation or evolution of spaces at some times than at others. This is
linked to political cycles and electoral outcomes, but also to the current state
of the power balance between central and local governments, donor agencies,
non-governmental actors and ordinary people. Further decisive aspects of the
environment are the source of demand for poverty knowledge (who needs
it and what for) and the state of debate in the national social science establishment (whether the time is ripe for a general breakthrough in understandings
of poverty knowledge construction, or whether advocates of conventional
and less conventional approaches are still 'talking past each other').[6]

The next set of factors concerns the nature of policy, and how policy
processes and actors are framed in a given context. Where policy processes
are viewed as linear and rational, policy spaces are not generally acknowledged
to spring into being autonomously, and those that do are sometimes viewed

as threats to the order. Where policy processes are understood to be fluid, dynamic processes involving multiple actors with various motivations, the same spaces are valued as an integral part of the whole and actions occurring in them have a chance of generating policy shifts. The complementarity between different kinds of space is well illustrated in this volume – how inter-relation enhances the effectiveness of advocacy spaces; how knowledge construction without inter-relation may represent an opportunity missed. Where key issues or actors are identified as being off-bounds for other policy actors to scrutinize or engage with, as occurs in many invited spaces, action is circumscribed and potentially controversial advocacy is avoided. If the dominant concept of poverty is as a multidimensional phenomenon involving processes of impoverishment and wellbeing improvement, there will be more scope for a range of interactions, advocacy and knowledge creation to arise from several policy spaces, and promote policy innovations on a range of fronts and levels, than if poverty is understood as simply consumption shortfall. Dominant discourses on knowledge, the poor and development institutions likewise affect the room for manoeuvre that policy spaces can afford.

The occupants of existing policy spaces shape what can happen therein. Is there a diverse policy community keen to enlist new entrants to enrich its understandings and sharpen the poverty focus of policy interventions, or is it homogeneous in terms of identity, disciplinary outlook and attitudes? Does it include poverty champions, people with influence who can pioneer innov-ative approaches to understanding or reducing poverty? Outside the policy community, is civil society actively demanding entry and demonstrating its ability to engage with those within? Are there easily identifiable targets among this community for advocacy actors to work on? Do the poor enter spaces for poverty knowledge creation as passive recipients invited in by government, or as autonomous citizens with a legitimate right and responsibility to exercise agency for improving their situation?

Internally, policy spaces are marked by complex power relations between different actors. Whether the space was brought into being from the top downwards or autonomously created; how the dominant institutional actors position themselves and exercise their dominance; whether they attempt to temper its influence through reflexive, self-critical practice or let it crowd out other actors' priorities and suppress their impacts on the knowledge-construction process; all these factors shape the dynamics. When the reconfig-uration of actors in a space involves power 'reversals' (Chambers, 1983), these are entry points for innovation and change. The biases introduced by power differentials can be offset by actively seeking to diversify the policy com-munity and forge new, strategic power alliances between groups of actors, and by skilful facilitation and use of participatory methods. However carefully offset, though, the tendency towards differentials will remain, with their inevitable negative consequences for the development of reflexivity among stronger actors.

The specific demands of policy-makers for national and, now, supranational-level poverty knowledge imply the need to generalize from micro-level spaces of knowledge creation, which in turn means imposing standardization and losing contextual information about the spaces or the dynamics therein. These knowledge spaces are further bounded by dominant notions about the 'validity' of different research approaches and prevailing attitudes to expertise, which 'push in on' new policy spaces or old ones in which new forms of knowledge, attributed little conventional 'validity', are arising.

Actors' capacities and attitudes are key determinants in ensuring that what takes place in policy spaces leads to pro-poor change. The commitment of dynamic, committed individuals is a crucial catalyst in several of the participatory poverty research initiatives discussed. Where these are powerful actors, their commitment can be the decisive factor in permitting invited spaces to be subverted by their occupants, or other spaces to grow up autonomously alongside them. Individuals' and groups' estimations of their own capabilities to effect change, the possibility of making a difference, their roles and responsibilities and those of other actors, and the accessibility of the 'policy community' all exercise empowering or constraining influences on actors' behaviour. The capacity to undertake participatory research or train others to do so, and the ability to develop advocacy strategies or engage with experts using technical language, determine which actors can be involved in promoting change and which will be able to override others in this process. The dynamic nature of policy spaces is such as to accommodate experiential learning by all involved if they wish it: in particular, the growth of self-knowledge, including awareness by actors of their own positions, motivations and influence, minimizes the risk of domination and maximizes the chance of strategic interaction between actors of differing capacities and powers.

IMPLICATIONS FOR PRACTICE: THE FRONTIERS OF PARTICIPATORY POVERTY RESEARCH

In sum, policy spaces and the scope they provide for pro-poor policy change are shaped and bounded by aspects of political and historical context, institutional imperatives, prevailing perceptions of the policy process and the nature of knowledge, existing configurations and capacities of policy actors, and the power relations between them. Many of these are beyond – or at best peripheral to – the sphere of influence of researchers attempting to gain purchase on the poverty policy process through participatory research. Yet, as several contributors remind us, researchers too have their agency. Process and method, two other critical determinants of what happens in policy spaces, are the special domains of participatory researchers.

Knowledge, action and consciousness brought together in a participatory poverty research initiative create spaces for policy to change in ways that benefit poor people. Recognizing these elements and managing them strategically enhances the potential for policy shifts to ensue. Researchers and activists[7] engaging in poverty research are in a position to influence both dynamics. From this analysis of policy spaces and what goes on within them, lessons can be extracted for researchers seeking to expand them or engage in them so as to promote pro-poor policy change.

This final section brings together these lessons in the form of a series of pointers designed to orient and challenge participatory researchers as they enter into engagement with policy processes:

- Including a participatory component in poverty assessments remains an effective way to spur pro-poor policy change, albeit through different channels from those originally pursued. The first point in a poverty research exercise at which researchers can press for pro-poor policy innovations is in the creation or extension of policy spaces through the instigation of participatory poverty research, as opposed to other approaches that do not foster participation at any level. The impetus for this kind of research has increased greatly since the first tentative efforts to legitimize it in policy circles (Norton and Francis, 1992; Norton and Stephens, 1995). From the perspective of decision-makers and institutions of influence, the core argument that a methodologically pluralist approach offers a fuller picture of poverty remains unchanged, but is rendered more compelling now that there is plentiful evidence to support it. What is new among participatory poverty researchers, including some in these same institutions, is the understanding that the fresh information is but one component to be located in a large, complex and still unfolding model of how participatory assessments can lead to policy change. The model is based on heightened consciousness along several axes, by researchers, policy-makers and those who participate.
- The process and methods of participatory poverty research are replete with policy spaces and opportunities to shape them, which participatory researchers can use strategically. The momentum for adopting a participatory approach can come from decision-makers' or researchers' acquaintance with emotive accounts of poverty arising from qualitative or participatory research elsewhere, or from a kind of methodological advocacy exercised by committed technocrats. Foremost among the lessons from this collection is that participatory methodologies themselves harbour many spaces in which there are more dynamics at work than simple knowledge construction; but that they can also lever open additional spaces, for

example through the combined use of participatory methods and a broad-based partnership including both existing and prospective new members of the poverty policy community, as in Uganda. The emergence of new perspectives from unexpected quarters both shakes the complacency of the adherents of standard methodological approaches, and legitimizes the entry of new actors into the policy community. The wide dissemination of participatory poverty research processes, as well as their findings, is favoured by broad, mixed partnerships, leading to further growth of interest in this approach and awareness of its possibilities and limitations.

- More needs to be done to bring decision-makers into the project of knowledge creation and chart this uncharted area. The first-hand exposure of decision-makers to situations of poverty nurtures the growth of experiential knowledge, increasing the levels and loci at which action for change takes place and, in the long run, engendering change in the institutions of which these individuals form a part. Examples of the transformative effects of exposure notwithstanding, much remains to be done to convince busy decision-makers of its usefulness. A step towards this has been taken in the form of the recently published *Rough Guide to PPAs* (Norton et al, 2001), which takes stock of almost a decade of experience with PPAs and offers guidance on appraising at the country level whether a PPA might make a useful contribution to improving the effectiveness of poverty reduction policy, and if so how to enhance its impact. Written for development practitioners in general, it is highly accessible to policy-makers and can be expected to stimulate not only support for PPA processes but also a desire to be personally involved in them.

- More ways are needed of facilitating policy actors to engage in structured self-critical reflection, to enhance their understanding and use of the scope for change that the policy process offers. Experience suggests that structured, self-critical reflection is key to good participatory poverty research and to ensuring that the process, its convenors and its consequences are fully accountable from the perspectives of all those involved, in whatever capacity. As yet, there are few experiences to learn from, and this require-ment is hard to reconcile with the enjoinder that senior policy-makers get involved. Practically speaking, diverse approaches will be needed to accommodate the different needs and imperatives of different kinds of participants in exposure visits or PPAs. The question of how to reflect self-critically emerges in this volume as a major frontier for participatory research, requiring urgent attention.

- Participatory research offers opportunities to shape and 'nest' emerging policy spaces, in such a way as to maximize the impact of what happens within them. Crucial to this is understanding the context and level of receptivity or rejection of civil society participation in policy research or policy processes themselves. Potential is maximized by treating poverty policy processes as having at least four entry strategies (the informational route; the stimulation of local-level action, including cooperation with others in pre-existing projects or programmes; the broadening of the policy community; and the experiential learning of decision-makers and re-searchers),[8] and critically appraising the viability of each.

- Policy impact is susceptible to the ways in which poverty knowledge is produced and treated, and may also be susceptible to how explicitly these issues are dealt with in accounts of the process. The production and treatment of knowledge arising in policy spaces is an area in which con-tributors have signalled several implications for researchers seeking to maximize policy impact. There is a constant demand for inventiveness in methods for gathering information and synthesizing findings: the use of participatory methods to generate numbers, while carrying risks of reductionism if applied insensitively, is one under-explored area in this regard. While we still have much to learn about analysing and synthesizing information from large-scale and complex participatory research processes, the timely production and dissemination of outputs remains pertinent, both as a basic principle for getting social research used, and as an ethical essential. Researcher agency is key in exposing the myth that PPA-type approaches constitute pure 'listening' to the poor, and influencing dominant actors to recognize this. Researchers can do this by making explicit the translation and filtering which have actually been part of the 'hearing' processes, as some of our contributors have, and/or by actively promoting a dialogical approach in participatory research, in which researcher involvement in the co-creation of poverty knowledge is viewed as a virtue rather than as an impurity or a hindrance to the public relations impact of the exercise.

- Participatory research alone cannot change the world, but depending on how it is designed and executed, it can contribute to transformation as part of a broader strategy. To have significant, sustained impact on poor people's realities, participatory poverty research has to lead to concrete action – be it policy implementation, NGO intervention or local consciousness-raising and self-help – and/or be linked to a process of gradual institutional change. The research can be approached in such as way as to lay the ground for action or institutional transformation, or it can be framed so as to limit the possibility or exclude it entirely, or it can leave both to chance. Those designing participatory poverty research need to be cognizant of this from the earliest possible stage.

This volume has reflected on both the opportunities and the risks posed by participatory poverty research. While the former are many and increasing, the steadily growing following of the approaches we describe suggest that it is the risks and qualifications which we now need to emphasize. Cornwall has argued that, although participatory policy research does hold the potential to lever open policy spaces for the articulation of alternative policy discourses,

> . . .to make effective use of public and political spaces,. . . a more deliberative process is needed: one that engages policy actors in critical reflection on pervasive policy discourses and the accepted wisdom of prevailing policy narratives, rather than simply in finding out about poor people's perceived needs. (Cornwall, 2001, p64)

This she characterizes as 'promoting dialogue, rather than listening' (Cornwall, 2001, p64). I conclude by reflecting on the role that actors' self-critique and consciousness can play in shaping the future application of participatory poverty research for greater effect.

Policy spaces, I have argued, are the nexus in poverty research in which knowledge, action and actors' capacities and attitudes can combine to bring about pro-poor policy change. Participatory poverty research for policy purposes deliberately sets out to open up policy spaces; policy research using participatory tools may not incorporate this as a direct objective but can achieve it incidentally, which is perhaps one of the most significant distinctions between this and fully participatory research.[9] While the spaces are of very different sorts and functions, it is in the interplay of knowledge, action and consciousness in and around these spaces that the potential for change lies. New poverty knowledge, or the quest for it, is frequently the catalyst for spaces to be created, by invitation or autonomously, by institutions, researchers or people. The catalysis occurs through the mediation of researchers, civil society pressure groups or champions for change within institutions. Once the spaces are there, actors in and around them engage with each other in generating or applying knowledge for poverty reduction, or take more direct action for change which, besides its policy-influencing possibilities and immediate practical benefits, offers a cycle of learning in itself.

Knowledge and action, then, have a relatively straightforward role as the driving forces behind progressive dynamics that deliver policy impact. But while some contributions to this volume testify to their combined and individual effectiveness in this regard, others bear eloquent witness to the need for a third driving force. Knowledge and action engaged in without consciousness of political, institutional and personal factors, can be ineffectual or even perverse – from a poverty reduction perspective – in their influence on policy. Unless apprehended and challenged by a critical and self-critical consciousness on the part of actors engaged in poverty research, those factors may turn out to overwhelm progressive dynamics with conservative or regressive influences, so that any change that results is at best cosmetic, and at worst is a front for the entrenchment of existing unequal political, economic or social relationships. Perhaps the single most important challenge this volume poses for participatory poverty researchers is that voiced by Rademacher and Patel when they argue for 'a critical imperative in research practice that takes our responsibilities as reflexive, knowledge-producing individuals seriously, and exercises informed caution [. . .]' (this volume, p167).

Concluding the book *Battlefields of Knowledge*, Long (1992) argues that any attempt to conceptualize knowledge processes in terms of information transfer without giving sufficient attention to the creation and transfer of meaning at the interface between different actors' life-worlds has simply missed the significance of knowledge itself (p274). Contributions to this volume have sought to advance understandings of these knowledge dynamics as a crucial dimension of contemporary poverty reduction efforts by providing insights into what Long calls the research 'interface'. We have shown that in each participatory poverty research venture, there is not just one interface but many, requiring the researcher to juggle several roles, sets of imperatives and possibly conflicting expectations. At the risk of sounding overly bellicose, I conclude that our reflections on participatory poverty research confirm the appositeness of the battlefield metaphor for the field of the construction of poverty knowledge. But I would stress that the usefulness of this metaphor lies in the heightened awareness that it provides of the range and nature of the options available to poverty researchers and of the trade-offs between them.

As an antidote to that negative image, I would point to the many positive developments in which our contributors have played parts: building bridges and establishing dialogue between different approaches to poverty assessment, increasing the credibility and reducing the hubris around participatory research, and narrowing distances between differently placed actors in poverty policy processes. Furthering the strategies they have developed, addressing the challenges they pose, and developing collective and individual self-critical consciousness should be at the top of the agenda for the next decade of participatory poverty research.

NOTES

1   Grindle and Thomas actually call them 'moments', which is confusing because they are not necessarily transient, nor only temporal in nature, nor, indeed, just spatial. 'Opportunities' is perhaps the best way of describing them.

2   'Policy spaces' in Grindle and Thomas's (1991) sense differ from the use of this or similar terms by other analysts. Majone (1989) uses the term more statically and categorically to connote a 'set' of policies in one sectoral or policy field, eg foreign policy. Gerston (1997, p23) writes of 'triggering mechanisms', which he describes

as 'a critical event [. . .] that converts a routine problem into a widely shared, negative public response' requiring a policy innovation of some kind. Wright and Shore's earlier (1995) use of the term 'spaces' refers to gaps in knowledge for policy; Shore and Wright's later (1997) use is after Grindle and Thomas (1991). Kingdon's 'policy windows', described by Gerston as 'the conditions for triggering mechanisms' which 'open and close in unexpected intervals' (1997, p23), are close to Grindle and Thomas's meaning, albeit more transitory and less susceptible to human agency.

3 Used here in the sense in which Chambers (1997) uses it in his concept of 'normal professionalism' (1997).

4 Ethiopia may be an exception.

5 The concepts of 'pushing in on' and 'pushing out from' are discussed in detail in Jones and Speech (2001), drawing on Kesby (1999). Jones et al use them to explain dynamics at the community level when participatory approaches are used in contexts in which social conventions and norms differ widely from those adopted in the 'participatory arena'.

6 The term comes from Kuhn (1970), writing about 'paradigm shift' and the nature of scientific revolutions.

7 In the rest of this chapter, 'researchers' is used in the broadest sense, including all those who engage in participatory research activities, or in research on poverty that deploys participatory methods. This includes poverty activists and also, sometimes, decision-makers who are championing change in their own organizations.

8 As discussed in McGee (this volume).

9 See Cornwall and Jewkes (1995) for an exploration of what constitutes participatory research.

REFERENCES

Brock, K, Cornwall, A and Gaventa, J (2001) *Power, Knowledge and Political Spaces in the Framing of Poverty Policy*, Working Paper 143, Brighton, IDS

Chambers, R (1983) *Rural Development: Putting the Last First*, London, Intermediate Technology

Chambers, R (1997) *Whose Reality Counts? Putting the First Last*, London, Intermediate Technology

Cornwall, A and Jewkes, R (1995) 'What is participatory research?', *Social Science and Medicine*, Vol 41, No 2, pp1667–1676

Cornwall, A (2001) *Beneficiary, Consumer, Citizen: Perspectives on Participation for Poverty Reduction*, Sida Studies No 2, Stockholm, Sida

Gaventa, J (1998) 'The scaling up and institutionalization of PRA: Lessons and challenges' in Blackburn, J and Holland, J (eds) *Who Changes? Institutionalizing participation in development*, London, Intermediate Technology

Gaventa, J and Cornwall, A (2001) 'Power and Knowledge' in Reason, P and Bradbury, H (eds) *Handbook of Action Research: Participative Inquiry and Practice*, London, Sage

Gerston, L (1997) *Public Policymaking: Process and Principles*, New York, M E Sharpe

Grindle, M and Thomas, J (1991) *Public Choices and Policy Change*, Baltimore, Johns Hopkins

Jones, E and SPEECH (2001) *'Of Other Spaces': Situating Participatory Practices – A Case Study from South India,* Working Paper 137, Brighton, IDS

Keeley, J and Scoones, I (1999) *Understanding Environmental Policy Processes: A Review,* Working Paper 89, Brighton, IDS

Kuhn, T (1970) *The Structure of Scientific Revolutions* (second edition), London, University of Chicago Press

Long, N (1992) 'Conclusion' in Long, N and Long, A (eds) *Battlefields of Knowledge: The Interlocking of Theory and Practice in Social Research and Development,* London, Routledge

Majone, G (1989) *Evidence, Argument and Persuasion in the Policy Process,* London, Yale University Press

Norton, A and Francis, P (1992) 'Participatory poverty assessment in Ghana: Discussion paper and proposal', unpublished draft, Washington, DC, World Bank

Norton, A and Stephens, T (1995) *Participation in Poverty Assessments,* Washington, DC, Social Policy and Resettlement Division, World Bank

Norton, A, Bird, B, Brock, K, Kakande, M and Turk, C (2001) *A Rough Guide to PPAs: Participatory Poverty Assessment, A Guide to Theory and Practice,* London, Department for International Development

Shore, C and Wright, S (eds) (1997) *Anthropology of Policy: Critical Perspectives on Governance And Power,* London, Routledge

Wade, R (2001) 'Making the World Development Report 2000: Attacking poverty', *World Development,* Vol 20, No 8, pp1435–1441

Wright, S and Shore, C (1995) 'Towards an Anthropology of Policy', *Anthropology in Action,* Vol 2, No 2, Summer, pp27–31

INDEX